McKinsey's
Marvin Bower

McKinsey's Marvin Bower

Vision, Leadership, and the Creation of Management Consulting

Elizabeth Haas Edersheim

WILEY

John Wiley & Sons, Inc.

Published by John Wiley & Sons, Inc., Hoboken, New Jersey
Published simultaneously in Canada

For general information on our other products and services, or technical support, please contact our Customer Care Department within the United States at 800-762-2974, outside the United States at 317-572-3993 or fax 317-572-4002.

Wiley also publishes its books in a variety of electronic formats. Some content that appears in print may not be available in electronic books.

For more information about Wiley products, visit our web site at *www.wiley.com*.

Library of Congress Cataloging-in-Publication Data:

ISBN 0-471-65285-7

Printed in the United States of America

10 9 8 7 6 5 4 3 2 1

To the memory of Marvin Bower

Contents

Foreword

Marvin Bower was a great leader and a great teacher. He did not believe leadership could be taught, but he did believe it could be learned. I had the opportunity to observe his deep personal influence on legions of business-people and colleagues one by one. For that was his way. One by one.

What I learned from Marvin Bower I brought to Harvard when I led the business school. It was very much about the need to invest in people and ideas—to become an intellectual venture capitalist. It was about creating an environment and a community that is so vital, so rich and fertile, and humane, that each of us will end up far better off than if we selfishly pursued our own interests. As Marvin would say, "If people are working at the things that really interest them, they are going to perform the best, make the greatest contribution, be the best family. . . ."

When Marvin joined McKinsey in 1933, it wasn't clear what was going to happen in the profession of management consulting. Business is not like science. Experiments cannot be conducted in 48 hours, or even in five years. Marvin created an industry when he defined the profession and identity of McKinsey in the way he did, and then he recreated it when he had the insight and courage to hire young people from Harvard and other universities and have them work with business leaders. He demonstrated that it is not necessary to send in a retired CEO to advise senior executives: Young, highly intelligent, and well-trained men and women of great integrity can get the job done, and do it very effectively. That was a huge leap.

In January 2003, we lost a great teacher and a pioneer. Marvin's ideas were founded in basic human attributes of respect for others as well as promotion of self-esteem and courage. What made him a pioneer was that he took basic values into the business world—a fairly novel approach—to help leaders create value-based compasses for their own leadership. He valued the imagination of youth and understood the power of new ideas. He had passionate convictions and he cared deeply about his "students." He never stopped innovating, learning, teaching, or caring.

As with all great teachers, his teaching continues far beyond his 99½ years of life. Each of Marvin's students is living some of those lessons, telling "Marvin stories," and teaching others. I, for one, am persuaded that his story deserves a full telling. His ideas and insights and human values are as applicable today as they were on the day he was born, a century ago. Time has shown how well they work.

—John H. McArthur
Dean of the Harvard
Business School,
1980–1995

Acknowledgments

In the two years this book has been in the works, the list of people to whom I am indebted for telling me their stories and giving me their encouragement, insight, and criticism has grown to unmanageable proportions. I hope I will be excused for singling out only a few of the many whom I have called most frequently for help, and for failing to name many others who have aided me.

To the people who connected me to Marvin:

My father, who introduced me to the myth and the man.

Steve Walleck, who fueled this book by taking the time to write his stories down, as well as Dietmar Meyersiek, and Fred Gluck, who all provided me the opportunity to work with them and Marvin at McKinsey.

To the people who helped me in this endeavor:

Sue Lehmann, who said go for it and reconnected me to McKinsey. Rajat Gupta, for opening the McKinsey files to me, and Bill Price, for being my escort, librarian, and traveling companion into the McKinsey world a decade after I had left it.

To everyone I interviewed, my thanks for your time, your enthusiasm, and your spirit. In particular I would like to express my appreciation to six individuals:

Warren Cannon, who told me it better be good, and when it wasn't, told me it wasn't and then had the patience to listen to me read it to him front to back.

Quincy Hunsicker, who gave me hour upon hour of his vacation time, just because he cared.

Jon Katzenbach, who took time to follow up his interviews with notes and many phone calls, always sharing his strong sense of motivation and pride in his association with Marvin.

Albert Gordon, who gave me invaluable insights into Marvin's enormously influential relationships with Harvard and its business school, was unbelievably precise in his recall of details from 30 years ago, and read Marvin's bio more thoroughly than I believe he read his own.

Mac Stewart, for just being Mac.

Ron Daniel, who never stopped giving me ideas, contributions, and corrections, as Marvin would have done.

I also offer my thanks to the following, who did so much to make writing this book possible:

Dick Bower, who encouraged me and embraced the effort, and Jim Bower, who graciously tolerated the intrusions into his life and gave me unique insights into their father.

Joan Wilson, who worked with me in the middle of many nights on many words and many drafts. Jim Wade and Paige Siempelkamp, who read, challenged, and made suggestions to help make the book better. Sara Roche, who long ago taught me the value of an editor and never ceases to amaze me.

Mark McClusky, Ron Blumer, and Kevin McHugh, who read and encouraged me when I was in doubt.

Brande Defilippis, Amelia O'Malley, Stephanie Nelson, and Kate Handley, who took fabulous care of Marvin in the last years of his life.

Maggie Neal, Marvin's assistant, and Joan Wallace, Marvin and Cleo's housekeeper, who never let me go.

Juliette "Lilita" Dively, Marvin and Helen's longtime friend, who had endless George and Marvin stories and always made me laugh at life.

Howard and Susan Kaminsky, my neighbors, who heard my head hitting the wall and made sure that Marvin's story got told. Alice Fried Martell, my agent, who believed in the book.

Ellen Harvey, who not only typed notes and draft after draft cheerfully and skillfully, but did fact finding, checked accuracy, and made suggestions.

Alvin and Violet, who put up with and supported a crazier and more frantic schedule than usual, and got involved in the effort—Alvin, who regularly asked me how the book was going, and Violet, who kept requesting to come with me to visit Marvin and recently explained to me that the fifth-grade newspaper was failing because it had too much hierarchy and people weren't having fun.

Steven, who never complained that I wouldn't take a commercial mind-set to the effort and kept telling me it was good, even when it wasn't. He offered valuable and perceptive suggestions as always.

I relieve all of these people of responsibility for what I have written; but I cannot absolve them of responsibility for providing the sources of inspiration from which the book was drawn.

Finally, my mother, for giving me courage—for teaching me not to let fear or habits ever stand in the way of doing something I believe is important.

PART I

Translating a Vision into Reality

Ideas are not enough. They do not last. Something practical must be done with them.

—Marvin Bower, 2001[1]

CHAPTER 1

Marvin Bower

*1903—Harvard University had no business school. The
New York Times cost one cent. Women could vote in 2 of
the 45 states. The Wright brothers made their first flight.
Thomas A. Edison's light bulb was already 24 years old.*

*2003—9,000 applicants competed for 900 places at the
Harvard Business School. The New York Times cost $1.
The majority of registered voters were women in 42 of the
50 states. British Air decommissioned the first supersonic
commercial airplane, the Concorde, after 24 years of active
use. The light bulb, after 124 years, was fundamentally
unchanged.*

Born in 1903, Marvin Bower lived in one of the few houses in this
country that had electric light. When Marvin died in Florida
almost 100 years later, he had become to the world of business and management what Thomas Edison was to technology. Both men were elected
to the Business Hall of Fame. When notified of the honor being conferred
on him, Bower said, "It must be a mistake. I'm not a businessman. I am a
professional."[1]

His profession was one that he virtually invented: top management
consulting. As the person who transformed McKinsey & Co. from a nearly
defunct accounting and engineering firm into a preeminent adviser to
senior executives throughout business and, on occasion, government, his
term of service was a remarkable 59 years, from 1933 to formal retirement
in 1992 at the age of 89.

What distinguished Marvin Bower was his dedication to values and
his personal integrity. As John Byrne noted in an article in *Business Week*
after Marvin's death in January 2003:

Bower was McKinsey's high priest, the man who made the partnership the gold standard in its industry. . . . He strongly believed
that, like the best doctors and lawyers, consultants should always
put the interests of their clients first, conduct themselves ethically
at all times, and always tell clients the truth—rather than what
they wanted to hear.[2]

Bower's ethical sense and values can be traced directly to his early
years. The firstborn child of Carlotta and William Bower, Marvin Bower
grew up in a family of modest means in Cleveland, Ohio. While the Bowers were not poor, they valued integrity and respect over money. Two years
after Marvin's birth, his brother, Bill, was born.

The Bower family's emphasis on learning was a major element of
Marvin's childhood. Required reading included stories and poetry, with
William Bower keeping track of the books Marvin and his brother read.
Marvin read every Mark Twain story twice; as he completed one, he would
initial it.

His father was the ideal role model because his work on complex matters of land title transfers had both intellectual and practical hands-on
aspects. It involved both technology and law, and required business acumen and very high ethical standards. William achieved national recognition in his field, just as his son would in later years. William Bower
regularly took Marvin and his brother on tours of different kinds of industrial plants in Cleveland so they could experience firsthand what each
plant was like. Marvin remembered these plant tours as fun and absolutely
special because his father sometimes even took off a day from work to tour
a plant with Marvin and Bill.[3] It is a fair guess that Marvin's desire to learn
something useful and important from any and every experience was
inspired by his father. As they would leave each plant, his father would ask,
"What did you learn?"

While ostensibly a conservative midwestern family, the Bowers did
not emulate the patriarchal structure typical of the time. More democratic in his approach, William Bower sought the opinion of all family
members when it came to important decisions. Marvin clearly remembered being included in the discussion when his family was considering
a move to the other side of Cleveland. In fact, the discussion itself over-
shadowed Marvin's memories of the actual move. As Marvin recalled,

"[It was] remarkable [that my father] continued to involve his sons in family decisions. Of course, my input did not necessarily influence the family decision—I can't even remember what I said—but I did speak up on that and other occasions when I was invited to participate."[4] Such events would have been Marvin's first introduction to a non-hierarchical management structure.

Marvin demonstrated his independent way of thinking early on. In high school he met Helen McLaughlin, the woman who would become his wife. He recalled that his father did not approve of his going steady with Helen: "Dad and I had a real struggle until he learned that I would not give in about going steady."[5] His memories of that time also included an influential English teacher, editing a school newspaper, and holding down a wide variety of summer jobs.

Laura Edwards was Marvin Bower's English teacher in high school. Even at the age of 99, Marvin continued to retain strong memories of her and the effect she had on him and Helen:

> Laura Edwards made learning fun. We came to like her, and soon she asked that we all get on a first-name basis. . . . No other teacher did that. In a funny way, simply doing that made us feel closer to Laura. . . . She lectured us all in a pleasant manner about getting good grades so we could get into colleges, as we all intended to do. I think we all took it to heart. She was an out-standing teacher and influenced Helen to go into teaching. Helen and I visited her when we returned to Cleveland after moving away, and wrote to her over many years.[6]

Marvin adopted this practice of dealing with people on a first-name basis and made it an integral part of his relationships with others, colleagues and clients alike. He was known to everybody simply as Marvin, and if someone called him Mr. Bower he would correct him or her.

His ability to communicate clearly and effectively was evident in his high school years, when he launched a school newspaper entitled *Home Brew*.[7] The school administration did not like the title (this was during Prohibition), but the first-rate quality of the reporting convinced them to allow the name chosen by Marvin, providing him with an early lesson in how powerful good communication skills could be.

Each summer Marvin would work at jobs obtained with his father's help. He worked as a surveyor's helper, an ice deliverer, a factory worker, and a Boy Scout camp counselor during World War I when there was a shortage of help. As Marvin recalled, "It was a good experience. I had some real responsibility and I had excellent teachers, so I learned a great deal [despite being only 15 years old]. I collected a tidy sum of money and Father taught me how to save."[8] In years to come, Marvin Bower would prove to be frugal not only with his own money but with the money of clients as well.

An industrious young man, he was also adventurous. One summer, he and a friend, John Hamilton, set out to take a bike trip to Buffalo and back.[9] They thought it would be good training for football. They rapidly found the trip boring—more hills and mosquitoes than expected. After about three days of boredom, they grabbed onto a slow-moving truck. The truck driver did not know they had hitched on and began going faster and faster. Marvin and John let go and smashed into the pavement, fortunately without injuring themselves. A few days later, they reached Erie, Pennsylvania and turned around. The next summer the tenacious Marvin and John again set out for Buffalo, this time using William Bower's outboard motor on a rowboat they had built. A storm set in over Lake Erie, the motor died, and Marvin and John were washed up on an island. They managed to swim to the mainland, call home, and alert the Coast Guard. That ended the boating adventure for the two high school students. The following year, still set on visiting Buffalo, Marvin came up with a more practical approach: He asked his father if they could go to Buffalo for their summer vacation.

After high school, Marvin Bower attended Brown from 1921 through 1925 at his grandfather's suggestion. When Marvin reflected on his time at Brown, he mentioned one of the few regrets in his life: "I isolated myself in my fraternity too much. I didn't take advantage and get to know the full campus of people."[10] At Brown he met Malcolm Smith, who became a close friend for life. He studied philosophy and economics, the latter having been a relatively new academic field at the time.

Two of Marvin's college professors made a lasting impression on him: One was an economics professor named Patton who used the outstanding text by Marshall to teach principles of economics so they could be remembered. The other was the psychology professor who was very good in dealing with people, and from whom he learned a lot about listening and people.[11]

Following Brown, on the advice of his father, Marvin went to Harvard Law School, while his friend Malcolm Smith went on to Harvard Business School. Marvin recalled:

> It wasn't hard to get in . . . I had an adequate but undistinguished record scholastically, but one didn't have to have top grades to get into Harvard Law in those days. The big problem at Harvard Law at that time was *staying* in, because they flunked people out.[12]

Marvin was able to self-fund his law school education—he had saved earnings from his many summer jobs, and by 1925 he had made enough successful investments in the stock market to pay for his schooling.[13] Almost everyone made money in the stock market in the 1920s, but it was very unusual for a 22-year-old to have been such a careful investor.

For four summers, starting in 1925, Marvin worked for the Cleveland law firm of Thompson, Hine and Flory (TH&F).[14] During the first summer, his assignment was to collect debts for clients of the firm, principally wholesale hardware companies in Cleveland. First the clients' salesmen tried to get the retailers to pay up, then the wholesalers wrote letters to the retailers; if this proved unsuccessful, they turned the bad debts over to TH&F. When Marvin went to see the retailers—"dunning" them, it was called—he found he had more punch in person than through a letter: His style was so effective that he could persuade many of the retailers to pay up. TH&F continued to use him in that role for the next three summers.

In 1927, in the summer before Marvin's last year at law school, he married his longtime sweetheart, Helen.[15] Over 70 years later, Marvin still remembered the details of that day—what it cost to rent an awning for the church, the problems of renting a formal suit, the dress Helen was wearing, and of course his friends who attended. *The Cleveland News* coverage singled it out as the "Wedding Event of the Week."[16]

Their honeymoon was by car—a "new" (secondhand) car.[17] In typical Marvin fashion, this trip was going to be an adventure, and there was no detailed itinerary. The couple started out late, ending up in Erie the first night. (There were no interstate highways back then, although most of the roads in highly populated areas had some sort of paving.) They had planned to tour Nova Scotia, but instead meandered around, visited many interesting places, and met a variety of people. After two weeks, they arrived in Cambridge, Massachusetts, just in time for Marvin to go back to school.

When he finished law school, Marvin was determined to work for a firm he knew he could be proud of. He targeted Jones, Day, Reavis & Pogue, a highly respected Cleveland law firm. As he told the story, he had not done well enough in law school for Jones, Day to make him an offer, so he decided to go first to the then fledgling Harvard Business School to strengthen his record. His friend Malcolm Smith had found business thoroughly absorbing and was convinced that business was more creative than law.

Once he entered business school in 1928, Marvin confirmed what he had already suspected—that he really enjoyed business. A member of *The Harvard Business Review,* he was particularly interested in marketing, statistics, finance, and public utility management.

While Marvin was in business school, Helen worked as a teacher (ultimately becoming a principal in Medfield, Massachusetts) to cover their living expenses, with schooling paid for by their stock market earnings. In the summer between his two business school years, Marvin worked for the law firm of Davis Polk in New York, staying in Malcolm Smith's apartment in Bronxville while Malcolm was away. Marvin's strategy paid off. After graduating from the business school in 1930, he joined Jones, Day in their corporate law practice.

In 1933, after three years with Jones, Day, Marvin left the firm, plunging headfirst into the business world after he consulted his friend George Dively, a Harvard Business School classmate of Malcolm Smith and a fellow Clevelander, who agreed that such a move was wise. Marvin joined what was then James O. McKinsey's accounting and engineering firm. Six years later he bought it, and oversaw its transformation into the premier firm in a new profession—management consulting.

Marvin Bower's foray into the business world would have far-reaching effects on business management throughout the world. He successfully built an eminent institution—and through it a profession—and simultaneously influenced thousands of leaders. His professional life was marked by his commitment to people, his caring about the success of client institutions and promulgation of important ideas, and his absolute integrity. During his almost 100-year lifetime, business went from a second-class profession (for those who even deigned to consider it as a profession) to the engine driving a global economy. Throughout this transition, Marvin was there, anticipating and envisioning the future and recognizing and serving the needs of senior business executives who were faced with huge challenges in a quickly changing world.

As he moved into consulting, Marvin had the opportunity to work with and advise many of the leaders of companies who would lead the charge into less hierarchical structures: Alfred Sloan, chairman of General Motors; Charles Mortimer, chairman of General Foods; Crawford Greenwalt, chairman of DuPont; Ralph Cordiner, CEO of General Electric; John Loudon, chairman of Royal Dutch Shell; Thomas J. Watson Jr., chairman of IBM; and even President Dwight D. Eisenhower, who, with Marvin's help, dramatically reduced the size of the White House staff and gave his key people an unusual degree of autonomy.[18] At that time, no Republican had been in the White House for 20 years. The Republican National Committee felt that a complete examination of staff functions was necessary, so Eisenhower did something unprecedented: He called in an "outsider" from management consulting to study the problems he and his staff members would encounter as his new administration took over. Eisenhower's decision to bring in Marvin's McKinsey team reflected the esteem in which Marvin was held by business leaders to whom the president turned for advice. By the 1950s, Marvin had firmly established his position as a professional who represented the gold standard in consulting—someone who merited unreserved trust and respect for his dedication to the needs of McKinsey clients. (See Figure 1.1.)

Marvin never believed in making money just for the sake of making money to keep score. His commitment to his clients, his partners, and his values was exceptional. He believed that a great service institution was built not only on skills and experience, but most importantly on the behavior and conduct of its people. He was well ahead of his and our time. In 1935, as a two-year associate, he wrote a note to James O. McKinsey stating that he did not believe consulting and accounting could be performed by the same firm without posing a conflict of interest.[19] In the late 1950s and 1960s, Marvin sacrificed a significant increase in personal wealth by

Survey Helped Eisenhower to Fill U. S. Jobs

Study of Policy Positions Ordered Months Ago to Speed Appointments Now

A scientific survey of qualifications required for policy-making jobs in the Federal government is guiding top-rank members of the Eisenhower administration in filling these jobs, a management consultant revealed yesterday.

Marvin Bower, a managing partner of the firm of McKinsey & Co., management consultants, said his firm was retained before Gen. Eisenhower's nomination for President last July to undertake the survey. The firm was given the assignment by a "group of forward-thinking Republicans under the leadership of Harold E. Talbot, Gen. Lucius D. Clay and Herbert Brownell jr. . . . to aid the Republican administration in selecting competent individuals for key positions—to get the right persons for the important jobs," Mr. Bower said.

Data Wanted Earlier

He explained that the objective was to make information about the positions available early to facilitate the filling of these posts in the short period between election and inauguration.

Gov. Sherman Adams, of New Hampshire, who will be Assistant to President Eisenhower after Jan. 20, confirmed last night that the Eisenhower organization has accepted the services of "selected research groups and management consultants who are preparing studies on the executive branch of the Federal government."

Gov. Adams said the studies are "directing careful attention to the current organization" of the executive department, its personnel and existing relationships between departments.

Immediate Gains Sought

Indicating that the studies are designed to make immediate improvements in the President's administrative set-up, as distinguished from the long-range reorganization study to be conducted by Temple University in conjunction with a special commission headed by Nelson A. Rockefeller, Mr. Adams said the studies are adapting recommendations of the Hoover report to present needs.

The studies also are "preparing further suggestions for realigning and reorganizing the agencies in the Executive department for more efficient and productive results," he said.

Gov. Adams and Arthur H. Vandenberg jr., the President-elect's secretary, will visit the White House at 2 p. m. today for consultation with John R. Steelman, assistant to President Truman, and Matthew J. Connelly, the President's secretary.

FIGURE 1.1   SURVEY HELPED EISENHOWER TO FILL U.S. JOBS
(*The Herald Tribune,* January 12, 1953 © The New York Times Company)

selling his shares to his partners at book value when other service firms were going public and their partners taking a lucrative payday. He did not believe that a service firm could consistently place its clients' interests first if it were a public firm also answering to shareholders. Marvin decided that in order for the firm to grow and survive, ownership should be broad. Because of his adherence to high standards, he was a model for four generations of leaders. In addition to his one-on-one working relationship with senior managers, he used his superb communication skills to reach out to managers throughout the world.

In 1966, Marvin wrote his first book, *The Will to Manage,* in which he discussed the practical application of his many revolutionary ideas for helping management exercise meaningful leadership in a changing world. In 1975, a letter from the book's publisher, McGraw-Hill, informed him that *The Will to Manage* was one of the best selling business books the firm had ever published.[20] In 2002, the book was cited as one of the 100 most important business books ever written in the reference book *Business: The Ultimate Resource.*[21]

Marvin's unwavering commitment to enhancing the welfare of business and the world in general included his involvement in a variety of business and community services. In 1955, he agreed to be president of the Joint Council on Economic Education. Marvin believed that the U.S. school system, including colleges, was woefully inadequate when it came to teaching economics, and that every citizen needed to have some understanding of economics. The council, founded six years earlier, provided state-of-the-art economic education through state councils and university-based centers. Marvin's impact in this role was not soon forgotten: Lou Gerstner, who assumed the council's presidency three terms later, was continually asked, "How's Marvin doing?"[22]

Marvin was also an active adviser to the Harvard Business School and was president and board chairman of the Harvard Business School alumni association. His Harvard-related services included close associations with five of the school's deans, spanning a 50-year period. Marvin provided advice to Dean Donald K. David on setting up a joint program with the law school. For Dean Stanley F. Teele, who had been an HBS classmate, Marvin was an informal adviser. For Dean George Baker, Marvin studied the school's organization. For Dean Lawrence Fouraker, Marvin served on the advisory board. For Dean John McArthur, Marvin was a key adviser and counselor. In addition, Marvin was quite active on the board of Case Western Reserve, and was one of the leaders in merging Case and Western Reserve into a single institution.

Marvin also felt he had an obligation to help improve education in the United States at the local level. While a member of the Bronxville school board, he decided that it was important for an outsider to challenge some long-established school practices.[23] Marvin and Helen established an organization in Bronxville with the mission of educating young people on the dangers of drugs—a pioneering version of the now widespread Drug Abuse Resistance Education (DARE) program. Marvin also encouraged others to give back to their larger and smaller communities. He was active in and supportive of the Volunteer Consulting Group, an organization of consultants providing pro bono help to nonprofit organizations. Finally, in his seventies, Marvin became an elder at the Bronxville Reformed Church.[24]

Marvin and Helen had three sons: Peter, born while they were still in Boston; Richard, born in Marvin's first year with McKinsey & Co.; and James, born three years later. While his sons were growing up, much of Marvin Bower's time was consumed by McKinsey & Co. Perhaps that contributed to his particular intensity when he did focus on his family. For example, when it came time to plan the family summer vacation, Marvin would ask one of his sons what he wanted to do. When Jim answered, "a trip to the Grand Canyon," that is what they did, donkey riding through the canyon.[25] When Dick hot-wired the family Cadillac, Marvin recognized the yen for adventure, perhaps recalling his own youthful mishaps in his quest to reach Buffalo, and grounded his son for two weeks. And Marvin was nothing if not loyal: After Peter joined Campbell's Soup in 1956, Marvin never touched a competitor's soup.

Marvin had six grandchildren and nine great-grandchildren. His grandchildren remember a wonderful grandfather who carried a dollhouse home on the train for Christmas, enjoyed watching *The Munsters* with them, and was an inspiration for their work and their lives, always sending them articles he thought might interest them.

Helen died in 1985 at the age of 81. As Marvin wrote to his family following her death:

She respected everyone. . . . Perhaps you can gain some meaning by understanding better the qualities that Helen had—from which you benefit by genes and blood or just from example. The large number of letters I received (perhaps 250) were a great tribute to her, and many were quite specific in describing her qualities from which you have benefited and still can benefit. . . . Let me share [one in particular] with you. Years ago when I was chairman of the Joint Council on Economic Education, the president [of the council] and I went to Washington with our wives. He writes:

"My most memorable recollection of Helen stamped her as a rare person and one I was privileged to know. You will recall one of our Annual Meetings in Washington when the students marched on the White House. Helen and Lois left the hotel and marched along with the students. Helen's response to 'why' was 'my son was in the parade.' Courage and forcefulness went along with her protectiveness for her family. She portrayed for me the model of American womanhood."[26]

Marvin continued: "Clearly you are all loved and have inherited from her, in one way or another, outstanding qualities and have high standards to live up to. It's hard to imagine a better role model. We share a sorrow we will never get completely over. But Helen would want us all to adjust to it in the spirit she would bring to that task."

In 1989, Marvin married Cleo Stewart, a neighbor in Bronxville and a longtime family friend. Together they moved to Delray Beach, Florida. In 2001, Cleo died on Marvin's 98th birthday, but not before she had set him up with round-the-clock care and a project—writing his memoirs.

As Marvin's 99th birthday was approaching, his son Dick called me to say that he felt it was important that Marvin have a quiet birthday dinner with a few family members. Two days later, Marvin's secretary called to invite 21 people to the 99th birthday party Marvin was throwing for himself. It was quite a party. Attendees included Fran Allen, the widow of Jim Allen (from Booz•Allen & Hamilton); Juliette Dively, George Dively's widow; Jack Bennington, the inventor of the Bennington electrical joint, and Marvin's Sunday breakfast partner; Mac Stewart; Suzanne and Bill Bower, Marvin's great niece and nephew; friends from McKinsey; and

Marvin's son Dick and his wife Neely. At the age of 99, Marvin continued to be in charge of his life: He was going to celebrate what turned out to be his last birthday in the manner he wanted.

Looking back on Marvin's long life, a quote from Thomas A. Edison seems appropriate:

> "I am long on ideas but short on time. I expect to live only about a hundred years."

CHAPTER 2

The Vision

Man is a problem-solving, skill-using, social animal. Once he has satisfied his hunger, two main types of experiences are significant to him. One of the deepest needs is to apply his skills, wherever they may be, to challenging tasks— to feel the exhilaration of the well-struck ball or the well-solved problem. The other need is to find meaningful and warm relations with a few other human beings—to love and be loved, to share experience, to respect and be respected, to work in common tasks.

—Herbert Simon, 1965[1]

Marvin Bower built and led the management consulting firm of McKinsey & Co. from a staff of 18 to a sustainable firm of over 500 consultants at the time he stepped aside as managing partner in 1967, and 2,500 by the time of his retirement in 1992.[2] Over these same years, management consulting as a distinct profession grew from a handful of pioneers to a wide spectrum of firms employing over 500,000 people with an aggregate revenue in the billions of dollars. During this same period, Marvin Bower boldly took on powerful individuals, such as Derek Bok, president of Harvard, over the Harvard Business School's mission; and Royal Little, president of Colgate, over the necessity to listen to the company's employees. What enabled Marvin's professional success, and the financial success of his firm, was an undeterrable will to lead coupled with a base of business values, strong leadership skills, and unemotional, absolute logic.

Marvin Bower's vision of and passion for what he later termed *management consulting* began during his career as a lawyer between 1930 and

1933 at Jones, Day, Reavis & Pogue in Cleveland. In 1930, the firm found its practice had largely turned to the cleanup of Depression-ravaged companies. Having done the legal work related to the issuing of industrial bonds by its banking clients, the firm inherited the chore of untangling the obligations of defaulters. Saddled with de facto company ownership through bondholders' and creditors' committees, the bankers called upon Jones, Day to help reorganize these companies, or at least wring some value out of the remnants.

Having much more to do with business management than law, these assignments were outside the usual range of a law firm's work. The 27-year-old Marvin Bower was among the first to hold both a master's degree in business and a law degree from Harvard, so the law firm put him in charge of these cleanup assignments.

Marvin's business degree paid off for both him and his employer. Over the next three years, he served as secretary to 11 bondholders' committees, including those of Thompson Products, Inc. (later TRW), Midland Steel Products Company, Otis & Company, and the Studebaker Company.[3] The committees took over the power of defaulting companies' boards of directors, and Marvin's role as secretary gave him considerable power.

In this capacity, Marvin investigated potential earning power and suggested recapitalization structures to the bankers and investment bankers. He typically began his search by interviewing the chief executive of the failed company, and then followed up by talking with any other staff members who might have insight into the causes of failure and the company's ability to recover from disaster. As amateurish and superficial as he later considered this early work, it nevertheless produced meaningful results. The fundamental problem, Marvin learned, was not that the presidents of the failed companies were stupid; in fact, all 11 of them were very smart men. The problem was that they lacked the information necessary for informed decisions.

From his front-row view of 11 business tragedies, Marvin was convinced that the chief executives had been shielded from information that could have saved them. He firmly believed that had the right anecdotes and data flowed to the top and been properly analyzed, 10 of the 11 companies would still have been operating and healthy despite the Depression.

The culprit, Marvin believed, was deference to hierarchy. Employees simply didn't dare tell the boss what was really going on. The isolation of the CEO, and Marvin's anger at its disastrous results, kept Marvin and Helen up many nights talking. This experience also strengthened Marvin's belief in the value of information from a frontline employee—the person selling in the field or building the product on the factory floor—and the value of that person's knowledge. More often than not, the critical facts that needed to flow to the CEO could be found at the front line.

Armed with this insight, Marvin set out on a mission to help CEOs become more effective by showing them the necessity of eliminating the barriers erected by corporate hierarchy that so severely constrained locating and mining the knowledge inside a company. He recognized that CEOs of companies concerned about basic policy or strategy had no independent, objective advisers to turn to. For legal problems, they could go to a law firm; to raise capital, they could go to an investment bank; but when it came to advice on organizing and running a company, there was no professional firm of the necessary stature.

Marvin gave a name to this needed professional discipline: management consulting. (He later said he wished he had called it "consulting on managing" since he felt that was a more descriptive name.)[4] In 1933, there were only two types of business advisers: the accounting and engineering firms and individual experts. Although the oldest firms in the field had already been founded—Edwin Booz & Company (now Booz·Allen & Hamilton) in 1914; McKinsey in 1926; and Stevenson, Jordan and Harrison (now out of existence) in about 1918[5]—their practices were still in relative infancy, and they considered themselves accounting and management engineering firms.[6] At that time, the only professional top management consulting was provided by individual experts (primarily academics like Frederick Taylor), not by institutions. In fact, it wasn't until 1950 that Booz·Allen & Hamilton modified the title on its marketing materials to *management consultants,* and later, in the 1950s, that Arthur D. Little began calling what they were doing *consulting.*[7] And it wasn't until the 1960s that Boston Consulting Group was founded, and the 1970s that Bain & Company, Monitor Group, and CSC Index were founded.

Marvin Bower
Meets James O. McKinsey

As Marvin was searching for a place to practice this new profession, the dean of Harvard Business School, Wallace Brett Donham, suggested that he talk with James O. McKinsey. McKinsey had seen a paper Marvin had written while at Harvard Business School and had called Donham to inquire about it. In a conversation with Steve Walleck, a partner in the Cleveland office at the time, and me in 1983, Helen Bower remembered the events leading up to her husband's move to McKinsey:

> Marvin and I were living right off Shaker Square, in a cold-water, third-floor walk-up. He had graduated from business school the year before and had come to Cleveland to work for Jones, Day, a law firm he very much respected.
>
> It was 1931, right in the middle of the Great Depression, and Marvin was working mostly on bankruptcies and reorganizations. Somehow, a paper he wrote for one of his clients, a clothing manufacturer, fell into Mac's [James O. McKinsey's] hands. Maybe it was through the Marshall Field connection, since that was Mac's largest client. Mac wrote to Marvin and offered to interview him for a position, if he would come to Chicago.
>
> Anyway, I didn't want to go to Chicago. I had read about the gangsters there, and I had been told the weather was worse than Cleveland's. So Marvin put Mac's letter away—I suppose he wrote him a polite "No, thanks."
>
> We were just about scraping by on Marvin's salary as a junior associate and what I was earning as a new teacher, when we received notice from Jones, Day that all salaries would be cut 25 percent the next month—I believe it was September. We worked it out, and figured that we could barely make ends meet. Marvin was a little bored with law and thrilled with helping businesspeople with their needs.
>
> So we went to a little ice cream parlor right around the corner from Shaker Square—we couldn't afford a restaurant—and talked about what we could do. I still remember the wrought-iron chairs and the printed paper tablecloths.

This was a turning point for both Marvin and Helen, but, as Helen recalled, the crucial decision was postponed. The world of management consulting might look considerably different today if Marvin Bower had ultimately not decided to take McKinsey's offer.

> Two years later, Marvin pulled out Mac's letter, and said he wanted to go to Chicago to meet Mac and see what his firm had to offer. I was afraid to let Marvin go alone. In addition to gangsters in

Chicago, our *Cleveland Plain Dealer* was reporting that bubonic plague had broken out, and people were dying on the streets. When we got there we didn't see any bodies, though.

The problem was we didn't have money enough for two tickets. And I told Marvin he wasn't going to go without me.

We solved that problem by sharing one Pullman berth. That kind of thing was frowned upon in those days, even for married people. But Marvin always was a good problem solver.

When we got to Chicago, Marvin parked me at a hotel near the train station and went off to see Mac. He told me he would be back in an hour or two.

Two hours passed. Then four, then six. I was about to go out on the street to look for Marvin's body when he came back to the room, all smiles.

"We got a job!" he shouted.

"You got an offer," I responded. "Let's talk about it." So, back to Cleveland in the single berth. But we were getting better at it.

And then back to the ice cream parlor around the corner from Shaker Square. Marvin was full of ideas and excitement. He said there was room in business for a professional firm, laid out along the lines of Jones, Day, that advised business leaders on their business problems, much as Jones, Day advised them on their legal difficulties. He said that working with Mac would enable him to use his Harvard Business School training as well as his legal degree.

He said there were some things about his legal job he liked and some things he didn't. He emphasized that Mac had said, "Why don't you join us and enjoy your work completely." The offer was fair, and even though it wasn't an increase over what he had been making, at least it wasn't a cut. So we agreed. We were going to Chicago.[8]

Looking back, Helen wondered, "what would the young people at McKinsey think if they knew this critical decision was made in an ice cream parlor!" "And I wonder how many would join," Steve Walleck responded, "if they had to pay their own airfare to come for a job interview, and, instead of wining and dining them, we offered them banana splits." For a moment, I doubted whether Helen heard Steve, since her eyes were closed. Then she opened her eyes and gave me a full smile. "Nothing wrong with banana splits," she said. "And I still prefer trains to air travel, especially in the right company, and with improper accommodations."

As it turned out, Helen's fears about Chicago proved to be needless, because Marvin went to Chicago only to be told that he was going to be located in the New York office.[9] A year later, he was running the New York office.

The McKinsey that Marvin joined in 1933 had been founded by James O. McKinsey, who had once been a professor of accounting at the University of Chicago and was a leading thinker in the importance of linking accounting to management. Founded in either 1926 or 1927 (there are conflicting reports), the original firm was opened in Chicago, with the addition of a New York office in 1932.[10] Self-defining his new business as an "accounting and management engineering firm," McKinsey offered advice to clients on how to use financial facts as an effective management tool and support for management decisions. McKinsey's initial staff included two industrial engineers and no one with explicit training in management.

In 1935, James O. McKinsey decided to join Marshall Field briefly to help implement some of his suggestions, and "temporarily" merged McKinsey with an accounting firm called Scoville, Wellington. From Marvin's perspective, the merger was not successful:

> The most important lesson of the McKinsey, Wellington period—
> and one for which we paid a high price—is that no personal service firm can long endure dissension among the partners; that it is never any stronger than the commitment of the partners to the firm and to each other. Differences of opinion are healthy because their resolution among people of goodwill leads to sounder decisions. But when the guiding principles, the fundamental purposes, philosophies, policies, values, and attitudes cannot be reconciled rationally and emotionally, the majority had better force the prompt resignation of the dissenters.[11]

Soon thereafter, in late 1937, James O. McKinsey died unexpectedly of pneumonia (see Figure 2.1). Marvin reflected on James McKinsey's death in his memoirs:

> In October 1937, he made an exhausting tour of the Marshall Field mills and returned with a severe cold, which turned into pneumonia. Since there were then no specific antibiotics for his

James O. McKinsey Dead at 48; Head of Marshall Field & Co.

Director in Many Firms, Former Professor and Author of Business Texts

By The Associated Press

CHICAGO, Nov. 30.—James O. McKinsey, chairman of the board of Marshall Field & Co., died of pneumonia Tuesday. Mr. McKinsey, who was forty-eight years old, contracted a severe cold recently and entered a hospital a week ago.

Made Chairman of Board

Before he became chairman of the board and senior executive officer of Marshall Field & Co., in October, 1935, Mr. McKinsey had been management counsel for many of the largest corporations of the country. He was the author of several works on business administration and accounting and from 1926 to 1935 was professor of business policies at the University of Chicago.

He was the organizer of the management counsel firm of James O. McKinsey & Co., which he headed from 1925 until his assumption of the Marshall Field post ten years later. At Marshall Field's he succeeded James Simpson, who had resigned in 1932 to become chairman of the Commonwealth Edison Company. Under Mr. McKinsey's direction Marshall Field reported a net income of $1,280,907 for the nine months ended last September 30, as compared with a profit of $225,510 in the corresponding period in 1936. This 1937 net did not include normal Federal income taxes or a credit of $313,929 paid to Mr. McKinsey.

Mr. McKinsey had been chairman of the board of directors of the American Management Association. During his years on the faculty of the University of Chicago, he lectured frequently at Columbia University on accounting.

He was born in Gamma, Mo., June 4, 1889, the son of James Madison and Mary Elizabeth Logan McKinsey. He obtained his Pd.B. degree from the State Teachers College, at Warrensburg, Mo., in 1912; an LL.B. from the University of Arkansas a year later, and a Ph.B. from the University of Chicago in 1916. He also received a master's degree from Chicago in 1919, two years after he had joined its faculty.

In 1919 Mr. McKinsey became a certified public accountant. Besides heading Marshall Field, he was a director of the Chicago Corporation, the Kroger Grocery and Baking Company, Selected Shares Corpora-

Underwood & Underwood photo
James O. McKinsey

tion and other companies. He also was a member of the board of trustees of the Armour Institute of Technology, a member of the board of managers of the Chicago Young Men's Christian Association, a director of the Central Y. M. C. A. College and a member of the transportation committee of the Chicago Association of Commerce.

He was a member of the American Institute of Accountants and the National Association of Cost Accountants. Other memberships included Delta Sigma Pi, Phi Kappa Sigma and Delta Theta Phi fraternities, and the Chicago, Attic, Racquet, Saddle and Cycle and Chicago Golf Clubs, of Chicago, and the Rookery, of New York.

During the World War Mr. McKinsey served as a lieutenant in the ordnance department of the Army.

Mr. McKinsey's books included "Bookkeeping and Accounting," "Budgetary Control," "Managerial Accounting," "Business Administration" and "Accounting Principles." He also was the author of pamphlets published by the American Management Association.

In 1930 Mr. McKinsey married Alice Louise Anderson, of Sioux City, Iowa. They had twin sons, Robert and Richard McKinsey.

FIGURE 2.1   JAMES O. MCKINSEY DEAD AT 48
(*The Herald Tribune*, December 1, 1937)

21

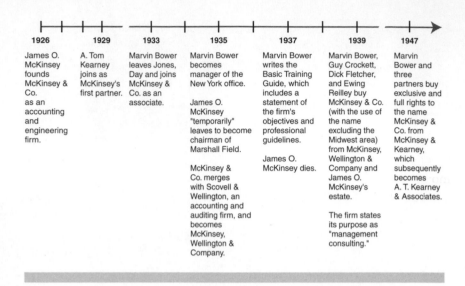

1926	1929	1933	1935	1937	1939	1947
James O. McKinsey founds McKinsey & Co. as an accounting and engineering firm.	A. Tom Kearney joins as McKinsey's first partner.	Marvin Bower leaves Jones, Day and joins McKinsey & Co. as an associate.	Marvin Bower becomes manager of the New York office. James O. McKinsey "temporarily" leaves to become chairman of Marshall Field. McKinsey & Co. merges with Scovell & Wellington, an accounting and auditing firm, and becomes McKinsey, Wellington & Company.	Marvin Bower writes the Basic Training Guide, which includes a statement of the firm's objectives and professional guidelines. James O. McKinsey dies.	Marvin Bower, Guy Crockett, Dick Fletcher, and Ewing Reilley buy McKinsey & Co. (with the use of the name excluding the Midwest area) from McKinsey, Wellington & Company and James O. McKinsey's estate. The firm states its purpose as "management consulting."	Marvin Bower and three partners buy exclusive and full rights to the name McKinsey & Co. from McKinsey & Kearney, which subsequently becomes A. T. Kearney & Associates.

FIGURE 2.2   CHRONOLOGY OF MARVIN BOWER'S PURCHASE OF MCKINSEY & CO.

type of pneumonia, he died ten days later, in November. Everyone was stunned. Certainly I was. My hero was gone. The degree of my admiration and affection for Mac is best reflected in the fact that Helen and I named our third son, born the following January, James McKinsey Bower. My personal loss was that the man I admired most was gone; my career loss was that I had had less than two years to learn from my mentor.[12]

Almost simultaneously with McKinsey's death, the firm's largest engagement, the U.S. Steel study, came to an end, and McKinsey, Wellington, went into a no-profit situation. That is when Marvin led a group in buying back McKinsey & Co. from the merged entity. (See Figure 2.2.)

Marvin and His Partners Buy McKinsey & Co.

In 1939, a mere six years after joining McKinsey & Co. as a new associate, Marvin Bower and his three partners—Guy Crockett, Dick Fletcher, and Ewing "Zip" Reilley—bought the then 18-person accounting and engineering management firm with a regional presence (primarily in the East), a 13-year history with now problematic economics, and limited use of the McKinsey name. Marvin continued to lead McKinsey & Co. until 1967,[13] and was active in protecting and syndicating ownership of his vision until his death in 2003.

How did the 35-year-old Marvin Bower, the distinctly junior member of this new partnership, convince his three co-investors[14] (two over 60 years old)[15] to leave their careers in established institutions, invest their money, risk their personal assets,[16] and embark on a journey to not only build an institution but also create the heretofore unknown profession of management consulting? Marvin was able to persuade his partners to join him on this potentially perilous journey by articulating a clear vision of a management consulting profession and the institution that would play this professional role. Marvin's concept included elements of James O. McKinsey's vision (e.g., bringing the facts to management, the importance of training, the desire to work for prestigious clients), but went well beyond Mac's original idea and was based on experience, values, and logic that were both convincing and transferable to others. From the moment of acquiring ownership until his formal retirement in 1992, Marvin lived and breathed that vision, always leading by example but never afraid to listen to and test new ideas.

Some 12 years after Marvin's departure from McKinsey, it is fair to say that the story of Marvin Bower as an institution creator, profession builder, and leader's leader can provide valuable lessons applicable to a variety of professions—lessons as relevant today as they were in 1939.

CHAPTER 3

The Profession and the Institution

*Our optimism about the future was based on a solid belief
in the need for our type of service and our capacity to
deliver it. We had seen the value of our work and had
observed that client executives recognized it. . . . Although
we made no formal declaration of our goal, we did discuss
these lofty ambitions almost constantly among ourselves.
Indeed, if we had not been ambitious, optimistic, and somewhat visionary, we would never have had the courage to go
ahead at all.*

—Marvin Bower, 1957[1]

With a high level of optimism and a clear vision of the target profession and target institutional vehicle for conducting management consulting, the four partners began their journey. (See Figure 3.1.)

The Profession:
Management Consulting

From the outset, Marvin and his three partners had a clear vision of the profession that would be management consulting and of the independent and unbiased posture that would be required to create the reputation needed to attract CEOs to their services. It was a revolutionary vision in all regards.

The notion of management consulting was virtually unheard of at the time. Ruth Neukom, the wife of one of the original 18 members of the firm, remembers the challenge faced by this firm and profession:

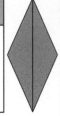

The Target Profession: Management Consulting	The Target Enduring Institution: McKinsey & Co.
The provision of highly respected, independent, unbiased advice to CEOs of all types of businesses and on all types of major management problems	A national firm with multiple offices Syndicated ownership of a strong firm personality as characterized by: ● Common values ● Common problem-solving philosophy ● Action orientation High-caliber, committed people Sensitivity to external factors/aversion to complacency Regenerating leadership

FIGURE 3.1   BUILDING AN INSTITUTION: BOWER'S TARGET VISION

You must realize in the '30s and '40s, the term "management consultant" was unknown. There were many years when it was almost looked on as something slightly nefarious. They would say, "oh, an efficiency expert" and that was the word that made all the men in McKinsey draw up in horror.[2]

Furthermore, many people in the United States regarded business itself as a job that was less desirable than working in professions like law or medicine—a bias that came up in a famous discussion between Marvin Bower and Adrian Cadbury of Cadbury Schweppes, during a lunch in New York in the late 1950s. Cadbury remarked, "I got into business because the legitimate careers were not open to a Quaker or third sons. I, like most of the explorers, am a third son. The first went into the military, the second into the ministry, and the third had nothing to do so he became an explorer. Exploration is no longer being funded by royalty, so I became a businessman. The more respected professions were not open to me."[3] Marvin laughed and disagreed, responding that, "Business properly conducted could be as high a calling as anything."

As if those challenges weren't enough, how likely was it that CEOs would open up to an outsider? At that time, it was rare for senior management to discuss their most critical business issues with third parties; when they did, they were usually faced with a disastrous business event or a specific problem that called for focused expertise—an accountant, an engineer, or a lawyer.

But Marvin had a passionate belief that CEOs in America had a real and unmet need for advice on policy and management and would be receptive to assistance from outsiders who understood issues from their perspective and who maintained high professional standards.

At Jones, Day, and during Marvin's six years at McKinsey prior to buying the firm, he had various experiences that validated the value of and respect for an outside professional adviser who could take an independent, unbiased view of the full business. Marvin often talked about an incident from his time at Jones, Day that illustrates the value and power of independence and the lesson it taught him. The head of a leading local investment banking firm requested that Jones, Day assist with a merger he wanted to bring about between Bethlehem Steel and Youngstown Iron and Steel. He expected antitrust action by the government and wanted the firm's help in defending the action. Mr. Ginn (the managing director of Jones, Day) studied the case and declined the assignment, convinced that the merger would violate the antitrust laws. The investment banker pointed out that fees might run to $1 million, that he was prepared to risk losing the case, and that he would take the case to another leading Cleveland firm if Jones, Day turned it down. Mr. Ginn still declined.

As Marvin put it, "The news swept through the firm. It made an especially deep impression on us young associates who were expecting our salaries to be cut (and they soon were). Our impression was further deepened when the law firm that took the case and fought it long, lost it. That news spread like wildfire through the business community. If the independence and professional stature of Jones, Day had not been established up to this point, Mr. Ginn's one brilliant and courageous professional decision established it then."[4]

Marvin also remembered James O. McKinsey as a role model for taking an unbiased, independent posture at clients:

> In client studies, Mac was always sensitive to the situations and viewpoints of the people in the client organization. He realized that

recommendations are neither accepted nor implemented on the basis of rational factors alone. But the trait that appealed to me most was Mac's independence with clients. He told them the truth as he saw it, even though it risked continuance of the relationship, and I noticed that clients appreciated his candor. This independence was important to me because it squared with my concept that a consulting firm should show the same independence that I had seen exercised at Jones, Day. I had observed how valuable that independence was to law clients, and I knew that it would also be valuable to consulting clients. I had expected Mac to be an independent person, and I was reassured to see that independence in action.[5]

Marvin firmly believed that the relationship with the client required working directly with the CEO. If the CEO were not involved in the issue, it was not important enough. If the client were not the CEO, the key messages might not get to the critical decision maker: "The chief executive is the integrative force in organizations; if we take his point of view, then we are solving problems with an integrating point of view." This philosophy stayed with Marvin throughout his consulting life, and he never feared the repercussions of holding to this requirement. John Stewart, a director who has been with McKinsey since 1961, relates an incident from 1982:

> General Motors did not like consultants. They did not use consultants, and they thought they were better than consultants or any other firm for that matter. It was just an institutional arrogance. Although the people themselves were not arrogant, they did have an institutional arrogance. They began to worry a little bit, so Roger Smith asked Marvin to come out and talk to him. Marvin interviewed 64 people on his reconnaissance of General Motors and reported to Roger Smith that when he had asked about General Motors' strategy to deal with the imports, the Japanese cars in particular . . . 63 of the 64 people said General Motors had no strategy. The only person who believed that General Motors did have a strategy was Roger Smith himself. It certainly wasn't clear to the next 63 people in the corporation. Concerned by this communication gap, Roger asked Marvin to start work on reorganization of North American operations. Not the corporate staff, not overseas, not R&D, but North American operations. . . .

North American operations reported to Jim McDonald, the president. So when Marvin went to talk to Jim and explain how he would go about doing such a piece of work, Jim said, "Of course, you'll report to me on this." Marvin said, "No, we won't. We only work for the chief executive and you are the president. We will work for Roger Smith." Later, Jim McDonald used to shake his head and say, "So many people have wandered through here who are more than happy to work for the president of General Motors, yet that man said he wouldn't work for me. He had to work for the chief executive." It did not diminish Jim's respect for Marvin. He had a way of doing it so earnestly that even those whom he might have otherwise affronted had respect for him.

That story about Marvin and Jim made it easier for us to work with the hierarchy in General Motors. . . . They did not resist help and really gave us a much easier time than they otherwise would have. Later they told us that.[6]

This is but one of many instances of Marvin's unwavering commitment throughout the years to the basic premise of management consulting that he and his partners had envisioned in 1939. As Marvin later confided to me, "I was not about to let the General Motors effort start without the CEO's commitment and involvement."[7]

During his early years at McKinsey, Marvin had also witnessed the downside of failing to address strategic problems. For example, as a sub-contractor to another third party at U.S. Steel, McKinsey had large teams solving tactical problems and thus was unable to address the more pressing CEO-level concerns.[8]

By insisting that McKinsey work with CEOs, Marvin felt he would greatly enhance the likelihood that the firm was focused on solving "major problems," a critical dimension of his vision of a professional firm. However, as he pointed out in his annual speech to the firm in 1953, this was a challenging, ongoing goal:

When I joined the firm in 1933, we were devoting most of our time to helping executives solve major management problems; auditing made up only a small part of our practice. In fact, nearly all of our engagements during the middle thirties were general surveys for banks, bondholders' committees, and directors to determine what could be done to put the company on a profitable basis.

It was during this period that we learned the basic importance of industry trends, competitive position, and other external economic factors. These studies gave us the raw material out of which we later fashioned the "top-management" approach.

The start of the European war in 1939 and the later entry of the United States into World War II gave our practice a definite stamp of techniques. For during this period, we naturally dedicated our efforts to solving production problems of any type at any level.

For these and other reasons, we are less positively dedicated to devoting our time chiefly to the solution of major management problems. . . . We have a long way to go in putting all of our man hours on major problems. Within twenty years—and probably within ten—we should have developed a reputation that will put us in a position, income-wise, to pass over all assignments that do not involve major problems.

That goal can be achieved, I believe, only as part of the overall development of our firm personality. It calls for our developing increased conviction, determination, courage, and skill in identifying and not accepting routine or non-major problems.[9]

Marvin did not just talk the talk. There are many anecdotes about how he took definitive steps to maintain independence and ensure that the firm's work primarily entailed solving major management problems. For example, he refused to work for Howard Hughes because the problem set forth by Mr. Hughes was not, in Marvin's opinion, the pressing problem for Hughes' business at the time.[10] And he did not believe that Hughes was willing to address what Marvin felt was the critical issue. All was not lost, however; Howard Hughes was looking for a financial adviser, and Marvin suggested that he talk to Malcolm Smith, his fraternity friend from Brown. Malcolm worked with the Hughes organization for the next 15 years.

In 1963, Marvin sent a strong signal to his firm that solving major business problems was at the heart of McKinsey's professional makeup when he fired an ostensibly successful partner in Chicago who worked often with Mead Johnson.[11] In fact, one of the primary reasons the partner was fired was for doing an excessive amount of work for Mead Johnson, much of which did not meet the "major problem" standard. Everyone in the firm knew about the firing almost immediately and knew the reasons behind the decision. How unusual was this type of action? Typically, in a service firm, firings would occur for the opposite reason—namely, failure to bring in enough business or revenue. As Marvin's action demonstrated, protecting the vision and reputation of McKinsey & Co. meant that the firm would resist temptation to seek business or revenue at any cost.

In communicating his vision of the profession, Marvin was precise in his use of language. Marvin made a point of articulating this precision. In a 1953 presentation, Marvin said:

> We are what we speak—it defines us—it is our image. We don't have customers, we have clients. We don't serve within an industry, we are a profession. We are not a company, we are not a business. We are a firm. We don't have employees, we have firm members and colleagues who have individual dignity. We don't have business plans, we have aspirations. We don't have rules, we have values. We are management consultants only. We are not managers, promoters, or constructors. And we are no longer executive recruiters. The big development in concentrating our efforts in our own field came in 1939 when we severed our affiliations with Scovell, Wellington & Company, then exclusively an auditing firm. At that time, we gave up calling ourselves "management engineers" and pioneered in using the designation "management consultants." Over the years, since 1939, we have resisted various excursions into side lines; and our convictions in this aspect of our firm personality are deep and well crystallized.[12]

And throughout the years, even as potentially lucrative opportunities arose, Marvin Bower stuck with the management consultant path. Any major deviations or sidelines, in his estimation, would undermine McKinsey's reputation and ability to perform as an unbiased, independent adviser to their clients.

Gary MacDougal, currently the head of the Illinois Republican party, the retired chairman and CEO of Mark Controls, and a partner who was with McKinsey from 1963 through 1969, remembers Marvin's negative response to one such opportunity in 1965:

We ended up in the L.A. office having two of the five biggest mergers in the country that year. . . . So we actually built a computer model that had the capability to evaluate acquisitions just like other capital investments—cash flow, et cetera. It was successful enough that Kidder Peabody wanted to buy it for $50,000. The word came back that Marvin said no, we were not in the business of selling software, we were a firm that did strategic consulting for boards of directors and it would be a conflict if we were building software to serve a client and sold it to somebody else.[13]

Because the vision of management consulting as a targeted profession was revolutionary, management consultants had to earn stellar reputations in order for the profession to be widely accepted and valued. This requirement presented somewhat of a circular challenge. A professional firm working hand in hand with top management executives to successfully solve major management problems would, by definition, develop a favorable reputation; however, at the same time, a professional service firm would be unlikely to gain access to top management without a favorable reputation.

To avoid getting in a cart before the horse situation, Marvin worked hard at building the firm's reputation throughout his time at McKinsey.[14] For example, in 1939 and 1940 he wrote several articles addressing organizational and financial issues with which U.S. companies were struggling at the time: "Untangling the Corporate Harness"; "Unleashing the Department Store—A Practical Concept of Department Store Organization"; "Beating the Executive Market"; and "The Management Viewpoint in Credit Extension." In 1939, he made a dozen speeches at professional organizations, played countless rounds of golf with prospective clients, lunched with executives at every opportunity, and encouraged everyone else at McKinsey to do the same.

Marvin's early experience at McKinsey had taught him that great consultants were not necessarily great salespeople and that selling a service was difficult even for the best salespeople. James O. McKinsey had hired great salesmen who, while having a track record of successful sales of physical products, were simply unable to sell professional services. Marvin did not view this as a disadvantage because he had also seen the pull created by Jones, Day's reputation.

As Marvin explained in a 1951 training program:

Genuine and sincere application of the professional approach must start with our approach to new clients.

It is our policy not to solicit clients or advertise our services—not because it is unethical but because to do so is inconsistent with the professional approach. We can't advertise our services or solicit clients without making implied promises of what we can do for clients. Since we don't, at the outset, know what we can accomplish, such promises do not meet high professional standards.

Furthermore, the professional approach to attracting clients helps get action on our recommendations. If we are *asked* to help (and we make proper arrangements), then the client feels some responsibility to aid us in our work and to act on our recommendations. There is a psychological but real difference in attitude between the client who has asked for our help and the one who has been "sold" and hence has a "show-me" attitude.[15]

In short, Marvin viewed management consulting as a profession, not a business. He believed that, as with doctors and lawyers, McKinsey & Co.'s reputation and its clients would come from putting client interests first, conducting themselves ethically at all times, only taking on work where they knew they could provide true value, and maintaining their independence by always telling clients the truth—not always the practice in the early days of consulting. Warren Cannon, a director who was with McKinsey from 1949 through 1988, says that Marvin "picked these principles, not believing they were God-given, but principles that he really believed in. In almost every case that I know of, he was absolutely right. They were in the long-term interest of the firm."[16]

The Institution: McKinsey & Co.

Early in his professional career, Marvin had seen many great institutions fail. He had also seen the power of Jones, Day, a high-caliber professional firm that respected its employees and gave them the opportunity to grow and achieve peak performance during the dispiriting years of the Great Depression. Bower knew that if McKinsey & Co. were to similarly empower its people, it could not be hierarchical—the cause of many business failures during the Depression and a barrier to the all-important flow of information to the CEO. Yet, virtually every organization in 1939 was structured as "command and control." Marvin recognized that his professional goal could only be met by creating an environment in which the youngest possible people felt free—if not compelled—to tell the truth, even when they disagreed with the boss. With this requirement in mind, Marvin conceived his vision of the institution as one firm with:

- *A national presence,* with multiple regional offices
- Syndicated ownership of a *strong firm personality* characterized by common values (including the right/obligation to dissent), and a common problem-solving/action-oriented philosophy
- *High-caliber, talented, and committed people* who were joining a career firm and would be active participants in the expression of the firm's personality and supported by sustainable economics
- Sensitivity to external factors/*aversion to complacency*
- *Regenerating leadership* so that the viability of the institution would never depend on a single generation of leaders

National Presence

To aspire to a national presence, when no other professional firm had launched regional offices, was a groundbreaking goal. The logic for a national presence was twofold.[17] First, professional respect in Marvin's mind was integrally tied to community involvement; therefore, for McKinsey & Co. to be involved with leading communities, local offices were required. Second, the targeted clients (major companies) were at that time increasingly national in scope themselves and could be better served if McKinsey & Co. had offices in close proximity. Having a single office serving a national marketplace would require sending teams to client sites for prolonged periods of time, increasing the likelihood that key associates would get burned out. This was a cost Marvin would not tolerate given the importance of people assets to the success of his vision. In fact, this desire for a national presence was the primary reason that Marvin parted ways with A. Tom Kearney, James O. McKinsey's first partner and head of the Chicago office in 1939. Tom felt that the firm should be Chicago-based, sending teams out to clients in any location in the country, no matter how distant. Although Marvin had great respect for Tom, this was a point of contention where Marvin was unwilling to compromise.

Strong Firm Personality

Defining, building, and syndicating the right firm personality was an absolute cornerstone of Marvin's vision of the institution. As he said at a staff conference in 1953:

> A distinctive and attractive personality is the key to building an outstanding reputation for a professional firm. And—except for its personnel—a good reputation is a professional firm's most valuable earning asset.[18]
>
> Marvin contended that the "personality" of a professional firm—like that of an individual—can be roughly defined as the total impression that the firm makes on those who come in contact with it or who hear or read about it. Thus the total impression that a firm makes depends on two principal factors: the collective personal impressions made by each individual, and the firm's objectives, major policies, and working approaches that guide (or should guide) each individual in what he or she does, writes, and says in carrying on firm activities.

Marvin then went on to say:

> Hence, the development of our firm personality is controlled by (1) our skill in selecting our consulting and operating staffs, (2) our skill in establishing objectives, policies, and working approaches, and (3) our effectiveness in communicating those objectives, policies, and working approaches to every individual and persuading him or her to follow them as positive guides to everyday action. We know our people make favorable personal impressions. Our major tasks, then, are those of communication and leadership.
>
> Just picture the power our firm could develop if the daily actions of each of us were really guided by the same objectives, policies, and working approaches. Day in and day out we would have people from coast to coast acting in unison and writing and saying words geared to the same concepts. Since our client executives and directors are the most influential business and government people in

America, we could rapidly become an even more potent force for good management than we are now.

Advancement toward that unattainable goal of complete unity has always been the underlying objective of these annual staff conferences. So we gather here again today to deepen our convictions about the firm personality and to further unify our actions in making that personality effective in daily action.[19]

With every passing year, Marvin's convictions about the power of a shared institutional personality only deepened, as he confirmed in 1974 when he wrote:

Any group of people that works together for years develops a philosophy, a tradition, a set of common values. One of the highest achievements in leadership is the ability to shape those values in a way that builds successful institutions. At its most practical level, the benefit of a managed value system is that it guides the actions of our people at all levels and in every part of our widespread empire; therefore, it permits greater self-control and self-governance. In a profession where service is all we offer, and where the majority of our professionals are relatively new, a strong culture that guides individual action is crucial. Our heritage [is] the ideas that have always guided our destiny.[20]

At Marvin's McKinsey & Co., the key characteristics that defined the firm personality were:

- Professional-value-based leadership by all. While Marvin provided important direction and constant reinforcement of all that was important to the success of the firm and the external embracing of management consulting as a valuable supplement to business management, he was not the "king." Rather, all in the firm were empowered to be leaders.
- A common problem-solving approach designed to rapidly get to the heart of the matter and spawn insightful, powerful solutions.
- A constant push (and creation of client pull) for meaningful action that took companies far along the path to success.

Marvin worked hard to syndicate adoption of the firm's personality by every new associate joining McKinsey & Co. Don Gogel, president and

CEO of Clayton, Dubilier & Rice, Inc. (a private equity investment firm), who was with McKinsey from 1976 through 1985, remembers his first encounter with Marvin:

> In the summer of 1973, before I went back to law school, I was invited to a lunch with Marvin, who routinely took out new associates. Marvin talked to us about the firm philosophy. He spoke so articulately you thought he was reading from a script. But, of course, he never had notes, and he went down the list of things that he thought made McKinsey & Co. a unique institution and why he thought they were important.
>
> That was really the first time I heard, from the source, descriptions of things like the one-firm philosophy and what it meant to always put the client's interests first, why language was important and the way we described our client relationships and our engagements was very important to him. He didn't like the more crass, commercial language that some of the other consulting firms used about customers as opposed to clients. He really didn't like people saying, "Well, I did this job for General Motors." He thought it diminished the quality of the professional relationship.
>
> He talked a lot about the importance of teamwork within the firm and why McKinsey & Co. was stronger because its engagement teams were able to function as a team. And, he really defined for me the essence of what it was like to work in a professional firm. It was great.[21]

Professional-Value-Based Leadership

Professional values are not personal values; they fundamentally differ in substance and purpose. In the legal profession, for example, of the nine canons of the law, five of them have to do with confidentiality, building trust, avoiding the appearance of impropriety, putting the client's interest first, and competence. The other four involve building the profession and protecting it from competition. However, Marvin Bower's example shows the power of living by business values with the same rigor and integrity as personal values. He believed that business values establish a mind-set and a compass for decisions made and actions taken. They provide parameters that define the business's objectives and means of competition and serving customers as they support the longer-term gain of the business. They involve a deliberate choice of means to achieve ends and serve as guidelines for all sorts of decisions in the pursuit. (See Figure 3.2.)

Professional values are not financial objectives. As Marvin often stated, while financial considerations cannot be ignored, business goals must not be financial; if they are, the business will fail to serve its customers and ultimately enjoy less profit.

Marvin incorporated business values and value-based logic and conviction in his work with CEOs, the analysis and resolution of business problems, and the creation of a self-renewing institution—McKinsey & Co. Business leaders have repeatedly talked about how they learned a lesson from Marvin on the essential importance of business values to their own leadership. Andrall Pearson, president and COO of Pepsico for 14 years, founding chairman of Yum! Brands, and with McKinsey from 1954 through 1970, credits Marvin with teaching him the importance of work environments, which he then focused on at both Pepsico and Yum! Brands.[22] Sir John Banham, former head of the English Audit Commission, credits what he learned from Marvin with influencing virtually all critical decisions in setting up and running the commission.[23] Joe Connor, the former senior partner of Price Waterhouse, credits the advice Marvin gave them in the early 1980s with being part of the reason that Price Waterhouse is not where Arthur Anderson is today.[24]

When every decision maker inside a company is making business decisions founded on a set of principles about what is important for the business and the way the business is conducted—or, as Marvin would say, "the way things are done around here"—the business has become a value-based institution that does not rely on a single leader.

Marvin's steadfast conviction that there was a need for integrity—and the respect-based business values that would be logically applied by all decision makers in a given company—was developed early, as we have seen from the role models in his family. The concrete form and specificity in the content of his business values resulted from his experience with those failing companies during the Great Depression in the early 1930s and other lessons learned while at Jones, Day, and during his early years as a McKinsey & Co. consultant.

Personality: Consultant Who Also Manages

Bower of McKinsey & Co. Gives Views on Giving Advice

By ROBERT E. BEDINGFIELD

The consultant is the man who helps the businessman with all the problems he himself has avoided by becoming a consultant.

That is the classical definition.

Marvin Bower acknowledges there may be something to it, saying that not all consultants would make good executives. Mr. Bower is both consultant and executive, because he is managing director of McKinsey & Co., the big management consulting concern.

Mr. Bower has been getting a great deal of mileage in recent months from a book he wrote last winter on his particular specialty. Its title, "The Will To Manage," suggests half of Mr. Bower's philosophy of management:

The executive must be determined to make his enterprise succeed regardless of outside conditions.

•

The other half of Mr. Bower's basic thesis, as it emerged in his book, as well as in a recent interview, is that the enterprise itself must have a formal structure. This, he explained in great detail, allows everyone to do his own job to the best of his ability, without stopping all the time to consider whether he is stepping into someone else's territory.

Mr. Bower's hero is the executive in the widget business in 1929, with 8 per cent of the market, who finds the widget market down by three-fourths in 1932 and goes after 32 per cent of what's left—or a little more. The Economist of London, in a review of Mr. Bower's book, intimated sadly that too many British corporations were satisfied with chief executives who would just tell the stockholders: "Sorry, chaps, people just aren't buying widgets."

•

As befits one who tells others how to do their jobs, Mr. Bower has the manner of a man well pleased with the way he has done his own. He does not flinch from a share of the credit for the considerable success the McKinsey organization has enjoyed. Thrust, on behalf of his new book, into the apparently unaccustomed role of interviewee, he did not fight the impulse to play consultant to the interviewer.

Mr. Bower has headed McKinsey since 1950. He was born in Cincinnati in 1903, but grew up in Cleveland, where his family moved while he was a youngster. He went to public grade school and high school in Cleveland and was graduated from Brown University in 1925.

At graduation, he had no fixed idea of how he wanted to make a living. His father, who was deputy county recorder of Cuyahoga County, Ohio, persuaded him to study law.

His wife, the former Helen McLaughlin, whom he had married in 1927, had been a classmate in high school.

"She was willing to work my way through college, so when I had my law degree and decided in 1928 to become a corporation lawyer, I felt a knowledge of business was necessary. I entered Harvard Business School, from which I got my M.B.A. in 1930."

Mr. Bower began his career with the Cleveland firm of Jones, Day, Cockley & Reavis. It was a fortunate time to start out, he recalled, because of the considerable activity in corporate law as a result of the number of corporate reorganizations that developed with the Depression.

With his business school education, his employers recommended him as secretary of a number of bondholder protective committees they represented. "Being the secretary of a bondholders' committee, I had plenty of opportunity of talking with the top officers of a leading corporation in reorganization," Mr. Bower remarked. He added that he was in a good position to determine why a corporation had gotten into trouble, "and I was able to help them reorganize their capital."

"In doing so, I found many corporations were operating without advisers at their top management level on some most serious management problems. I realized that many top corporate executives needed someone on the outside in whom they could place their trust and with whom they could discuss problems which they couldn't talk over with their own people because of career problems."

By 1933, Mr. Bower said he was convinced there was a future for him as a consultant. He got an interview with the late James O. McKinsey and got a job as the third man with the McKinsey firm's New York office. His initial assignment was to come up with recommendations for the bondholders' committee of the former Savoy Plaza Hotel here.

"I was doing exactly what I thought should be done—working on the management problems of the hotel corporation rather than its legal problem," Mr. Bower said. He told how he made an exhaustive study of the hotel's operations, how the hotel could be restored to profitability and how much of a capital structure a reorganized hotel company could hope to sustain.

•

Mr. Bower's second assignment with the McKinsey firm required his returning to Cleveland to help with the merger of three steel companies—Republic, Corrigan McKinney, and Otis. In the summer of 1934, he got his third assignment, which was to help prepare a study for Marshall Field & Co.

"By then, I was Mr. McKinsey's first lieutenant," Mr. Bower recalled. The firm, in its study, recommended the liquidation by Marshall Field of its wholesale business and the sale of some of its mills as well. Marshall Field invited Mr. McKinsey to carry the program through as chairman.

In 1937, after Mr. McKinsey died, Mr. Bower was made manager of the McKinsey New York office. He has held the largest participation in the partnership since 1940. He is now 63 years old, but Mr. Bower says he has absolutely no plans for retirement.

"We have an architectural plan for succession of management here," he said. "It's all on our drawing board. From age 65 to 70 each partner must be re-elected at the end of each year for the next year and at 70 we are required to retire. But I don't plan to retire from business. I will be a consultant as long as I can."

•

Their three sons having long ago grown up and established homes of their own, Mr. Bower and his wife live by themselves in a comfortable home in Bronxville, N.Y.

The one art object that he owns is integrated into his business. It is an abstract painting he bought several years ago in a London flea market. What persuaded him to buy it was the fact that the artist had titled it "Forces at Work."

It hangs in his office and Mr. Bower says that when he looks at it, he doesn't see a lot of graceful strokes of the brush. Instead, it reminds him, he said, "that there are a great many forces at work within and without" the corporation he advises. And he sets forth each day to make those forces work for him instead of against him.

Tommy Weber

Marvin Bower, managing director of McKinsey & Co., before abstract, "Forces at Work"

FIGURE 3.2   PERSONALITY: CONSULTANT WHO ALSO MANAGES
(*The New York Times*, July 23, 1967 © The New York Times Company)

Marvin's value-based leadership qualities that were admired and emulated can be summarized as six sets of characteristics, some of which may
seem paradoxical; but Marvin was able to strike the right balance in his
leadership, thus interlocking these puzzle pieces into a coherent, cohesive
pilotage. Had WorldCom, Enron, and other recently failed businesses
been guided by Marvin Bower's business values, they would not have
imploded. Marvin's success and the success of those who learned from him
came from the following value-based leadership qualities.

1. Put the client's interests first and separate yourself from the job. In a letter on leadership that Eisenhower wrote in 1967, he commented on advice
Marvin had given him, "an admonition of a man whom I admired greatly."
Eisenhower wrote that Marvin had said, "Always take your job seriously,
never yourself."[25] This capability enabled Marvin to understand his flaws
as well as his strengths and do what was best for the client. For example,
when a client was a particularly sensitive individual and not amenable to
being "beaten up by the facts," or was arrogant in style, Marvin recognized
that he was not the right person for such situations and would ask Everett
Smith or Carl Hoffman, two of his early partners, to step in and manage
the relationship. On the other hand, Marvin never held back the truth
from a client: That would not have been in the client's best interest. As
Harvey Golub, the retired chairman of American Express and formerly
with McKinsey 1966 through 1973 and 1977 through 1983, remembers
from his early days with McKinsey, if there was one thing to always keep
at the top of his mind, it was to serve clients well:

> When I joined the firm, I went out to lunch with Ron Daniel,
> who was then a group leader in the New York office. During
> lunch, I said to him, "Ron, can you tell me what it is I have to do
> to make it around here?" I was really asking, What are the impor-
> tant things? And he said, "Serve clients well over an extended
> period of time." I said, "Come on, Ron, tell me what you really
> have to do to make it here." And he said something like, "If you
> believe anything else, you won't be successful." He didn't tell me
> how to serve clients well. He didn't tell me what the other things
> were. But I believed him. How did he pick that up? He picked
> that up from Marvin, and from Gil Clee [the managing director of
> the firm who followed Marvin], and other early partners at that
> time. There are very few CEOs who have ever created something

that will outlast them for that kind of period of time. You know, Alfred Sloan, Thomas Edison, but it is not a long list.[26]

2. Be consistent yet open-minded. Marvin Bower was consistent in his values, in culture, in mission, and in the respect he accorded others. He knew who he was, what he believed in, and what he could or could not accomplish. Every individual he encountered during his long life met the same Marvin Bower, a man who never told people what he thought they wanted to hear and who ignored ephemeral management fads and fashions. But, according to all those who knew him, he unfailingly recognized real change, learned from it, and mastered it. Al Gordon, who was with Kidder Peabody from 1931 through 1994, and chairman from 1957 through 1986, saw Marvin "as someone who was listening to learn—he wanted every fact and view he could collect to better understand. He wasn't listening to attack. He was listening to learn."[27] Another observer cited an apparent contradiction: "He was a very conservative man and still open-minded. He really was."[28] In a training program in the early 1950s, Marvin explained his philosophy: "Perhaps the most important requirement of all for seizing our opportunities is the maintenance by firm [McKinsey] members generally of open-minded, broad-gauged, and flexible attitudes. Our internal resistance to change has been, at times, exasperating and frustrating. Although we should of course avoid hasty decisions and ill-considered moves, we must also cultivate a greater internal willingness to do new things and to try new ways."[29]

3. Center problem solving on the facts and on the front line. Marvin's reverence for facts is legendary. He always insisted on assembling the essential facts, including external facts, to create a context for a business's behavior; analyzing where the facts pointed; and having the determination to follow the fact trail wherever it led. He was a master of making sure the right facts were captured and of weaving concepts and details together in a way that was compelling and action-driven. He also recognized that business problem solving is often about externally driven change and that the need to change is often first understood and can only be brought about by those on the front line—the salesperson interfacing with the customer, the machine operator struggling with a difficult design, or the demanding service requirement. In 1992, while advising McKinsey & Co. on revamping its value statement, Marvin began by interviewing the firm's frontline associates to capture their sense of the values and related issues.

4. View problems and decisions in the context of the whole and in terms of the immediate actions to be taken. Although Marvin valued the importance of facts, he also believed that isolated facts do not lead to solutions; rather, having imagination and context to see where the facts lead creates solutions and paths. During Marvin's 59 years with McKinsey, there wasn't a business meeting he attended that didn't begin with his asking about how a problem fit into the bigger picture and how this should be factored into an action plan. The value and reputation of management consulting can be diminished by analyses and recommendations that lie idle on the shelf. The inventor of this profession was committed to making sure action did happen—action that was consistent with the mission of the company and that had fast payback both emotionally and financially.

5. Inspire and require people to be their best. Somehow or other, Marvin managed to make the firm and its work extremely important to each member. It became, for most, the largest, most important thing in their working lives. Marvin, more than anyone else, created that environment by working at it endlessly and in countless ways: in casual comments, in training meetings, in staff conversations, in memoranda. Simultaneously, Marvin could be ruthless. For example, he believed that no moment should go to waste, and that consultants should use their lunch time to meet with and touch base with old and potential clients. Associates in New York were afraid to go out for lunch with a friend to a restaurant Marvin might patronize, because if he saw you there, he might remind everyone in the office that lunch was not a social hour but another opportunity for people at the firm to use their time effectively. And he might cite you as an example of poor time management.

6. Communicate the values of the company over and over again to ensure that people in the firm will understand them, embrace them, and translate them into action. Marvin tirelessly and constantly preached the values that formed the firm's personality without the message becoming stale and heard but ignored. Warren Cannon remembers how Marvin always managed to bring the firm's values to life: "He did it in a way that I never found repetitive or boring because he seized on instance after instance that illustrated either the power of the message, the way in which we could do what we set out to do, or the mistakes that we were making. Far more often, he would talk about good things and name names. He never passed up an opportunity to celebrate success. Every time somebody negotiated a study the way he thought it ought to be negotiated and he found out about it, he would tell people and give credit and praise for it. When people took risks with clients because they were doing what they thought was best for the client, and he found out about it, he would talk about it in detail."[30]

When the firm's fundamental values were violated, Marvin took swift and decisive action, as he did in 1959, sending a clear message to his organization. Chuck Ames, the retired chairman of Acme Cleveland, and a partner of Clayton, Dubilier & Rice, Inc., who was with McKinsey from 1957 through 1972, remembers one such instance:

> The best performing associate in the office was Gerry Andlinger. He was very smart and viewed as key. He was working with Stromberg Carlson on a top management organization study. He had recommended an organization change and the creation of a new officer's position, and recommended himself for the position. I don't think he recommended himself in writing, but in discussions with the client he recommended himself for that job. He was doing work for Dawes Bibby who was a good friend of Marvin's. [Dawes] called Marvin . . . and told him what had happened. Marvin asked Gerry if this was true, and Gerry said, "Yes." So Marvin said, "You have 30 minutes to clear out. You're all done. And if you need some help, I'll be glad to get the building services to help you get your things out, but you're out." That was it.
>
> Gerry was clearly the smartest, if not one of the two or three smartest guys in the firm. He was a real loss to the firm, but that didn't make any difference to Marvin. His position was that you live by these principles or you're out of here. Marvin made a point of communicating that what Gerry did is not how we run the firm. I think this was on a Friday, and Gerry had a dinner party that night. My wife and I were there. I said, "Gerry, I'm sorry to hear about this." Gerry said, "No, he did the right thing. I violated principles, I got caught, it's the right thing—throw me out."[31]

This event left its mark on a number of people. As Ron Daniel, managing director of McKinsey from 1976 through 1988, and currently active with McKinsey and a member of the Harvard Corporation, described it: "I always remember the time Marvin was willing to sacrifice one of the most talented resources in the firm when we needed talent—it didn't take him five seconds to make the decision. When I asked him about the loss, Marvin responded, 'If you are not willing to take pain to live by your principles, there is no point in having principles.' "[32]

As Everett Smith, an early partner, described listening to Marvin speak: "I used to sit there and say, 'That son of a bitch. He's going to do it again.' He'd charm them right out of their socks again, give them the old pitch and the boys would go away just all pepped up, including me. I began to believe it. I said, 'He's got the vision and we can do it.' "[33]

Marvin was able to live with these apparent paradoxes and garner respect and trust from virtually everyone he knew or worked with. As Jack Dempsey who joined McKinsey in 1987, described Marvin:

> He was plenty smart and plenty stylistic. But what I admired most was his absolutely compelling, unemotional logic, absolute disarming candor, a directness that was completely untainted by self-interest, and an unwillingness to mince words. [I also admired his] unbelievable precision in communications, and yet simple style, almost monosyllabic . . . every word concise, simple, well chosen. The last thing you came away with was that Marvin was just absolutely relentless in constantly thinking about how to make us better.[34]

Integrity-based business values and the discipline to adhere to them are more important today than ever before. As businesses grow and increasingly cross and link cultures and countries, and as communications change in scope and speed, so grows the importance and power of adhering to a meaningful and enduring set of business values as a compass that can keep a firm on course through challenging and increasingly complex situations.

As noted in John Dewey's *Ethics,* published in 1908 (a book that was still on Marvin's shelf at the time of his death), ethics and culture are connected etymologically: "The terms 'ethics' and 'ethical' are derived from a Greek word ethos which originally meant customs, usages, especially those belonging to some group as distinguished from another, and later came to mean disposition, character."[35] Thus, it is the business values that create the culture of a given company. And, as history shows, an institution's culture determines its success or failure.

Common Problem-Solving Approach

The firm's values constituted the glue holding the firm's personality together, with the overarching value to always put the client's interests first. And the common problem-solving approach was crafted with the client's best interests in mind.

In order to best serve CEOs, it would be necessary to adopt a top management mind-set that considered critical external factors while simultaneously mining important information from deep within the organization that typically did not flow up to senior executives. This would enable the consultant to focus on the right problem(s) and solve problems in a prioritized fashion.

As described by Marvin in a 1941 training program:

> The top-management approach calls for consideration of external factors, such as industry trends and competitive position. If we are to establish a reputation as solvers of major management problems, we must be able to identify and evaluate the impact of economic, social, and political trends; we must consider these forces in formulating policy and organization recommendations.
>
> Thus, the top-management approach has these essential characteristics:
> 1. We make an overall diagnosis before we decide on the specific problems to be solved.
> 2. We determine the order in which problems should be solved. We try to persuade the client to let us put first things first.
> 3. In the solution of problems, we take an integrating approach and recognize that: (a) external factors are usually important in the solution of internal problems; (b) very few problems can be solved in any single department or section of the business or government agency.[36]

What Marvin wanted to avoid was an institution that did a good job of answering the wrong question. He constantly advised his teams of consultants to make sure they were answering the right question and not [simply] fixing a signal of the problem. He said, "The most frequent cause of failures in business is not people who answered the right questions incorrectly, but people who answered the wrong questions correctly. I have seen many companies "incrementalize" themselves into a corner, through a series of small—what appeared optimal—decisions, often based on erroneous assumptions."[37]

Marvin also was quick to remind his organization that, as consultants, they were often better positioned than client personnel to uncover the right questions. He maintained that being in an organization [as opposed to being an external consultant] is an advantage, because you understand the power structure. But, it is also a disadvantage because you take, as given, things that are really only assumptions.[38]

Pinpointing the right problem was crucial if McKinsey & Co. was to help its clients avoid failures—and Marvin's early experience at Jones, Day and at McKinsey & Co. had brought him face to face with numerous business failures. He believed that such failures stemmed from top management's disconnect with reality—not only the reality of internal signals from the front line that something big was amiss, but also the reality of external changes and trends. In stressing the importance of external factors, Marvin often told the Pierce Arrow story:

> In 1934—about a year after I joined the firm—I was assigned to a study of the Pierce Arrow Motor Car Company, which had closed down and was in bankruptcy. The purpose of our study, which was made at the insistence of creditors, was to determine whether the company should be refinanced.
>
> The "Pierce Arrow" was the "Rolls Royce" of its day—outstanding in engineering, distinctive in styling, and highly prized. The reason for the failure quickly became clear—the car had been priced out of the market and the less expensive line that had been developed came too late to save the business. We recommended immediate liquidation; but the local banks (in Buffalo) pumped in another million dollars before the company sputtered and died.
>
> . . . That close look at the agonizing death of a business giant is seared in my memory. It stimulated me, as a student of management, to discover for myself what has been discovered by others:

The success of any enterprise requires that it be kept effectively responsive to its environment.[39]

Marvin could see that the rate of external change was accelerating, creating major challenges for many businesses. During the 1950s, Marvin often quoted Sir Charles (C.P.) Snow's *The Two Cultures and the Scientific Revolution:*

> During all human history until this century, the rate of social change has been very slow. So slow, that it would pass unnoticed in one person's lifetime. That is no longer so. The rate of change has increased so much that our imagination can't keep up. There is *bound* to be more social change, affecting more people, in the next decade than in any before. There is *bound* to be more change again, in the 1970s.[40]

An integrated approach would be required to solve business problems created by an ever increasing rate of external change. Marvin's basic concept of integration was derived from James O. McKinsey, whose book *Budgetary Control* is credited with being the first book on budgetary accounting—using accounting as a holistic, integrative mechanism to help manage a business, and the general survey outline, a consulting tool originated by McKinsey to look across a business before diving into a problem.[41] McKinsey is profiled in *The Golden Book of Management* by Lyndall F. Urwick, which describes the life and work of pioneers in management.

> Having grasped this unifying principle, he [McKinsey] had one intellectual advantage over the majority of his contemporaries in management who had been trained as engineers; his basic education in law and accountancy had taught him to look at a business as a whole. From this appreciation of every business as a unity, coupled with his practical experience as a management consultant, flowed his special contributions to management thought and practice.[42]

Action Orientation

Solving the right problems with the right perspective was at the core of the problem-solving approach that Marvin promoted. However, at the end of the day, a great solution was of little value sitting on a shelf unimplemented. Shortly after joining McKinsey & Co., Marvin had an encounter that he would never forget in his drive to move clients to action:

> Back in 1933, I took the train from Cleveland the night before I reported for work in New York. On the train I met Aims C. Coney, then a vice president of a Cleveland bank and now a vice president of the Mellon Bank in Pittsburgh and a director of two client companies. Aims asked where I was going and I told him I had joined a management engineering firm, as the field was then known.
>
> Aims's comment still comes clearly to mind. "The trouble with management engineers," he said, "is that they write up improvement programs in nicely bound reports and then go on their way. In my desk are at least six reports containing what seem to be sound recommendations about which nobody is doing anything. If your new firm can get its clients to adopt its recommendations, I predict a brilliant future for it."
>
> Naturally, when I reported for work the next morning, I began to explore our performance in getting action on our recommendations. I was disappointed in my findings. That aspect of our firm personality did not shine forth. In fact, we were guilty as charged.[43]

Getting clients to adopt recommendations requires client ownership of recommendations. From this, the notion of working in partnership with the client was born. If the effort were perceived as being isolated from the client, no matter how right or applicable the recommendations were, they would likely be viewed as threatening or not relevant. Harvey Golub remembers how, as a partner at McKinsey & Co., he had to stand firm to establish the right working model with Gulf Oil:

> I was invited to go to visit Gulf Oil in Pittsburgh. I met with the president, a fellow named Tommy Lee, about a strategy project that he wanted to undertake for one of the four major businesses within Gulf Oil. . . . He indicated that the man who was currently head of it would be stepping down in about a year and retiring and somebody else would get the job. And having laid out the strategy, the new person coming in would be well prepared and have the

blueprint for going ahead. I explained to Tommy that I did not think that was the right way to go . . . he ought to figure out who should be the replacement and have him work on the team so that the strategy [was] his and therefore would get implemented. Tommy said he didn't think that was right and he didn't want to do it.

I was disappointed. I went back to New York. Marvin asked me how it went and I explained the situation. Without any hesitancy at all, he said, "You did exactly the right thing." And he wrote a memo to the firm, explaining why not doing the work at Gulf Oil was the right thing.

About three months later, I got a call from Tommy saying they had rethought the issue and had concluded that I was correct. He asked if I would now do the study as they had identified the person who would take over the unit and work with me as the project manager. I said, "Sure." And we started the work. I told Marvin about that. And he said, "Marvelous." [He] wrote another memo that started out, "Remember when I told you what Harvey did with Gulf three months ago; well here's what's happened since."[44]

This need for client action was something Marvin continually emphasized. In a speech in the 1950s, he said:

> Our greatest opportunity for personality improvement during the next 20 years is found in stepping up our effectiveness in getting clients to adopt our recommendations. We have much to learn in the techniques of getting action. We have even more to learn in developing the courage and skill to become better negotiators and better persuaders.[45]

High-Caliber, Talented, and Committed People

Marvin's early professional experience at Jones, Day had convinced him that the two most important assets a professional firm could possess were its reputation and the caliber and professional standards of its people. Certainly, these assets went hand in hand, since reputation would be, in a large part, determined by the aggregate of individual impressions made by each member of the firm.

Marvin needed to create an institution that would attract and retain high-caliber people and grow and harvest their professional skills, enabling each one to contribute to a positive reputation for the firm. Such an outcome would reinforce the firm's external reputation, growing its client base, thereby increasing McKinsey & Co.'s ability to continue to attract high-caliber employees.

Attracting and retaining the best people meant creating a firm in which smart people could be proud of the culture, their work, and their impact in the business world and could be part of an externally legitimate, valued profession. And Marvin envisioned a significant investment in training and in his personal commitment of time to people, in return for which firm members would not live for the moment, but rather have a genuine concern for the ongoing viability and sustainability of the firm for their successors. The consultants also had to make reasonable money—not as much as an entrepreneur, but, like a lawyer or doctor, enough to make a good living. Beyond that, Marvin needed to create the very best group of collectively energized talent—not just good individuals, but people who could work effectively together within the context of the firm's personality and work well with clients. This, in turn, meant hiring raw talent, right out of school, rather than experienced "experts." Based on what he had seen in the law, Marvin valued imagination more than experience.

Alignment with Firm Values/Culture

Marvin sought individuals who were comfortable with both the CEO and the frontline employees, and who believed in and would be committed to the firm's values: The more those values were articulated and adapted, the stronger the pull for both new, high-quality employees and new, high-quality clients.

In linking the culture and the people, Marvin said in a 1954 speech:

> The professional approach—when skillfully and personally applied
> *on the job* by partners and principals—cuts people turnover in these
> ways:
> 1. Seeing good work done by "pros" builds confidence all
>   around.

2. If associates see the office making solid growth accomplishment based on good performance, they gain confidence in the firm and are less likely to be receptive to outside offers.

3. A true concentration on the professional approach gives real "tone" to the office; and this builds good morale in the staff.

4. Turning down assignments that cannot be properly negotiated shows confidence of the firm in itself—and this helps build morale that holds associates.[46]

In fact, the culture/value system was key to retaining people and building their commitment to the firm and to a profession that was relatively new and, in the early years, unproven. As John Stewart describes his experience:

After three or four weeks with the firm and on a study looking at a possible merger for Harris Intertype and Itek, we met with Marvin at his round table.

We began going through the draft document. I was really just a fact finder. I had had very little experience. I had been in a merger but had never done one and Marvin started making statements about Itek that didn't ring true to me, and having been brought up in a hierarchical corporation, I felt you didn't talk back when you didn't know someone. But I'd been told that at McKinsey you had to call things as you saw them. I heard him rework positions with other team members earlier in the hour, searching for what was right.

So, finally at one point Marvin said, "Isn't that right?" I then said, "Mr. Bower," and he interrupted me and told me to call him Marvin. I said with great trepidation, "No sir, it is not right," and I explained why we ought to conclude something different. And Marvin said, "Oh, thank you," and crossed out what he had written and wrote out what I said. I thought, "Wow, this is different, this is really different." So, here it was in living color and I was impressed. As you can tell, 1961 was 41 years ago and I still remember it. Because here was someone who was doing what he said we should do and demonstrating to a young associate what the firm was about. That was impressive.[47]

Fred Gluck, managing director of McKinsey & Co. from 1988 through 1994 and currently advising McKinsey, describes how the firm's values became very clear and attractive to him during his first study experience in 1967:

> I was on an R&D strategy study for Owens Corning. The team was not delivering the right value. On my way out one night, I ran into Marvin and he asked me how things were going and I told him. The next morning when I arrived at my desk at 8 A.M., there was a note to see Marvin. I thought, "My God, I won't have any work." When I arrived in Marvin's office, Rod Carnegie, the partner in charge of the study was on the phone. They were discussing what was the right thing to do. They decided not to charge the client for the effort to date and to modify what we were doing over the next few months. I walked out thinking this is a firm I want to be part of.[48]

Mac Stewart, who joined McKinsey & Co. in 1952, captures the uniqueness of being a part of McKinsey:

> The first delightful experience I had was that I had no boss, that I was not a boss. And having been in the army for six years and having worked for an advertising agency, and having had an executive job at a paper company, this was just delightful. No boss. And this obligation to dissent. This was Marvin's principle. It came directly from him. If you read his principles, he dissented on his first study, right in the beginning, and laid the groundwork. And very few people have the guts to dissent.[49]

Not only did Marvin respect the right to dissent, he let others learn from experience by giving them the freedom to try things that he did not always believe in. Quincy Hunsicker, a now retired director who joined McKinsey in 1963, offers a powerful example:

> Rod Carnegie, a new partner at the time, and I suggested taking stock rather than fees for a company that was in the process of reorganization. And Marvin was quite open. He said, "I wouldn't do it. Because I don't think it is the way we ought to consult. I'm opposed to it, but if you guys think it's a good thing and want to

try it, try it." He was very remarkable—for someone who was so innately conservative to be able to take so many risks. His idea [was] that if you get disappointed, you will learn. You will learn better than you ever would if I told you and didn't let you try. It was a controllable situation. And it didn't work. And we both learned a lesson. No matter how smart you think you are, sometimes there are things you can't turn around and don't overestimate your ability to work miracles.[50]

Clearly, the lack of a hierarchical structure in the McKinsey & Co. culture was both novel and compelling for its employees. From the beginning of his ownership of the firm, Marvin promoted the notion of "hiring people with knowledge we didn't have and who are better than ourselves." David Hertz, one of the pioneers in the field of operations research, remembers being hired by Marvin in 1962:

Marvin was a little bit scared of technology—I was a technologist. He recognized the need for problem-solving tools. When I first met him, Marvin wanted to know what we did in this strange world of operations research. Marvin was a curious guy—he was easy for me to get along with. He was very curious about what I knew and why I knew it. What did I know that Marvin felt that he ought to know, and how could it help management . . .[51]

Training and Commitment of Marvin's Personal Time

Not only did Marvin want to start with a base of raw talent that exceeded his own, he was willing to make a major investment in that talent not only through formal training but also through commitment of his own time.

When Marvin first joined McKinsey & Co. in 1933, there was only one formal training tool—James O. McKinsey's General Survey Outline. However, Mac [James O. McKinsey] valued training. In fact, attendance at a training session was typically the first exposure to the firm in those days. Marvin remembered being trained in the use of the General Survey Outline three weeks before his formal start date:

I can still see and hear James O. McKinsey describing the complexity and interrelations of business problems and the use of the General Survey Outline in solving them. I vividly recall paying close attention for fear that Mac would call on me for a spot answer to a case problem—and although I was a new associate I was not passed over.[52]

This early training was not lip service: Marvin and others at McKinsey's original firm routinely applied this tool to quickly analyze a client's existing situation and potential within a full context before defining the real problem at hand.

In designing a more expansive training program, the General Survey Outline continued to play a central role. As Marvin noted in a 1941 training session:

> The General Survey Outline is still the primary instrument for applying the top-management approach. Under the philosophy of the General Survey Outline, we do consider external factors and we don't start working on procedures before we have considered policy and organization questions.[53]

From 1949 through 1957, effecting change was the focus of the monthly training sessions. Marvin insisted that this was the most critical capability to be learned and often Peter Drucker would come in and lead part of the session. According to Harvey Golub, the leader of McKinsey & Co. training several years later, the training activity of the firm was designed at different stages to bring people who didn't know how to consult to become consultants and then to become managers of consultants and then leaders of consultants, and that was the focus. But it was also more than that—it was to inculcate values so that you could go anywhere in the firm and people would approach things, think about things in a similar way and you would recognize that way to think about it. So that if you were in New York, you could go do a study in Japan and it would be the same firm. It would not be a Japanese branch. It would be the same firm doing things in the same way. Not doing things in the same way in a mechanical sense, but doing things in the same way in a broad-thinking sense. And that was the strength of the firm. As Harvey put it, "The training program was not just a skills development program, it was an acculturation process. One of the things that McKinsey did was have the leaders of the firm do the teaching, and that is one of the things I did at American Express as well. The training programs that we did were all at least started by and the initial ones led by the senior leaders of the firm."[54]

A key measure Marvin used to determine the success of training was this acculturation process, or "organizational socialization," as defined by Edgar H. Schein, a leading organizational behaviorist at MIT:

> Organizational socialization is the process of "learning the ropes," the process of being indoctrinated and trained, the process of being taught what is important in an organization. . . . The concept refers to the process by which a new member learns the value system, the norms, and the required behavior patterns which, from the organization's point of view or group's point of view, it is necessary for any new member to learn. This learning is defined as the price of membership.[55]

Teaching was not limited to formal training events. Marvin constantly coached and encouraged others to coach, and, as shown by the following story, he was extraordinarily willing to invest his own time in his people. Carel Paauwe, chairman of Rekkof (the successor to Fokker), and with McKinsey & Co. from 1970 through 1998, has a vivid memory of an incident some 20 years ago, when he was hospitalized during a partners' conference in Holland. At that time, Marvin was 80 but was still attending all of these conferences. Paauwe was stunned when Marvin walked into his hospital room over 100 kilometers from the conference location. After warmly expressing his concern and best wishes for a speedy recovery, Marvin asked Paauwe, who was the partner in charge of recruiting, how things were going.

> Marvin stayed for over an hour and a half, stressing just how important recruiting was for McKinsey's future, making it a responsibility that could not be delegated to junior members of the firm. It was amazing how he . . . gave me the Ten Commandments on recruiting, in a very nice way. He said, have you thought of this? Do this. And all these good things that we now all take for granted. The importance of hiring, the importance of rejecting someone and how you do that, the care and carefulness that is needed in these decisions. The following morning, a note from Marvin arrived, underlining and expanding on some of the points he had discussed.[56]

Paauwe realized that this visit conveyed a message:

> [While] he demonstrated so personally what it is to really care about [people], I realized myself that this warmth and this care—

that there was a price tag on that. That at the end of the day there was no nonsense. It wasn't just all nice and fuzzy and friendly and stroking. It was stroking with a purpose. It was, "Yes, I care about you *but* I want you to perform." Perform in the study sense, or perform on the intellectual scene, or perform in terms of firm values. So, it was goal oriented. Very much.[57]

Career Firm

Succeeding at McKinsey required a level of commitment and an identification with the firm and its personality associated with a career mentality. Marvin credits James O. McKinsey with beginning this orientation. He believed that James O. McKinsey clearly had the vision that a firm like McKinsey can best be built with people who are strongly motivated by the opportunity to make a permanent career with the firm.[58]

Marvin embraced the career firm concept and, over time, the firm strengthened personnel policies and programs and its own economics to make this concept increasingly effective. Marvin took pride in saying, "I am confident that no other firm in our field comes even close to ours in real dedication to the career concept or to a sound administration of that concept."[59] It is interesting to note that, despite that fact, only one in six hires stays with McKinsey & Co. for five years or more (the firm has a well-publicized "up or out" policy); a number of partners estimate that over 80 percent of today's new hires view McKinsey & Co. as a career firm within six months of joining.[60] The numbers suggest a level of employee commitment that perhaps would not be expected in a business environment in which companies of all types were competing for highly talented people. As Marvin emphasized, commitment is two-way. When people are hired, it is expected they will make it at McKinsey. When separation occurs, it is expected that a lifetime relationship will follow. On the other hand, committed employees are likely to work that much harder. For Marvin's part, he always made a point of making sure that, when people left McKinsey, they always went on to great jobs.[61]

Sound Economics

Establishing sound economics was essential to creating a career firm and building an enduring institution, but it was never an explicitly stated characteristic of Marvin Bower's vision of the target institution. This was a conscious decision on his part because he felt that he could rely on a sterling reputation and outstanding people, and that being beholden to specific financial goals would undermine the firm's ability to maintain the independence necessary to provide valuable services to its clients. And, as usual, Marvin remained true to this belief throughout his life.

In 1990, at the age of 87, Marvin attended a McKinsey & Co. directors' conference. One of the senior directors began a discussion on how to improve the economics and the firm's business system. Marvin asked Fred Gluck, then managing director of the firm, "Although I'm not a director of the firm, may I say something?"[62] Fred said, "Of course." Marvin stood up and said, "How can a professional firm have a business system? I don't think the partners of this firm ought to be talking about how to improve the economics to the partners. I think the only topic that the partners of this firm ought to talk about is how to serve clients better. If we serve clients better, we will have handsome incomes. If we focus on our incomes, we will have neither clients nor income." And he sat down. As Fred Gluck remembers, ". . . and the conversation ended. Because he was absolutely right."[63] As Lord Norman Blackwell, current chairman of SmartStream Technologies Ltd. and with McKinsey from 1978 through 1995, remembers, "It is a memory emblazed in my head. It was a time when a lot of focus and peer pressure in the world and even at McKinsey was on economics and commercial aspects of business. While the discussion on the firm's business system was happening, I was uncomfortable but didn't feel I had the tenure to object. When Marvin stood up, I was cheering. He relieved a lot of pressure in the room. It gave me courage."[64]

Although Marvin aspired to a value system in which the ultimate, most important measure of success was stellar service to the client, he was also pragmatic. When he and his partners bought McKinsey & Co., the economics were not sound. Steve Walleck, a former director of McKinsey who worked on several client engagements with Marvin, recalled the importance Marvin placed on economic stability. When he asked Marvin why he had not changed the name of his firm to Bower & Co., Walleck remembers that Marvin smiled and winced as he responded:

> When Mac left the firm to go to work [as chairman] for Marshall Field, Mac took the cash with him. There wasn't enough money in the bank account to pay next month's salaries. The rent was due.

And I don't remember what our client situation was specifically, but I do remember that it wasn't robust.

My partners and I had to go out and convince clients to keep us on, even though we had lost our principal partner. I had to seek out new engagements as the head of the firm, even though my name was not McKinsey.

I resolved right then that I would never place my successor in the same position of having to explain why his firm wasn't named after him. So we kept Mac's name on the door, and I've never regretted it.[65]

Given the strained financial position of the firm, Marvin had to move quickly to stabilize the firm's economics. And he had to do so in a manner that would be compatible with the maintenance of independence and other critical values of the firm. Within a year after he and his partners assumed ownership of McKinsey & Co., Marvin established and began to charge value-based fees to clients. This approach was at odds with the dominant practice of billing on a per-diem basis, but, in Marvin's estimation, was a fair billing method for the value received by the clients. Expenses were to be managed carefully, with consultants directed to act as if it were their own dollars being spent, not the client's.

Marvin had seen value-based fees work effectively at Jones, Day, and he was of the belief that, as a professional firm, McKinsey & Co. should do the same. In 1985, Marvin explained his rationale:

We started out in 1939 billing on a per-diem basis. That was common among accountants and other consulting firms. You'd just multiply the number of days by the rate and that's the bill. In about 1941, I said, "This is ridiculous and we've got to change it. You cannot measure value by hours. Lawyers don't and we shouldn't. [At least that was the case in those years.] If we run up hours that aren't valuable, we shouldn't charge them." And so we had quite a struggle among our partners to change fees to either a fixed lump sum decided in advance or a monthly fee with no per diems and an estimate of how long it takes. Lump sums ... was a risky way because we couldn't tell what the problems were, but after a struggle in the firm we got away from per-diem rates.

Some partners were afraid that clients wouldn't go for it. . . . And it turned out to be an unfounded fear. This is a matter of the courage of the consultant, the partner and his confidence in the value, and his confidence in himself. This came from the law.

Now the law has slipped back to by the hour, not by the day, but when I was practicing law in Jones, Day my mentor, Mr. Ginn, would say, "Now, you've been doing quite a lot of work on Industrial Rayon, and here are the hours. These hours come out to $80,000 dollars, with annual billing. How much would you bill them? Then I'd say, "Well, we worked on this and we worked on that," I said, "I think those are pretty valuable pieces of work for them and I don't see how time can measure it." He said, "You're right on target now. Just tell me, what figure you would put up?" I said, "I'd put up $90,000." He said, "You're wrong. It's going to be $100,000." He sent out the bill, $100,000 dollars annual fee for legal services. Then he said, "If they come . . . and argue about that," he'd say, "You just take a pen and scratch out that bottom figure and put in what you think is fair, and we will accept it within reason. If you were to put down $25,000, we'd say we'll never serve you again, but if you put down something that you think is fair in your opinion, we'll accept it and no questions asked because we want our clients to be satisfied with their charges, to believe that we're giving them value." And he didn't have many arguments.[66]

Marvin lived by the value billing rule, always concerned that the client should feel that the fee was reasonable. John Stewart remembers a negotiation Marvin had with George Dively (a fellow Harvard alumnus and chairman of Harris Intertype) that illustrates this philosophy:

The negotiation between George and Marvin went something like this: "Well, Marvin, over the next two or three months can you let me know whether we should merge with Itek?" "Sure, George." "Now how much is this going to cost me, Marvin?" "Well, we are going to have a couple of people here and a partner and this is valuable work, so I think the study will cost $10,000, the whole study." George said, "Gee, Marvin, I thought it would only be about $5,000 for the study." Marvin said. "Well, George, why don't we meet in the middle and we will do it for $7,500." I thought this was a peculiar kind of world. I would never have given in that easily when I was negotiating with the Army Ballistic Missile Command, but then I probably wouldn't have charged that much either.[67]

Marvin took a very practical approach to ensure that the company was successful at managing expenses. He purposefully hired people who would have that cost consciousness—in particular Everett Smith, who was well respected and demanded a justification for every expense, and Gil Clee, who had a finance background and played a very important role in designing the financial underpinnings of McKinsey & Co. when it became a privately held corporation in 1956.

In addition, Marvin seized every opportunity to remind consultants of their responsibility to keep costs down on behalf of the client. Don Gogel provides an amusing anecdote on the occasion of a new associates' luncheon when Don was a summer intern at McKinsey:

> Marvin said, "Now, remember, when you are out with a client for lunch or dinner, it would serve you and the firm well if you always ordered the blue plate special." He went on: "Remember, even though we separate our professional fees from our expenses, the client looks at the total bill. And the value that we deliver, of course, is greater the lower the total cost the client pays. There is no excuse at all to order expensive things off the menu when you are with a client, and a blue plate special is perfectly acceptable." Well, of course, everyone was looking at the menu to see what the cheapest possible thing was . . . even though there was no client. If I think of the hundreds if not thousands of dinner menus I've looked at, and I always think of Marvin and look at the blue plate special, asking myself "What would Marvin say?" "Get the blue plate special, forget the Dover sole. It's too expensive."[68]

The combination of value-based billing and expense control proved to be successful and provided the firm's members a reasonable income without elevating the quest for revenue over freedom and independence. As Marvin has often noted, while obviously the firm must have the economics required to keep it running, there is a harsh downside to pursuing revenue goals and accepting assignments where a professional management consulting firm (or any professional firm, for that matter) cannot deliver value—namely, the destruction of the firm's reputation to the detriment of future generations of employees, and possibly, the firm's longevity.

David Ogilvy, a founder of the advertising firm Ogilvy & Mather, remembers learning this lesson: "Marvin Bower . . . believes that every company should have a written set of principles and purposes. So I drafted mine and sent them to Marvin for comment. On the first page I had listed seven purposes, starting with 'earn an increased profit every year.' Marvin gave me holy hell. He said that any service business that gave higher priority to profits than to serving its clients deserved to fail. So I relegated profit to seventh place on my list."[69]

Aversion to Complacency

Having witnessed the demise of major business institutions that had become complacent and disconnected from the realities of their changing external environment, Marvin knew that McKinsey had to avoid the same pitfall. As he wrote in 1960:

> Our profession is not static, and it serves our interest to keep pushing the state-of-the-art in the technology of management. In doing so, we will not only ensure our ability to deliver quality but will continue to meet our own needs for excitement, intellectual stimulation, and personal self-reward. We are the most natural bridge between theory and practice of management, and we should exploit that.[70]

Not being complacent or static also meant a willingness and ability to respond to criticism without adopting a defensive posture. Clay Deutsch, a director with McKinsey & Co. who has managed the Cleveland office from 1993 through 1999 and the Chicago office from 2001 to the present, recalls:

> Marvin was coming to Cleveland to visit Case Western Reserve, with which he has had a very long association. They worship him. And he said that he'd love to stop by, and I said, "Marvin . . . I'd like to get the whole partner group together, and let's have a dinner. I would like for the partner group to have the privilege of hearing your thoughts the way I have . . . about leadership, what it means to commit to the firm, what it means to make the firm better, what it means to build and lead an office." So then he got engaged. He said, "Great."
>
> [By coincidence], the day he was coming *The Wall Street Journal* ran kind of a hatchet piece, nonsubstantive. They were saying that as the firm grows rapidly and becomes more complex and expands internationally, that we run the risk of losing sight of our values, run the risk of creeping hierarchy, run the risk of

entropy and centrifugal force eroding our one-firmness. I think there was even a hint in there about increasing commercialism, commercial pressure.

When I picked him up at the airport, he quickly got into how we should discuss the article. I hadn't really thought about it. So we got to this very nice restaurant where all the partners were gathered chatting over cocktails. About 10 minutes into the evening, Marvin said, "Ahem, gentlemen. I trust you've all read *The Wall Street Journal* piece on the firm this morning. I'd submit to you that we have our agenda for the evening, and I think we ought to be seated and just get right into it." Silence in the room. So we all sat down. And here's what I marvel at . . . rather than proceed to completely defang the article, in a defensive fashion, he took all the allegations very seriously. And he basically said, "Gentlemen, whether it's right or wrong, take it as a warning. We need to be activist and vigilant. And constantly opposing all the risks that they are portraying. And, therefore, I think we need to talk about how all of us stand tall, and lead the way, not just stand against, but lead the way out of hierarchy, out of commercialism, into values, into one-firmness."

Basically, what he said was that, as a partner in the firm, you have only one obligation . . . it's to make the firm better. Our obligation is to perpetuate the firm and not just kind of keep it going. We must perpetuate the firm by having every partner make the place better.[71]

Regenerating Leadership

As was the case with many elements of Marvin Bower's vision, his emphasis on the need for regenerating leadership was based on positive and negative experiences early on in his professional career. In the positive category, he could understand the benefits of providing leadership opportunities for others because he himself had been granted such opportunities at Jones, Day and by James O. McKinsey. In the negative category, he had witnessed painful business failures because new leadership was not in place to take over the helm—many law firms had perished with the death of their owners.

From these experiences, Marvin knew that he had to ensure that there would always be a new generation of leaders in place in order for McKinsey & Co. to survive and thrive. Underlying this was a need for a facilitating structure. As Bob Waterman, currently chairman of The Waterman Group, coauthor of *In Search of Excellence,* and with McKinsey from 1964 to 1985, says:

> Marvin had incredible foresight, probably because of his legal background and experience in seeing how often partnership organizations self-destruct. One partner, or partner group, gets too much control or too much wealth. They find no easy way of passing it on to other generations, and then the young, who are the organization's future, become resentful. It's a common and deadly pattern. Marvin had the wisdom to put a set of organizational arrangements in place at McKinsey whereby nobody, not even Marvin, could have that much control. It was reelecting the managing director (our CEO) every three years, limiting the number of terms one person could hold that office, limiting the amount of ownership any one person could have. It was putting systems in place that fostered a meritocracy—systems that recognized that even being a director, lofty as that position seemed, was no sinecure. The culture valued performance, not favorite sons. Marvin, Gil Clee, and others had all that figured out, at no small cost to themselves. Late in my career I remember hearing Ron Daniel urge that our fundamental strategy had everything to do with the way we managed ourselves. It sounded a little, well, wimpy to many of us; but it was pure Marvin and it was dead right.[72]

For the company to provide the right value to clients, it had to become, in effect, a leadership factory that could help ensure that the businesses consulted had developed their own next generation of leaders as was required to secure their respective futures. So it was not surprising that Marvin viewed building and support of leaders as one of the most important tasks in running a business. He wrote in 1960:

> Leadership skills are so personal and so rare that people don't talk about them easily. Certainly, the true leader has so much humility that he does not call himself a leader. And since leadership, unlike authority, cannot be assigned, the superior ordinarily does not like to point out to his subordinates their failure to

display rare personal skills they may not have and may not be able to develop. For these subtle reasons, leadership—the greatest resource that any business can have—typically gets inadequate attention unless there is an organized program sponsored by the present top leaders.[73]

In Marvin's experience, the critical task of leadership building was made less daunting by starting out with the right high-caliber people. He believed that outstanding executives are produced from good individual material to start with. This material must then be given an opportunity to grow in a healthy working atmosphere.

He went on to assert that the next critical element was to leverage this foundation of "good individual material" by means of a well-run company. He asserted that a company that is well run naturally produces good executives without any special effort—the special effort just increases the number developed and the rate of growth. And the development of executives results principally from:

1. Feeling the real weight of supervisory or executive responsibility
2. Good leadership and direction, including coaching by his or her immediate superior
3. The atmosphere of a well-run business that in itself encourages the growth and development of executives.[74]

Marvin went out of his way to provide individuals the opportunity to lead, be it offices, practices, high-visibility conferences, or simple projects within an office setting. This was an area in which he routinely took risks: He bet on people and actively supported initiatives that were within his vision of the firm. For example, when Rod Carnegie needed to return to Australia, Marvin didn't require too much convincing by Gil Clee to let Rod, only a three-year associate at the time, open the first McKinsey & Co. office in Australia. In 1962, when Andy Pearson wanted to build a marketing group, Marvin encouraged him. Andy and the newly created marketing group worked with General Foods and created the concept of direct product profitability and then developed the now ubiquitous universal product code (UPC) system. Marvin was skeptical but supportive. He thought both were old industrial techniques being applied to consumer products. It was a huge success, and is still used 40 years later. In both cases, Marvin had real doubts, but, once having authorized each endeavor, he actively supported Rod and Andy and helped them win by backing them emotionally and encouraging the best resources to join them.

Marvin was personally committed to developing the next generation of leaders, whether they be a part of McKinsey & Co. or a part of some community or other organization. Don Gogel remembers Marvin's persistence in this regard:

> I had left McKinsey and was working in an investment bank, Kidder Peabody. Marvin heard that I was moving to Bronxville. . . . This is pure Marvin. He called me . . . and said, "Don, I heard you were moving to Bronxville. Let's talk about Bronxville." (Marvin had lived in Bronxville for over 50 years.) So we had lunch. Blue plate special lunch. "Let me tell you about Bronxville." He told me about the town. He said, "Let me tell you the areas that I think you and Georgia should get involved in in Bronxville." There was no, "Are you interested in community service?" "What are the areas of interest to you?" His assumptions were, "Of course you are going to participate in the life of the community and of course you will want to get involved in the areas that are most important." Forget what your interests might be. I'm going to tell you what's most important. How can you say no to Marvin?
>
> . . . He said, "Either you or Georgia has to get involved with the school board, but you don't have to do that for a couple of years because you have to know the community a lot better." Well, five years after we moved to Bronxville, Georgia joined the school board; she served for six years, three of which she was president of the Bronxville School Board. Marvin was right. Bronxville revolves around the school.
>
> . . . Marvin said that the most important thing for the future of Bronxville is that each leadership group in the town recruits the next generation of younger people to understand what community service and public-spiritedness is all about because these are lessons that have to be taught. . . . Marvin's sort of civic-mindedness wasn't just something that he thought applied to him and that people should do. He really had a model of how it sustained us—how it has to be sustained. I think that, at least my experience in a community like Bronxville has worked largely because people take

seriously what Marvin was talking about; they recruit the next generation of people who were 10 years younger—whether they participate in the school, the church, the United Fund, or whatever. So there's more intergenerational participation in a lot of these activities than I think in a lot of other towns. And Marvin certainly was aware of this and encouraged us to do that.[75]

In a 1955 speech, Marvin succinctly expressed his beliefs about what constitutes good leadership:

> If our leaders confuse leadership with the need to control, we will destroy collaboration and true leadership. . . . Running a business well means developing executives. . . . The rewards for learning to run a business well more than compensate for the difficulties. The rewards are more than a growth atmosphere for executives. They include growth for the business itself—growth in competitive position, size, and profits.[76]

Marvin understood that new leadership could not exist and thrive if the old leadership did not step down and make room for the new. If the old leadership lingers, it is difficult for an organization to look to its new leaders for guidance. Consequently, in 1967, when nearly 64, Marvin stepped down from the position of managing director despite protests from his partners, who believed that they could not find anyone as good as Marvin and wanted him to stay on. Having stepped down, Marvin actively supported the new leadership of Gil Clee, and the new rules that limited the age and tenure of each managing director of McKinsey, as well as the time period that any individual could hold shares, thus helping to ensure that others would assume leadership roles. Only by opening up an opportunity for his successor was Marvin able to prove his partners' fears unfounded.

Marvin often recalled how Abraham Lincoln responded when asked by a young man about the best way to become a lawyer. Lincoln told him that half the job was a "firm resolve" to become a lawyer. It might be said that Marvin had a firm resolve to create a distinctive service and build a professional institution founded on the excellence of the people who worked in it. In the late 1950s, Marvin asserted that:

> One of the great advantages of any professional type activity is the freedom it offers the individual to work in a non-structured

situation. Within the limits of meeting [their] responsibilities to clients and to the firm, our consultants have freedom of action, independence of thought, and an opportunity to pursue activities of personal professional interest. This contrasts with the typical corporate or governmental position where most individuals have prescribed duties and specific limits of authority.

As we increase the size of the firm, we will have to make particular efforts to ensure that our consultants retain these basic freedoms of a professional person. We avoid substituting "control" for freedom of action based on a high degree of self-imposed personal responsibility of the consultant to clients and to the firm.

The best way to accomplish this is to ensure that we continue to place a high degree of personal responsibility in every consultant. It has been traditional in our firm that we expect the consultant to impose higher standards of performance, self-discipline, and responsibility on himself than the firm could reasonably impose on him. We must resist every effort to substitute firm discipline for self-discipline.[77]

By setting clear values and living by them throughout his long professional career, Marvin Bower, with the help of his partners, was able to create a profession and an institution in defiance of the conventional wisdom in that era. Mac Stewart sums up the interlocking nature of Marvin's original vision that gave life and endurance to the profession of management consulting and the institution that was McKinsey & Co.:

The guiding principles were all designed to differentiate ourselves, enhance the quality of what was delivered and our reputation, and make us successful. And the values are designed to gain the trust of our clients and the commitment and excitement of our associates. Without the trust, you have no clients that are any good. Without commitment, you won't sustain an institution.[78]

Mac Stewart goes on to explain how Marvin and his partners, during these early years at McKinsey, worked together in an environment of commitment and trust:

Marvin was the jet engine. He drove the organization. He pushed the plane, kept it moving ahead fast. Breakneck speed sometimes.

But not always. He knew when to slow down. And particularly when it came to this period when others were going public.

Everett Smith[79] was the flaps that you put down when you want to slow down, always disagreeing, slowing everything down. It was remarkable that Marvin would tolerate someone like that who was always finding something wrong with everything he wanted to do. Marvin found that this was a way of exposing all the weaknesses that had to be answered before he went ahead and did it, which was a very insightful concept.

Alex Smith, who was one of the most decent people I've ever known, was the gyroscope—he kept the whole place from crashing. He did. Marvin was tough medicine for a lot of people. Gil was a visionary, the navigator. And Zip Reilley was the company conscience. He was the control tower, the airplane conscience. He always made sure that, in terms of dealing with people, we did the right thing.[80]

According to Theodore Levitt, a retired professor from Harvard Business School and author of *Marketing Myopia,*[81] Marvin set the benchmark for the now mature profession of management consulting:

I have always heard about Marvin Bower, considered around here as sort of the inventor of management consulting as we know it. He set the standard, not by articulating the standard but by practicing the standard—both by the kind of people he selected and how he worked with them. Everybody feels a strong sense of his leadership—he does that very much by example.[82]

CHAPTER 4

Defining Moments
of Leadership and Influence

*"I find the great thing in this world is not so much where
we stand, as in what direction we are moving: To reach the
port of heaven, we must sail sometimes with the wind and
sometimes against it—but we must sail, and not drift, nor
lie at anchor."*

—Oliver Wendell Holmes, 1894

Since he was a stickler for action and a role model for leading by example, it is not surprising that Marvin Bower stayed on at McKinsey &
Co. for 59 years[1] to ensure that his vision of the profession and the institution came to fruition. It was an extraordinary and sometimes contentious
time with Marvin as the effective head of the firm (1939–1967) and as an
occasional but influential factor in firm behavior and decisions (1968–1992).

During Marvin's long tenure with the firm, he made, advocated, influenced, and/or adopted thousands of decisions that were the natural enact-
ment of his original vision, yet accommodated a changing world. From the
start, he had a sense of what firm values ought to be and all his decisions
were consistent with that vision. This chapter focuses on nine points of key
decision-making spanning a 60-year period. (See Figure 4.1.) In describing these decision points, many of which broke new ground in the business
world, it is impossible to separate them from Marvin the man: They speak
volumes about the makeup of his character while bringing to life his professional and institutional concepts.

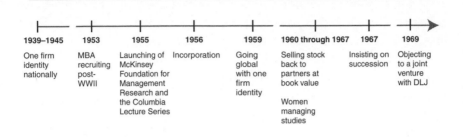

FIGURE 4.1   DEFINING MOMENTS OF MARVIN BOWER'S LEADERSHIP/INFLUENCE

One Firm Identity Nationally: 1939 to 1945

Marvin's insistence on a single identity for the firm was not a capricious mandate from above. He had good reasons for working so hard to create and for demanding that others adhere to a common image that would manifest itself across all aspects of the company: the look of the physical office space, the mode of employee and partner dress, the appearance of McKinsey & Co. products (reports and other documents), appropriate terminology, how consultants were compensated, how clients were served, and so on. The one-firm concept was a distinctive idea. Warren Cannon credits it with being the most important aspect of building McKinsey:

> If you are in the LA office, you are primarily employed by McKinsey. If you are in the Mexico office, you are a member of McKinsey and have met the same hiring standards as a German associate. I cannot imagine McKinsey developing the way it did without this. We could not have served clients or developed people the way we did without this one-firm orientation.[2]

First, to validate the new profession of management consulting Marvin knew it would be necessary to project a professional image that would instill confidence in clients and attract the best and the brightest to join the firm. Consulting could not be perceived as a part-time job for out-of-work people or retired sales managers; rather, it had to be understood as the valuable professional enterprise it was. This meant clients not customers, a profession not a business.

Second, for the firm to effectively meet the needs of clients that were national firms, McKinsey & Co. also had to have a national presence, meaning that a multitude of offices would be required. A common firm identity would be a key mechanism for linking these autonomous offices without imposing the command and control hierarchical structure that Marvin was striving to avoid.

Third, in order for the firm to be consistent in how individuals and teams served clients, Marvin was a sponsor of procedures and policies as well as training that would help consultants. Marvin called the policies *guides* because he believed that in most circumstances they would be helpful, but it was critical to leave room for judgment in exceptional circumstances. A lot of time was spent preparing the guides (the organizational guide, the management information control guide, the manufacturing guide, the firm policy guide, etc.) and in training.

Finally, Marvin wanted to create an actual brand image for McKinsey—quite a challenge for a professional service firm with no conventional physical product to offer its customers. Marvin felt that "physical manifestations were important in creating a wholly distinctive identity." If the client had a stack of reports, he or she should know instantly which one was a McKinsey report from the look of the cover. While the content of each product would obviously differ, the same look should hold true of all written communications to the client, whether a letter, a report, or a memorandum, and regardless of the author. As for McKinsey's ultimate product—the implementation of its recommendations at the client company—the firm's image would be created by successful execution and quantifiable positive results.

Taken in isolation, many of the "little" things Marvin insisted on may seem like taking small pains to the extreme. While the firm's image was derived from Marvin's distinctly conservative nature, he always had a compelling rationale for each requirement, and, taken together, all rules added up to a strong, professional identity for both management consulting and McKinsey.

In justifying his dress code to Quincy Hunsicker, Marvin said:

> If your job is to help a client have the courage to follow the trail indicated by facts, you need to do everything you can to minimize the distractions and deviations the client is likely to take. If you have revolutionary ideas, they are much more likely to be listened to if you do not have revolutionary dress—the CEOs must have confidence in us. If you were an airline passenger, and the pilot came aboard the plane and he wore shorts and a flaming scarf, would you have the same confidence as you did when he came on with his four stripes on the shoulder? Basically, the dress code all has to do with what you want to do, when you want to build confidence and an identity. You want to be as *unauffällig*, which is as unnoticeable as possible.[3]

In espousing this dress code (from head to toe, as it turned out), Marvin meant business, and the organization was always kept on its toes. Deviations from the code were unlikely to go unnoticed, as Quincy still vividly remembers:

> We were sort of quaking in our shoes whenever we'd get in the elevator with Marvin. There were all sorts of stories of people who rode up with him and he noticed that they had their handkerchief out of line or that they had a blue shirt or didn't have dark socks, and he was the master of instant feedback.[4]

Not only did associates have to project a professional image through their dress, they had to blend in with or at least not stand out from the prevailing dress conventions in the business world. To Marvin's mind, any visual appearance that might distract the client's attention from the matter at hand (solving major business problems) must be avoided. So his notion was, if everybody wore hats, you wore hats. This way, the fact that you didn't wear a hat would not be an attention distracter. Such was his rationale for long black socks, for blue suits, for white shirts, and so on. (Note that Thomas J. Watson Sr., whose leadership overlapped with Marvin's, had the same idea: IBM's employees would dress the way their customers dressed, as a sign of respect and parity.)[5]

The hat and sock anecdotes are numerous and often amusing. Roger Morrison, with McKinsey from 1953 through 1991, believes he was hired because he wore a hat:

> Marvin had approximately 45 minutes before he caught his normal 6:11 train to Bronxville. I was ushered in and he looked at me and said, "What is your background?" I explained to him that I had been in the Navy, acted as an accountant during the summer in summer hotels, managed some small businesses on the side, but basically had no experience. You could see that his interest lapsed very quickly. He then pursued various academic questions in terms of subjects that I'd studied and professors that I'd had, but basically didn't seem to be all that interested. Then he got up and said that I could walk to the train with him if we wanted to continue chatting because he was short of time. As we walked out of the door Mrs. Carpenter, who was the receptionist for many years, handed me my hat. Marvin's eyes lit up, because I had heard that everyone in McKinsey wore a hat. I had bought the hat the day before for $5 in Filene's Bargain Basement, if I remember correctly. Marvin clearly became more animated in his discussions as we went down, and was beaming happily as he got on the train. I subsequently received an offer. I've always thought Filene's Bargain Basement probably had as much to do with that offer as the Harvard Business School credentials and other achievements that I'd had.[6]

Certainly everyone recognized that Marvin was serious about the hat issue and other aspects of the dress code. Nevertheless, they were still able to have fun with this, albeit at the expense of others. Lee Walton, the managing director from 1968 through 1973, remembers how he became the subject of an office prank after his first encounter with Marvin in 1952:

> Marvin invited me to lunch and we went down to the Board of Trade which contained a nice business restaurant. It was cold as I recall, snowing, so we put on our overcoats. I had acquired a hat because I had been told by Warren Cannon [the Chicago office administrator] that I needed a hat. My hat was very fashionable for the time. It had a very narrow brim with a Homburg crush in the crown and the bow on the hatband was in the back of the hat.

There was a little yellow feather sticking out of the bow. A gray hat with a black headband and a little yellow feather. I was very proud of my new hat. We went down to lunch and checked our hats and coats. After lunch I had recovered my hat and coat and I put my hat on my head so I could shrug into my overcoat. As I was struggling to do that, Marvin came over to help me with the overcoat. All of a sudden I heard this stage whisper from Marvin, "You still have the hatcheck in your hat." So I took the hat off, looked at it and said, "No, Marvin, this is a feather." And all he said was "Oh."

I put the hat back on my head and we walked back to the office and had a good chat. I thanked him for lunch and when I passed Warren Cannon's office on the way to my own I dropped in to tell him the story of the hatcheck feather. I was laughing at Marvin mistaking the feather for the hatcheck and Warren said, "What did he say?" I said, "Well, he didn't say anything he just said, 'Oh.'" Warren said, "Oh, my God. He said just 'Oh'?" I said, "Yes." He said, "Lee, you've got to get rid of that feather." I said, "Now, wait a minute. I'm not going to. I've done a lot of things to accommodate myself to McKinsey in the last few weeks but I am not going to get rid of the feather. This is my brand new hat. It's very stylish, everybody is wearing them—with a feather. I like the feather." He said, "No, no, you don't understand. You really have to get rid of that feather. Marvin has obviously taken offense at it." And I said, "Aw, come on." He said, "Yes, really, I'm sorry." "I'll pull the damn feather out," I said, "that doesn't bother me that much. It's against my principles but I'll remove the feather." "Oh, no," he said, "You don't just pull the feather out." I said, "I don't? You just told me to get rid of it." He said, "Yes, but you've got to do this very subtly." I said, "Oh?" He said, "Yes, each evening when you go home, take the scissors and cut a little bit of the yellow feather off. And over a period of about a week it will disappear. That's the way to do it." And I was naive enough to think he meant it.[7]

Some years later, after hats were no longer in style, Marvin stopped wearing one. As the story goes, an associate in the New York office noticed and asked his office manager what he should make of Marvin's bare head. The office manager replied that this was an indication that Marvin believed wearing a hat had become a distraction as it was now counter to the norm. However, just to be sure, the office manager cautioned the associate to wait a few weeks before abandoning his own hat. After several weeks of watching a hatless Marvin, the firm followed and eliminated this "distraction" from their mode of dress. In 2002, Marvin remembered the day 40 years earlier, "Kennedy had set a new style, and CEOs were no longer wearing hats."[8]

Marvin's sense of appropriate professional dress was so ingrained in the members of his firm that it transcended generations. In 1994, as head of my own firm, New York Consulting Partners, I experienced this phenomenon firsthand.

While flying with a new associate to a client meeting at Colgate in Canada, I noticed that he was not wearing socks in the middle of January.[9] I looked at him and said, "You are going to have to buy socks in Toronto, before you go to the client." He turned red. He was the son of a former McKinsey director, Fred Searby, and explained that when he got into the taxi that morning, he noticed that he was wearing argyle socks and that his father had sworn that you were never to wear argyle socks to a client, so he had taken them off. I laughed thinking how Marvin's legacy lived on in strange ways, and actually found myself seriously considering whether it was appropriate to break Marvin's rule. I told him the history of the rule. Marvin had been to a meeting at DuPont with an associate. During that meeting, Marvin noticed Crawford Greenwalt's eyes were repeatedly drawn to the associate's argyle socks. They were distracting. From this experience, the 1966 McKinsey policy prohibiting argyle socks was born—and it was not in jest. Marvin went so far as to write a blue memo [the distinctive color of memos to the entire firm from Marvin, when he was managing director of McKinsey] explaining his rationale for all who chose to read it, and he held a Saturday training program on characteristics of socks that were acceptable and those that were not. Needless to say, after relaying this history, I told Fred that, in 1994, the rule was dated and he could put his argyle socks back on.

But, in 1994, Marvin was still concerned about appearance. When Fred Gluck, then McKinsey's managing director, returned from vacation with a red beard, Marvin commented, "Fred, that's a beautiful new beard. How many of your clients have beards?" Fred shaved it off that night.[10]

Marvin's concern about the look of the firm did not stop at dress: He was determined to extend this notion of brand to the product left behind at the client's office (typically reports, letters, and memoranda). As Warren Cannon, the administrative partner of McKinsey from 1960 to 1988, explained:

> Marvin was concerned with the appearance of written communications. I know because, at his request, I wrote the writing guide for the firm. He was a bear about this. We had formal reports, informal reports, memorandum reports, letters of proposal, memoranda of proposal, and so on. Every one of those had a full and logically sufficient set of rules. Every office of the firm, no matter where, had to use exactly the same typeface on typewriters. We had custom-made platen rolls, so that all our reports were not single or double spaced, they were one and a half. When you ratcheted the ratchet wheel it automatically gave you one and a half lines instead of one or two lines. The indentation was specified to the number. We had rules for numbered paragraphs, lettered paragraphs, block paragraphs, et cetera. All of this was to create an absolutely consistent, distinctive image so that anybody anywhere opening a report would know it was a McKinsey report. We established standards of how a firm report should look, in order to promote uniformity when we had different people writing reports and writing them in different offices.[11]

Beyond creating a writing guide, Marvin took some very concrete and, at the time, unusual steps to help ensure this uniformity. He made a decision to invest in discrete production or report-generating capabilities separate from secretarial and from consulting. Marvin's justification for this investment was both:

> Quality-driven . . .
>   In many ways our reports are our signature. It is what we leave behind at a client. When they pull it out of an old drawer or off a shelf, I don't want them to be pulling out that old consulting report, I want them to be pulling out the McKinsey report, a memory, something to look at and to think about. I want them to look at it and see how much we care about the quality of the work we do. That is our signature.

And strategic . . .

An executive at Eaton pulled a 10-year old report off his shelves when he was moving, flipped through it and called me to tell me what a good job the team had done 10 years earlier. Following the phone call, a lunch was arranged, and following the lunch, there was new work for McKinsey.[12]

Marvin's success in creating a common firm image and terminology/language facilitated the opening of regional offices to provide the national presence required to properly service national clients. When Marvin and his partners bought the firm in 1939, it had only two offices—New York and Boston. With the United States' ongoing participation in World War II, for the next several years, McKinsey & Co. was preoccupied with war-related work, such as helping H.J. Heinz and Food Machinery Corp. (FMC) convert their manufacturing facilities to play a support role to U.S. troops. Primarily for that reason, a third office—San Francisco—was not opened until 1944.

Alf Werolin, the first McKinsey manager of the San Francisco office, describes the events leading up to the decision and his move to San Francisco:

Some people of the firm had performed consulting assignments on the West Coast. At one of the partners' meetings, around 1943, it was decided that we ought to explore opening an office on the West Coast. Marvin said: "Why don't we take our own medicine and hire someone to determine the need and the desirability of opening a West Coast office." The consultant we hired was Dean Hugh Jackson of the Stanford University Graduate School. . . . and it was determined that there was a need for a high-grade management consulting firm on the Coast. There was no one else out here at the time other than George S. May Company, which we really didn't call a management consulting firm.

Opening a McKinsey office would represent an opportunity for us to enter the market early and possibly preempt it. On the other hand, [the investigation indicated that] many of the businesses on the West Coast were still in the hands of the original founders or sons of the founders and they typically felt that since they had started the business, had made it what it was then, they didn't need outside consultants to help them. Therefore, it would require a substantial amount of business development work to develop client engagements on the West Coast. The investigation also mentioned the rivalry between Los Angeles and San Francisco. The partners decided to set up a West Coast office in San Francisco . . . I agreed, albeit reluctantly, to go out to organize the office.

FMC was a bridge [for us in San Francisco]. During Marvin's visits to the Coast, he made a number of speeches, and Paul Davies, the president of FMC, who had a wide acquaintance, was generous in his praise of the firm. So a number of new clients were soon added to our ongoing work, and the office got off to a good start, giving better service to clients than we could from our East Coast locations.[13]

In 1947, after the affiliation with Kearney and McKinsey was terminated and the McKinsey name belonged entirely to the firm, the Chicago office was opened. Chicago was a coveted location. As Marvin put it:

I wanted to be in Chicago because Chicago is such an important center. We've got to move into Chicago if we're going to be a national firm. I held back, I don't know how many years, but two, three or four, in the interest of having harmony within our own firm.[14]

More offices were opened: in 1949 and 1951 Los Angeles and Washington, DC, and in 1963 Cleveland. As these offices were launched, Marvin attributed the firm's success in becoming a distinctive U.S. national firm to New York's willingness to seed these new offices with seasoned professionals who were well imbued with the one-firm culture:

Throughout all this period and under the leadership of all these managers, it was the role of the New York office to provide personnel for other offices as they were established or needed strengthening. This was a natural role because in 1939, except for our small Boston office, there was no other source unless we went outside and violated our policy of developing our own leadership.

But what came naturally soon became a matter of strategy. New York office managers and other partners recognized their responsibilities to help open new offices and strengthen all offices. As a participant in the transfer process and an observer of it at work, I can testify that this responsibility was not approached as discharging an obligation but as capitalizing on an opportunity.

So New York became the principal supplier of leaders and experienced associates to new offices. The office was able to play this role not only because of its historical position as our largest and best-established office but because it sought—as a matter of strategy—to recruit, train, and develop a surplus of leaders. And that strategy was possible because of its location in a management center of great potential.

As the firm moved nationally in the United States . . . it was always recognized that New York paid a high price for giving up scores of consultants—many of them our strongest leaders. That price was slower growth for New York. When other offices became established and began growing their leaders, they also contributed to the transfer process—and their contributions continued to increase.

What is more remarkable, however, is the fact that the New York leaders contributed these resources without grumbling or fanfare. Along with leaders elsewhere in the firm, they simply realized that if we were to have a strong, unified, national . . . firm, we must pay the economic and human costs of transferring leaders and potential leaders from our largest and strongest office.

The New York example, which other offices soon emulated, gave reality and vitality to our one-firm policy. That is how McKinsey became a single national firm, not a collection of offices or a collection of people.

Although there are many facets to our one-firm policy, i.e., many ways of showing support for, and constructive attitudes toward other offices, the critical test is: (1) the willingness of the leaders of one office to transfer to another a proven leader or an associate of high potential in order to serve the interests of the firm as a whole; and (2) the willingness of firm members to make the sacrifice of moving and of others to fill the voids they have left.[15]

So, as the number of offices grew, so did the importance and value of the one-firm policy. People were not just transferred to offices; there was lending and borrowing people too. For example, when the Chicago office was started, they went through some rough times and other offices were willing to borrow associates as well as provide experienced staff where it mattered. In 1955, about one-third of the work was done by borrowed or loaned staff. This required developing accounting that accommodated supportive lending and borrowing of resources. Marvin describes how critical this policy was to McKinsey's ability to grow quickly and smoothly:

> This policy grew naturally out of the firm's history of differing opinions among partners before 1939, and the closeness that developed thereafter. As we struggled together to overcome losses and build an outstanding firm, from 1939 on we almost instinctively treated all consultants as firm members, not office members. We want a truly unified firm—"one firm," not a federation of offices or a collection of individuals. To help ensure this unity and cohesiveness, we try not to make decisions or develop attitudes that put the interests and profits of an individual office ahead of those of the firm as a whole. For by thinking in firm terms, adhering to firm concepts, and following firm philosophy, standards, and policies, we can offer clients throughout the world a uniform standard of service by consultants of uniformly high caliber. Such service has special value to national and international companies with widespread operations.
>
> Our one-firm policy has had an important and continuing influence on keeping the firm unified. Without this policy, we would never have been able to develop the firm as a national firm with the same effectiveness or speed. For only if our consultants and earnings were regarded as part of a common firm pool would the individual office have been willing to transfer some of its outstanding personnel to new offices in the interests of expanding the firm as a whole.[16]

MBA Recruiting: 1953

In 1953, Marvin Bower made one of the most innovative decisions in his long career: to recruit young MBAs fresh out of school in lieu of the conventional experienced hires. Marvin was taking a calculated risk since clients might be unwilling to accept advice from consultants who looked to be almost the same age as their own children or grandchildren. Yet the advice they would receive from these bright associates who had been educated in business analysis and still maintained the imagination of youth was likely to be more valuable than that coming from some experienced "expert" who operated on the basis of experience rather than analysis (e.g., the 30-year career salesperson). Further, the firm's ability to inculcate its values and identity in its new hires would be greatly facilitated by hiring young people who were not already set in their ways. At the time there were 84 consultants on staff, 31 of whom had attended Harvard Business School, but none who had been hired directly from the school.

This decision grew from Marvin's long-standing desire to change the essence of consulting from experienced-based "experts" to analytically driven top management problem solvers:

> When I first joined the firm in 1933 I felt very strongly that we should not hire mature executives, which James O. McKinsey wanted to do. Of course, this I brought from the law. All law firms build their own staffs, take them right out of law school and train them. And most companies are quite welcome to the fact that they will deal with lawyers who themselves have never been in a company. James O. McKinsey would hire a vice president who was out of a job and believe that because he had been a vice president, the client would accept that person better. His rationale was greater acceptance by the client, whereas I was in favor of the young pups because I had seen them grow and develop. I had been one of them in the law. It took us some years to get there.[17]

The MBA Hiring Policy

Although some MBAs had been hired in previous years, the explicit policy was not formulated until 1953. World War II and the limited availability of resources had passed, and a large number of veterans were graduating from business schools. Simultaneously, the firm began to concentrate on solving problems faced by top management. With companies now growing in the postwar era, top management focus was shifting to new problems revolving around organization, divisionalization, and delegation in lieu of historic functional issues (production layout, sales force efficiency, and cost reduction). At the same time, McKinsey's reputation was growing.

Frank Canny, who was the personnel director for the firm at that time, suggested formalizing recruiting at Harvard. It was a logical step forward because Marvin had a strong affinity for the Harvard Business School, maintained regular contact with the institution, and kept abreast of developments there. But it was a very risky decision. The transition took place in stages—first hiring MBAs with experience, and then hiring MBAs with little or no experience. Warren Cannon, who had just become administrative officer, describes this phased transition in hiring policy:

> The first thing I had to address was to move from experienced hires with some applicable experience, probably moderate ability, and unimpressive academic credentials. And the firm was populated by those people because that was all you could get during World War II. For one thing, it was hard because so many people, young men, were off to war one way or another. But probably the revolutionary thing that [Marvin] did was to recruit young people.
>
> Bringing in inexperienced staff was really an extraordinary thing to do because people thought clients weren't about to take advice from some young fuzzy-cheeked associates. And Marvin was the one who started and pressed for these hires. He was the one that took them on studies. . . . The big swing was when we started moving toward hiring the very best with little or no experience from the leading business schools. It took a while because the numbers were so small in the beginning compared to the whole firm. I mean it took a while to salt and change the character of the firm.[18]

John Macomber was one of the first MBA hires in 1953, and stayed with McKinsey until 1973, subsequently becoming chairman of Celanese and president of the Export/Import Bank. John describes his pioneering experience at McKinsey:

> He hired people like me and Roger Morrison, who had had some military experience, and we'd all had good records as kids. Clearly, we were doing things that were interesting when we were growing up, in summer jobs, so we were not an unknown quantity. But we had no industrial experience to speak of. He went ahead and started by hiring the two of us and then a few more and a few more.

. . . It was over as far as ever hiring experienced people. . . . Every time we hired somebody . . . who had great experience in this industry, he was a flop. And why was he a flop? Because Marvin hadn't gotten his hands on him and trained him on these basic, simple ideas at a malleable stage. They came in with their experience. Marvin had people come in with their future potential. And there's a huge difference. Roger Morrison might have been the greatest CFO, but if he had come back to McKinsey & Co. as an expert in finance, he wouldn't have been nearly as effective as he turned out to be—an enormously effective man by being trained by Marvin and everybody around Marvin in these basic, simple concepts. An amazing thing.

He put me to work on the Texaco study with himself, in the research and development area of Texaco. First of all, I knew nothing about the oil business, although I had been a roughneck as a kid as a summer job, which, incidentally, went over pretty well with Gus Long who ran Texaco in those days. "Ah, you know something, don't you, kid?" Furthermore, it was working in research and development. What the hell do I know about that? Well, there were a couple of us on that. And the end result was an unbelievably successful program. We helped Texaco think through a whole new way of going about research and development.

The recommendations were to quit making research and development an examination of the different properties of lubricating oil and start figuring out how you can extract oil and minerals out of the ground at less money. Start getting into what was then electronics seismology. Sure, keep on going doing this very important work for your customers, but that's customer service that you're doing over here. If you're really interested in development that's going to help the company in new areas, we ought to look at what we can do in exploration and production . . . to open up new areas and reduce the costs and reduce the risk.[19]

Roger Morrison was the other MBA of 1953, and he stayed with McKinsey until 1991 including a stint as the head of the London office from 1972 to 1985. Morrison notes how important analytical skills that were honed at a good business school were to the success of top management consulting:

> There were a lot of people at McKinsey who had been to Harvard Business School. At that time, Harvard was essentially a finishing school for those who had not had any practical training at university, and therefore, provided them with a vocational training to go into business. Frank Canny [personnel director for the firm] was very interested in two or three people at that time, and invited us down to interview . . .

> I did my undergraduate [work] at Minnesota. Out where real people are. Business is hard. We have to recognize that the smartest people in the world do not go into business . . . they go into medicine . . . they go into all sorts of things. The only reason I was in business was that I found that the classes I was in, in engineering and physics, were full of people that were smarter than I was. I had to work a lot harder to get decent marks.

> Over in the business schools, including Harvard, it's a "lead pipe cinch." . . . I had started out going to Harvard on the basis that I wanted to be a consultant; the reason being that I got bored with anything after six months. I liked changes in people and problems and constant changes in scenery. The only thing I could think of that met those requirements was consulting. In seeking an opportunity in consulting, I obviously covered most of the major consulting firms—Booz·Allen & Hamilton, ADL, Cresap, McCormick & Paget (which was considered one of the better firms), and McKinsey & Co. Of these, Booz·Allen & Hamilton and ADL would not interview or even talk to anyone without experience. Cresap was more broad-minded and were interested enough to offer jobs to a number of people who approached them and had no experience. Clearly the opportunity at McKinsey was more attractive; basic professionalism, basic policies, and the strength of the firm was greater than the other institutions.[20]

What made McKinsey more attractive was, to Morrison's mind, the following:

> Firstly, Marvin supported recruiting at Harvard. And secondly, when people started working on studies they obviously knew how to

analyze things. The industry company analysis approach to studying a company was the heart of the thing that Harvard was teaching at that time. It was ideal. Now, many of the consultants that
came from industry understood how to look at the economics of an
industry, a successful competitive position, et cetera. They immediately found with MBAs a new source of cannon fodder that actually
knows something about the things we're trying to tell people. . . .[21]

This did not mean, as Morrison goes on to point out, that MBA hires
did not require any training:

With that transition came a more explicit recognition of the notion
that there needs to be a discrete set of skills. We used to have a
handbook that Marvin would keep up to date all the time. A handbook of consulting skills—how to analyze problems, how to look at
organizations. . . . Looking back it was kind of simplistic, but it
was basically based on the body of common knowledge—that's
what he called it. And he felt very strongly that [the handbook] is
the consultant's bible. Today, you would look at it and say it is not
necessary. But at the time, when you are trying to create a new field
it was very important. . . . [At the time] consulting was generally
not held in high regard by anybody.[22]

Everett Smith remembers his first study with Roger Morrison and his
initial trepidation:

I can tell you I had Roger Morrison on his first assignment and I
was sweating blood. It was Chrysler and those boys didn't play
games out there. I was worried sick about Roger. I put him on the
whole question of standard costs in the costing and controls sec-
tion of Chrysler, which is not a child's job. Roger was about 26
years old, and we struggled along for a while. I got happier and
happier because I began to realize what that guy's mind was like.
One day I was talking with the financial vice president. He said, "I
want to talk with you about Morrison." I thought, "Oh Jesus, here
I go." What he wanted to tell me was he thought that Roger was
the damnedest fine kid he'd ever seen in his life. He called him a
kid, but he had great respect for him. I sank down into the chair
and the next 15 to 20 minutes were very pleasant.[23]

The challenges presented by hiring new MBAs did not end in 1953, despite early recruiting successes. Henry Strage, currently with H.M. Strage & Associates and with McKinsey from 1962 through 1991, remembers a client questioning the youthfulness of the team during one of his first studies:

> The study was quite interesting because ICI, which had been a kind of royal treasure for Great Britain, made a stunning decision of the board to appoint an outsider. His name was Paul Chambers. It was stunning not only because he was an outsider to the company, but because he was not from the industry. And that was a kind of no-no in those days. If you hadn't been in the company for 30 years and gotten acid burns, gassed by caustic chlorine, you weren't eligible for the board. Anyhow, it was really quite dramatic.
>
> The other thing that happened with Paul Chambers which is quite interesting is that when Marvin began to introduce people on the team to Paul, . . . this was so-and-so and he has had this experience, et cetera, Paul turned to Marvin and said, "Mr. Bower, this is a very young team, and we are a very important company and this is a very important study. Are you sure you want to assign all these teenagers on this very important study? They are going to be working with leaders and captains of industry who have been in the industry for 20 or 30 years." Then Marvin said, "Paul, you know, if you look at the history of thought, and the history of inventions and innovations, you would be hard pressed to find anything of great significance that anybody has been able to produce after the age of 35." Which I'm sure is not 100 percent accurate. Then he sort of rattled off Michelangelo, Albert Einstein, et cetera.[24]

As Strage goes on to point out, with the advent of such a young group of associates, it was fortuitous that Marvin had instilled a disciplined dress code:

> I guess Marvin had to have an answer for these questions [about the youthfulness of the associates] because it must've come up quite often. Hence, the long black socks, dark suit, and hat syndrome. I think that was part of it. He didn't want [young] people coming in T-shirts and gym shoes.[25]

In the end, this hiring philosophy had a tremendous effect on the firm. McKinsey no longer sought out people with 15 to 20 years of experience; it relied on younger, better-trained, and, as Marvin emphasized, more imaginative, staff. This transition fit with and reinforced the firm values and competitive differentiation, as John Stewart notes:

> I think Marvin made silk out of a sow's ear by maintaining that these young people were trained to be professional, implying that firms that hired experienced people could never retrain them to be professional. And one of the things that does differentiate McKinsey today is we've got the best and the brightest and no one can come close.[26]

The firm's focus on hiring business school graduates had a significant impact on the firm's national expansion between 1952 and 1959. As Ron Daniel recalls:

> We opened offices in different parts of the U.S. . . . . We were taking advantage of the rapid growth in the U.S. and the world economy. . . . . And in hindsight, the most consequential step the firm took in that era was to discover that smart young people could do this kind of work. That discovery was important because it opened up a whole new pool of talent for the firm, which permitted growth.[27]

McKinsey's policy evolved with the times. For example, some years later when business schools changed their policies and started to require MBA candidates to enter with some experience, rather than coming directly from undergraduate studies, the firm changed its own hiring policies and began recruiting undergraduates as analysts. After these analysts accrued several years of experience, the firm would send them off to business school with the prospect of returning to McKinsey as an MBA associate. In 1993, in line with changing client needs, McKinsey also began formally recruiting people with advanced professional degrees (e.g., PhDs, MAs, JDs, Rhodes and Fulbright Scholars, and so on) from the best universities.

Marvin was confident that analytically capable, imaginative people supported by standards for problem solving could learn the business particulars on the job and deliver high value to clients. As Marvin stated at a 1998 partners' conference:

Einstein said that imagination was more important than knowledge. Today's problems cannot be solved by thinking the way we thought when we created them. Coming from Einstein that's quite a statement. Imagination is an important feature of the consultant. If he can't imagine, there's no use analyzing. And I'm afraid that we spend too much time analyzing and not enough on imagination. We can't really shape things without imagination.[28]

The Subsequent "Up-or-Out" Policy

The up-or-out notion that McKinsey was wrestling with essentially recognized that a large number of the people starting with McKinsey would ultimately move on to do something else. At the time, the issue was exaggerated because a number of the people had been hired during World War II and were not of the targeted caliber, and with the entrance of MBAs, more disciplined processes were being put in place. Realizing that 9 out of 10 people were not going to make their careers with the firm, Marvin began to build policies around this fact of life—policies to help people grow, minimize pain, and enable the organization to always move forward.

At the time, a number of institutions, including law firms, accounting firms, universities, and the U.S. military, had adopted some form of a policy under which, if members were not on a promotion track, they were asked to leave. Marvin formalized this concept and removed any element of arbitrariness by ensuring that all up-or-out decisions were grounded in facts that were gathered from a standard evaluation and feedback system that was applied throughout the firm, thus paving the way for a true meritocracy.

Launching of the McKinsey Foundation for Management Research and the Columbia Lecture Series—1955

In the late 1950s, the business world was in something of a transition. Large companies had emerged and were struggling with divisionalization/ organizational issues and with aspirations to become international. At the same time, business schools were entering a rapid growth phase with all the attendant turmoil and were wrestling with finding sources of funding for research. By now, the stigma of consulting had largely disappeared—it was no longer a service only for "sick" firms—and McKinsey & Co. was working for a number of top companies in the United States. With its growing base of young MBAs populating its client teams, McKinsey had developed strong relationships with the top business schools, the source of its new hires.

This environment was ripe with opportunity for McKinsey to expand its influence on the business world and move beyond the particulars of a client situation. Marvin saw that McKinsey was in a unique position to bring business leaders, academics, and expert business consultants together to connect the theoretical with the practical, and he did just that when he launched the McKinsey Foundation for Management Research in 1955. The brainchild of Zip Reilley, the foundation had two main missions: funding research and providing a forum for executive discussions. Flawlessly executed under the guidance of Marvin Bower, the foundation was an enormous success and spawned and published a multitude of important lectures by major business figures of the time. The money for the foundation came from each partner's compensation; 5 percent was donated. It was essentially a form of tithing.

Zip Reilley's rationale for creating this institution was very persuasive. First, he believed that the senior partners of the firm had a professional obligation to make a contribution to their field. Second, he thought it would be an interesting and personally satisfying thing for him and other senior members of the firm to be involved in. And third, he felt it would be a commercially desirable thing to do because it would add to the distinctiveness and luster of the firm and would repay the investment of the partners' time many times over. As a service firm, McKinsey (like lawyers and public accountants) was not an "inside" member of the business establishment. Creating meaningful relationships with senior executives would be greatly enhanced by providing a forum in which ideas could be shared and discussions could be held. Zip's concept was warmly supported by most of the partners, and Marvin Bower was probably the strongest proponent.

The McKinsey Foundation for Management Research took McKinsey from being just a practitioner to an organization supporting business-related research. At the time, virtually no one, outside of the Office of Naval Research, was providing money in support of management research. Neither the Ford Foundation nor the Carnegie Foundation had begun any significant funding in this regard, making the McKinsey Foundation the largest single private source of funds. The foundation provided a number of small grants ($10,000 to $20,000), including the Management Research Design Contest, the Management Book Award Program in collaboration with the Academy of Management Science, and the McKinsey Article Award Program. There were two criteria used to select grants: the topics had to be of interest to general management, and some member of McKinsey would be personally involved.

McKinsey's reputation in combination with its new role as a funding source for management research enhanced its relationships with business school faculties and resulted in significant joint accomplishments.[29] For example, Ewing W. ("Zip") Reilley and Eli Ginsberg from Columbia coauthored a book called *Effecting Change in Large Organizations,* one of the earliest, if not the first, books on change management.

The executive discussions (the McKinsey/Columbia lectures) were nothing short of a home run. The then dean of business at Columbia, Courtney Brown, was a key figure in the discussions. Leaders of American corporations would come to Columbia's Lowe Library on three successive Wednesday nights to speak to 800 people and describe the management philosophy of their respective firms; then a select group of 60 would have dinner with the speaker. This series of lectures was compiled in book form and distributed by the foundation with McKinsey's name on it.

The lectures covered important topics and were delivered by very prominent people. The first lecture, on managing expanding enterprises, was delivered by Ralph Cordiner, the CEO who had divisionalized General Electric. In subsequent years, speakers included Thomas J. Watson Jr. of IBM ("A Business and Its Beliefs"); Crawford Greenwalt of DuPont ("The Role of Marketing in a Large Industrial Corporation"); Frederic Donner of GM ("The Challenge and Promise of Worldwide Industrial Enterprise"); Roger Blough of U.S. Steel ("Free Man and the Corporation"); and David Rockefeller of Chase ("Creative Management in Banking").[30] Throughout the 10 years of the lecture series, the Lowe Library auditorium was packed; and each year 30,000 to 50,000 compilation books would sell, unprecedented for business-related writings.

Through its foundation, McKinsey & Co. became integrally linked with the generation's important business leaders, their ideas, and emerging research and knowledge. Later, the foundation did a lot with the Institut Européen d'Administration des Affaires (INSEAD) and enhanced

McKinsey's links into the European business world. All of this had a very positive effect on the firm's reputation, which, beyond its people, was McKinsey's single most important asset in Marvin's view. And, although significantly less active today, foundation elements (e.g., the McKinsey Article Award Program in *The Harvard Business Review*) still exist.

Marvin Bower's unwavering belief that all people have a responsibility to contribute to society drove him to embrace and execute Zip Reilley's foundation concept. In his retirement speech in 1992, Marvin reiterated this responsibility for future generations of leaders at McKinsey:

> We are, without doubt, the organization that has the most opportunity for leveraging methods. We can take theory and apply it all around the world. No other organization has the opportunity to develop a new system of managing. And so I hope that the firm is ready to do that, and all around the world—sprouting up within the firm—are opportunities to make a great contribution to society. And it is underway. I want to suggest that you continue it.[31]

Incorporation—1956

As Marvin's vision continued to take concrete form, new considerations and needs would continually arise. By 1956, the growing size of the partnership coupled with the assumption of responsibility and liability under the terms of the partnership forced Marvin to step back and reevaluate the wisdom and practicality of continuing in this mode.

Despite Marvin's desire that McKinsey remain a partnership, he was ultimately convinced, albeit not without a struggle, that it was in the best interests of the firm to incorporate. Only by incorporating would the firm be able to provide a tax shelter for retirement funds, reduce personal liability, and fund continued growth and expansion. Everett Smith, who had a reputation as the practical partner, remembered this struggle:

> The incorporation came about, to be honest with you, because when I became a partner, I was handed the Partner's Agreement . . . and realized that we had made no provision for the future whatsoever . . . We were a partnership at the time, and a partnership has a different tax basis than a corporation, and I went to Mr. Crockett (one of the original partners and the first managing partner after the

buy-out) the next day, as a matter of fact, after I had read the Agreement and said, "My God, have we ever thought of incorporating?" "Oh, yes, oh, yes, we have," said Mr. Crockett in his nice way. I found out later that we had hired a consultant to make a study of the firm, tell us whether we should be a partnership or be incorporated, et cetera. . . . He said there was no point in incorporating, we ought to continue as a partnership. I think really what he did was he found out what Bower thought and then decided what to tell us.

Bower wanted to be a partnership. He was terribly proud of being a partnership. We all were, as a matter of fact, because every nickel we had was at risk, you see. If anything happened to the firm, we all lost our money. We were big, brave boys. It took me two years . . . and an awful lot of pushing and shoving. Bower finally got into the act. It was the only way I could get him to face up to it. So he and I went head to head on that and he disagreed with me 100 percent, but finally, he said it was worth thinking about seriously.

When you stopped and looked at it, you realized that we always had to have about three months working capital. When I say three months working capital, I mean, everybody would give you this, three months of our billings in working capital. So if we billed $100,000 a month, we needed $300,000 worth of working capital, and boy, we were on the edge at that . . . If we were to grow, let's say, instead of $100,000 a month of billings, supposing we had $300,000 a month. That would mean, let's call it $1 million we needed in capital. We didn't have it. How were we going to get it? The only answer that I could think of was that we had to incorporate the firm and not pay individual taxes . . . on the money we were reinvesting in the firm. . . . When I joined the firm we were probably doing $4 million a year. Okay. If you wanted to grow and do $100 million dollars a year, you knew perfectly well how much money you had to have. You had to have three months of that, and where was it going to come from? We were all poor boys, including Marvin.[32]

Marvin fought incorporation because he believed that it would dilute the concept of partnership in which he so strongly believed. He considered partnership to be of enormous benefit to the firm—it instilled a strong commitment to the firm; it provided a means of limiting ownership by any individual or group, thus preventing the formation of power blocs and fostering a partnership style of management; and it permitted a mechanism for transferring ownership to the next generation of McKinsey leaders. His desire to protect those benefits kept him from addressing some of the more practical financial considerations. However, as the benefits of incorporation—the ability to fund growth and the ability to set up a profit sharing and retirement plan for members of the firm—became more clear to Marvin, and as he reflected on Gil Clee's essay distinguishing between the statutory structure and the operating structure of an organization, he realized that formation of a corporation with the partners as sole shareholders need not discourage broad ownership by the partners and might, in fact, facilitate it. At that point, he became more supportive of the need to make this move. In Marvin's own words:

> My attitude towards the corporation was that we shouldn't have it unless we could maintain a partnership philosophy and just deal with corporate shares as we did with partnership shares. In our many discussions, Guy [Crockett] and I remained skeptical, still concerned about the potential change in the character of the firm and its management style. But fortunately Gil [Clee], and especially Ev [Smith], maintained their strong advocacy.
>
> Finally, Guy and I became convinced that all the partners would make determined efforts to maintain the firm's professional character and partnership style of managing and that with their determination, we need have no fears. Another reason for our change in attitude was the fact that incorporation and funding would wipe out the disincentive of the large partner claims and thus facilitate the transfer of ownership to incoming partners and the accrual of a capital gain to sellers of shares if growth continued. The then partners concluded that such a step was essential for the long-term success of the firm.
>
> Incorporation brought valuable management improvements to the firm, and all of its prospective benefits have been realized. Profit-sharing plans that included partners were made possible. The accrued claims of partners were funded. Our shareholders

were (and are) protected against personal liability for claims against the firm, which was not the case when we were a partnership. Finally, we had the capital for our great international growth, which began the very next year. In fact, the accumulation of capital turned out to be the most important benefit of incorporation. The firm had been growing steadily in the United States, but unexpectedly—and over a short period—the growth in Europe became explosive. Yet we were able to finance it without adding new capital. I think it has worked out very well.[33]

In fact, there was virtually no change in the operating structure, including how partners were elected, how they selected clients, and how they were reviewed. Core policies remained in place—one vote for each partner; no single ownership beyond 5 percent; and standardized ongoing performance evaluation. There were some slight modifications to compensation. From the perspective of the more junior partners, these changes, particularly the profit-sharing plans, strongly signaled that ensuring the endurance of the firm for the next generation of leaders was a priority. Lee Walton, who was a junior partner when the decision to incorporate was made, remembers being very appreciative of the older partners' commitment to his generation:

> These older partners permitted incorporation of the firm to establish a profit-sharing retirement trust and a supplemental retirement program to help make up for the fact that the partners up to that juncture had had no retirement provision other than what they saved and invested out of their own current compensation. So, in effect, they were providing what was projected to be a significant contribution to the wealth of the forthcoming partners while recognizing that their own participation in that program would be very short because they were headed toward retirement. Sacrifices like that have been instrumental in keeping this firm together. So the current partner group owes a debt of gratitude to these individuals.[34]

In looking back on the decision to incorporate, although the financial and tax practicalities faced by the growing partnership may not have been at the top of Marvin's list of priorities, he was a reasonable man. So, after some heated and prolonged debate, he could see that the legal liability assumed by all members in a partnership, while unlikely to become a problem in the normal course of operations, could become one if highly qualified people regarded it as a reason not to join or stay with the partnership.

Marvin understood that growth was required, not for the sake of growth itself and not at the sacrifice of the firm's reputation, but to create the right "room" and environment for attracting and retaining the best and the brightest people. Such growth demanded that multiple leadership be more valued than a single leader at the top. The rule at McKinsey & Co. was one person, one vote, so, with Marvin's ultimate concurrence, the incorporation went through and has been maintained. In 1971, with the opening of the Tokyo office, incorporation was tested. McKinsey management would not change its legal structure to accommodate Japanese political demands. As a result, the opening was delayed for six months before it was accepted. McKinsey was the first service firm opened in Japan with such an ownership structure. In fact, the firm did grow substantially after incorporation (see Figure 4.2).

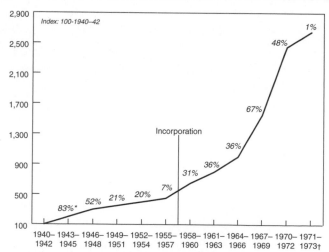

*Indicates percent increase over previous triennium.
†Overlaps preceding triennium.
(Source: John G. Neukom, *McKinsey Memoirs: A Personal Perspective,* 1975.)

FIGURE 4.2   MCKINSEY & CO. GROWTH FROM 1940 TO 1973
(Number of Consultants)[35]

With the incorporation and the transition to MBA hires, the firm entered a new phase of growth, more than doubling in size from 1950 to 1959, with its constituency shifting from about 20 percent MBAs to over 80 percent MBAs, reducing the median age of the McKinsey consultants by almost 10 years.

Going Global with One-Firm Identity—1959

In 1953, Marvin and his wife Helen took their first vacation outside of North America. Whereas most people would view a vacation as an opportunity to temporarily exit from their professional life and concerns, Marvin was a distinct exception. He took advantage of every vacation to reflect on McKinsey & Co. and think about the challenges ahead. As Jim Balloun, current chairman, president, and CEO of Acuity Brands, and with McKinsey from 1965 through 1996, heading the Atlanta office from 1979 through 1993, noted: "Marvin had more persistence than anyone else I've ever met . . . and Helen had more patience than most spouses, including my own."[36]

It was during this 1953 trip to Portugal that Marvin became convinced McKinsey needed to become an international firm. As he described his logic:

> During World War II, America had begun to think internationally. This thinking was heightened by *One World* (1943), a widely read book by Wendell L. Wilkie, dynamic Republican candidate for president. He pointed out that America is ". . . now changing completely from a young nation of domestic concerns to an adult nation of international interests and world outlook." . . . Men and women all over the world are . . . beginning to know that man's welfare throughout the world is interdependent. . . . Our clients needed to think globally and to service them properly we needed to think and understand more than America. . . . I felt that if we looked at it from the standpoint of the clients, the American companies would want us to help them move into Europe. I felt that if we wanted to be a leading firm we had to be able to help out clients that way . . . I felt that just as we had become a national firm, so we must become an international firm.[37]

Around the time of Marvin's trip, momentum for global expansion was building in the business world, with American companies establishing their own subsidiaries and on occasion buying up companies in Europe. Not surprisingly, clients were beginning to value McKinsey's consulting services for their interests outside the United States.

Although Marvin was a strong proponent of McKinsey's global expansion, there was significant resistance from some of the partnership group, and he recognized that reaching a consensus would require listening carefully to the opposition. In order to play the necessary role of an unbiased arbitrator, Marvin made a conscious decision to turn over the job of public advocate to Gil Clee, who, like Marvin, felt it was of critical importance that McKinsey & Co. open international offices.

Six years passed from the time Marvin and Gil first proposed global expansion to the opening of McKinsey's first European office in London. This was probably the longest period of debate in McKinsey's history. Marvin was not a patient or an indecisive leader. A lot was at stake and a lot was at risk. During those six years, Gil never let up on his advocacy through his memos, proposals, and plans. U.S. clients continued their pull for McKinsey to extend its services to Europe while the partnership debated the wisdom of the move and tested policies and procedures that would ensure that the single-firm identity could be maintained while serving Europe.

The Debate

The debate as to whether or not to expand internationally centered around a compelling set of both pros and cons. The pros included an ability to respond effectively to the increasing demand for overseas services from McKinsey's existing globalizing client base and proactively addressing the fact that the times were changing as communications, transportation, and so on were more and more enabling a global economy. The cons included the fact that McKinsey's U.S. activity was profitable and growing as fast as could be accommodated by the firm, so why drain off resources from this growing, successful operation to start up offices overseas instead of allocating those same resources to open offices in new U.S. locations (e.g., Detroit, Atlanta); moreover, European companies would balk at the fees and, as family-run businesses, were not ready for the top management approach that had become McKinsey & Co.'s signature. Marvin recalled the partnership resistance and credited the success of McKinsey's European model to the long process of debate:

> In fact, we couldn't be successful in moving overseas unless nearly everybody was in favor of it. We had studies made. Out of these disagreements came some very good things that would not have happened if there hadn't been disagreement.
>
> For example, Everett Smith kept raising issues that he thought might keep us from making a decision to become international. He said we shouldn't have a different kind of practice in Europe than we have in the U.S. After quite a few months of study, we formulated a policy that we would have the same kind of practice, the same caliber of people, the same general level of fees, and if we couldn't succeed we would pull back. The alternative of that would have been to take small studies for small companies and sort of work our way up. So the differences of opinion resulted in our adopting a strategy that was very difficult to carry out but which we did carry out.[38]

The Client Pull

At a management meeting in 1954, Gil Clee suggested that, "for the present, everybody should learn all he can about problems our American clients have in connection with their overseas operations. In a comparatively short time we should have a clearer understanding of what our future should be in this field."[39] To this end, McKinsey hired Charles Lee, an expert on business in Europe to work with Clee in studying and formulating McKinsey's expansion plans. Clee also wrote a piece for *The Harvard Business Review* called "Expanding World Enterprise."[40] It was a seminal article in an influential publication and attracted the interest of potential clients.

That same year, with globalization in its infancy, American clients were starting to pull McKinsey & Co. outside of the United States and a number of studies were under way on the continent. This work included a global organizational study for ITT, strategy work with Heinz in the United Kingdom, global expansion efforts with Food Machinery Corp., and an organization study for IBM World Trade.

These early studies proved to be good launchpads for McKinsey & Co. consultants to broaden their own thinking and adopt a more international perspective. According to Mac Stewart, with McKinsey from 1952 through 1996:

> The IBM World Trade study gave us an understanding of a major multinational corporation. We have since been told that the regional organization structure that we worked out contributed substantially to IBM's success in taking over the European computer market. Tom Watson Jr. told me at dinner one night that the study laid the groundwork for IBM World Trade Corporation for many years.[41]

In the spring of 1956, Gil sent the partners another memorandum on the opportunity and the need to move rapidly:

> In this situation, American management consulting firms are faced by an opportunity and a challenge. It is an opportunity for them to obtain gratifying and important rewards by doing on a worldwide plane what they have done or are doing in the United States to aid business in accomplishing its task successfully. It is a challenge in that it means making a greater contribution of effort and time, in accordance with America's new world role, to carry the know-how and techniques of management consulting to other countries. . . .
>
> Foreign industry needs and wants American management consultant assistance. American industry operating abroad has this same need and desire. Finally, a proper understanding today of American industry's problems, as its foreign activities become more and more complex and extensive, requires the dedication of adequate time and knowledge to the solution of its foreign management problems as an integral part of the total picture that determines a company's success or failure.[42]

Later that year, a key opportunity to work with a European company opened a number of doors for McKinsey. John Loudon, one of the managing directors of the Royal Dutch Shell Group from 1952 to 1965 and chairman from 1965 to 1976, became aware of McKinsey & Co. and Marvin Bower through Gus Long, chairman of Texaco.

A subsequent phone conversation between Loudon and Marvin launched a study in Venezuela that was essentially an organizational study and, as it turned out, a test of McKinsey & Co. Hugh Parker, who was with McKinsey from 1951 to 1983 and was the first head of the U.K. office, and Lee Walton, who was with McKinsey from 1956 to 1973, both relocated to South America. Marvin, in his capacity as engagement director, would go down for about two to three weeks at a time.

As Warren Cannon recalls, the results were very positive and propelled the firm to a new level of visibility outside of the United States:

> It was so successful that John Loudon brought the firm to London for a worldwide organization study and from there it just exploded. Marvin played a really critical role. He introduced Royal Dutch Shell. He assembled the team for Royal Dutch Shell. He directed the study, developed the client, was instrumental in cementing its success, and moved it to the U.K.[43]

During the course of the Shell study, client pull continued to increase and other forces were swinging the pendulum of partner support. In particular, in 1957, a *Business Week* article described McKinsey & Co. as an American firm with a sizable foreign business that still operates abroad by sending consultants out from its U.S. offices, in contrast to Booz·Allen & Hamilton, which had already opened European offices.[44] The management consulting world was as competitive as the next, and this article surely fueled some concern about lagging behind Booz.

It was shortly after the *Business Week* article appeared that McKinsey's work with Shell expanded, based on its initial success.

The London Office

In early 1958, Gil Clee sent out a memorandum recommending the opening of the London office, based on the following rationale:

1. Although we have deliberately moved cautiously since April 1953, the opportunity in Europe is substantial. With the advent of the European Common Market, which became effective January 1, 1958, many U.S. and European companies will be compelled to reexamine their basic operations.

2. Since January 1957, we have served 23 clients on purely international problems either outside or in the United States. This work has taken firm personnel to 19 countries.
3. A number of firm members have become interested in overseas assignments. Hugh Parker has the capacity to serve as resident manager of a London office and is in residence there. We have other associates now in residence in London and The Hague.
4. Our reputation for overseas work has been enhanced by seven articles written by Charles Lee and about as many speeches.[45]

The result was growing partnership support for international expansion. When McKinsey & Co. did expand to Europe, it was done in a manner similar to the successful national expansion some 20 years previously. Just as McKinsey had seeded its national office launches with the best and the brightest from its New York office, some of the strongest domestic resources were transferred to Europe—not an easy sacrifice for McKinsey's U.S. operations. In addition, consistent with Marvin's vision for national growth, McKinsey took the single-identity, one-firm concept to Europe. This meant, among other things, salaries and fees relatively consistent with U.S. practices.[46] As Lee Walton, one of the first associates in Europe and subsequently McKinsey's managing director from 1968 through 1973, points out, this was a particularly challenging goal: "We had to be able to justify what in many cases was as much as 10 times fee differences with local competitors."[47]

At the next management meeting, the proposal was discussed, and finally, some six years after the international concept was initially raised, the partnership voted to proceed. Marvin remembered that meeting:

When someone suggested further study, I decided that we had studied the problem long enough and asked for a show of hands on Gil's proposal.[48]

Once agreement was reached, Marvin and McKinsey moved quickly:

The next day we announced that we would become an international firm and open an office in London as soon as legal, tax, and physical arrangements could be made.[49]

The visibility that the Shell study afforded McKinsey & Co. greased the wheels for the successful 1959 launching of the firm's first office outside the

United States. On January 15, 1959, John Loudon made a worldwide announcement that Shell had adopted McKinsey's recommendations. Loudon also published an important article about the new Shell organization structure in Britain's prestigious publication *The Director.* He wrote: "A leading United States firm of management consultants, McKinsey & Co., was invited by the managing directors to assist them in the study."[50]

Despite such prestigious publicity, the move to London was challenging, as Hugh Parker, the first manager of the U.K. office, remembers:

> Lee Walton and I were asked if we would like to open an office in London. And, of course, we did. We were told, "Here's $25,000." That was our starting working capital. That was the first offshore office that McKinsey opened. Very shortly after that we opened an office in Geneva and subsequently Paris and in Düsseldorf.
>
> So, Gil was instrumental in setting up the financial controls. He dealt with the lawyers and generally did the administrative establishment of our practice in London while Lee and I were out looking for work, scrambling for work. . . . It could have been lonely sitting in James Street. Marvin called almost every day to see if he could do anything.
>
> We had several things going against us which we had to overcome. One was the fact that we were simply not known. . . . Secondly, we were American and there was still, even in the late 1950s, residual resentment against Americans. Not anti-Americanism overtly, but there was sort of a "we've had enough of you guys" sort of thing. Thirdly, management consulting, although it existed [in England], and there was in fact an association of management consultants comprising the four well established firms [Associate Industrial Consultants, Personnel Administration, Production Engineering, and Urwick, Orr & Partners] at the time in England. They were perfectly respectable firms. They were certainly not doing McKinsey-style management consulting as Marvin had then developed it, and people didn't know what kind of management consulting we were doing.
>
> It was believed that probably our earliest work would be doing work for the British subsidiaries of American client companies, like H. J. Heinz or Massey. We did do some work for ITT [and] Hoover U. K. But ICI was a huge bell ringer. They were the biggest

industrial company in Britain. Thanks to Paul Chambers [now Sir Paul Chambers], they gave it a lot of publicity. I don't think anyone in England knew we were working for Shell, but they sure as hell knew when we were working for ICI.

Marvin negotiated the study. He was a very persuasive guy. He shone integrity. I think that's what made people trust him and accept him readily.[51]

Once having added ICI, a huge European company, to McKinsey's roster, the staff of the London office grew to eight. John Macomber, the head of the continental office from 1961 to 1964 and in 1967, subsequently chairman of Celanese and president of the Import/Export Bank, remembers Europe in 1959:

We forget about the fact that the war absolutely ruined Europe. When I first went to England, there were rubble piles as I went to work in front of Royal Dutch Shell where the bombs had been. Still hadn't been cleared up—in 1959. And bread was still on price control in Paris in 1961. So, it was a much different kind of an environment in a sense that it was not nearly as rich, and significantly less sophisticated.[52]

Roger Morrison who led the London office from 1973 through 1983, remembered how the Shell and ICI engagements parlayed into multiple clients in postwar England:

We were strongly endorsed and supported by a number of influential people in the U.K. business society largely because we had been retained by Shell and ICI. It became almost fashionable to call in McKinsey. In a relatively short period of time, we were called in by Vickers, which at that time owned British Aerospace, the shipyards, and the steel works in England. We were then called in by the British Post Office as a result of the work we'd done at Vickers. We were called in by Rolls Royce in aerospace and subsequently, in the motor car field; and we were called in by United Biscuits. So McKinsey became a household word, which was capped ultimately by the BBC and the Bank of England deciding to retain us.[53]

Bank of England Plans Operational Changes

Efficiency Experts Advise 'Old Lady' to Grow Slimmer

By JOSEPH COLLINS
Special to The New York Times

LONDON, Feb. 3 — The Bank of England, the leading symbol of London's financial power, will shortly make changes in its operations on the advice of American efficiency experts.

McKinsey & Co., management consultants, have had a team at the bank for nearly a year. Last night it was officially announced that their suggested reforms would be made.

They are neither radical nor revolutionary changes. The bank's messengers will still wear tall silk hats in carrying polite suggestions from the Governor that have the force of law in the close-knit financial community here.

Experts To Stay a Bit

A spokesman for the bank said today that the recommendations of the McKinsey experts, dealing in good part with planning methods, had mostly been accepted. The McKinsey men will stay until the end of this month so that the changes can be made in consultation with them.

The Old Lady of Threadneedle Street, as the bank has been affectionately known to generations of City bankers will, among other things, get a little slimmer.

A statement from the bank on the proposed changes said: "Economies in manpower are likely to flow from some of the recommendations, but none of them appears to imply sudden or drastic cuts in the present level of staffing." The bank has 4,500 employes; the 2,500 who work for the bank's printing plant were excluded from the investigation.

One of the most important of the recommendations was the establishment of an Internal Policy Committee under the chairmanship of the Governor, Sir Leslie O'Brien, "to concentrate on long-term issues of policy and to promote the studies that these long-term issues require."

At present there are several ad hoc committees doing high-level thinking for the future on such matters as the role of monetary policy.

Another change will be the formation of a new department that will bring together the work on computer development and the work can

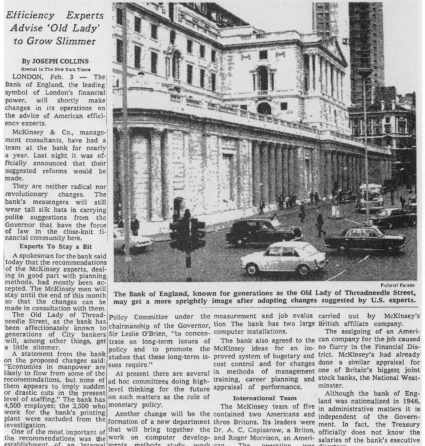

Pictorial Parade
The Bank of England, known for generations as the Old Lady of Threadneedle Street, may get a more sprightly image after adopting changes suggested by U.S. experts.

measurement and job evaluation The bank has two large computer installations.

The bank also agreed to the McKinsey ideas for an improved system of bugetary and cost control and for changes in methods of management training, career planning and appraisal of performance.

International Team

The McKinsey team of five contained two Americans and three Britons. Its leaders were Dr. A. C. Copisarow, a Briton, and Roger Morrison, an American. The operation was

carried out by McKinsey's British affiliate company.

The assigning of an American company for the job caused no flurry in the Financial District. McKinsey's had already done a similar appraisal for one of Britain's biggest joint stock banks, the National Westminster.

Although the bank of England was nationalized in 1946, in administrative matters it is independent of the Government. In fact, the Treasury officially does not know the salaries of the bank's executive directors.

FIGURE 4.3   BANK OF ENGLAND PLANS OPERATIONAL CHANGE
New York Times, 2/4/70

With the Bank of England study in 1969, the London office could say with confidence, "We've been accepted." Sir Alcon Copisarow, then a member of the London office, vividly remembers this breakthrough:

Lord O'Brien called me to do the Bank of England study. I said, "For nearly 300 years, since 1694, you have kept your secrets away from the Chancellor of the Exchequer, and now you are asking

private consultants, and American ones at that, to come in when
the government does not have this information?"[54]

A remarkable achievement in and of itself to have penetrated England
with American business experts, the establishment of the London office
was, in the words of Lee Walton, "one of the most significant events in
firm history as the first step of making the firm a truly international
body."[55] By late 1966, the U.K. office had become the second largest in the
firm after New York. (See Figure 4.3.)

The Evolution of McKinsey in Europe and Migration to the Continent

By 1961, it was time for McKinsey & Co. to expand further into Europe.
Marvin Bower proposed a plan that entailed a somewhat methodical evo-
lution, beginning with an office in Geneva and studies generated from that
location for foreign holdings of American companies (e.g., DuPont and
General Foods). The partnership supported Marvin's plan.

However, it soon became clear that the firm had not fully anticipated
the dynamics of the expansion. Again, as it had in London, McKinsey
experienced a greater demand for its expertise from European companies
than from international operations of U.S. corporations. Moreover, with
Europe an appealing growth platform, McKinsey's somewhat competitive
partners began tripping over one another in the rush to open new offices.
Mac Stewart remembers how, contrary to the plan to take it one step at a
time, the expansion exploded:

> We had this one funny situation where the strategy was to collect
> a series of functional and language skills in Geneva under John
> Macomber. Then in about 1967, when we had about 30 or 40 of
> them and a few tested clients in different countries—Italy,
> Switzerland, France, Germany—we would begin to open an
> office. But because of the good relationship with John Loudon—
> who introduced us to Prince Bernhard of the Netherlands (who
> introduced us to KLM and then SHV; SHV is not well-known,
> but is a very big oil company in Holland)—all of a sudden, we had

two clients in Holland and no office. So, bingo, we opened an office in Amsterdam to the surprise and horror of the McKinsey people in Geneva. They panicked. They went ape. And four of them rushed off and opened the office in Düsseldorf, and five more went to Paris under John Macomber. The whole theory of our European movement was to be able to serve foreign subsidiaries of our U.S. clients, which has amounted to about 3 percent of our billings ever since. So we went there for all the wrong reasons and had all the right policies.[56]

John Macomber (who opened the Paris office) reflects on the challenges, excitement, and rewards for those involved in this migration:

When we went to Europe . . . there was no other firm in the world that had this idea of building a professional firm that was really owned throughout by the people in it. And there was no other firm in the world that treated it like a profession. When I went to Europe, everybody advertised. We didn't advertise. It was just . . . like most operations in those days, there was no real body of knowledge about how European business worked. There was no understanding of the way the decision-making process worked, or the way people behaved, what value systems were, other than what we learned rather superficially in school and college. So it was a little bit like diving into a swimming pool, and you didn't know how deep the water was. So I am not disdainful at all at people who were a little chary about the firm going into it. It was a big decision on top of that. There was some financial risk. But it was really those other two risks of being associated with a rather unsavory group of people, point one, and point two being our lack of knowledge.

In the beginning [in France], we were not particularly well accepted. And then . . . a series of events . . . got us on the network. de Gaulle was very much in. He was terrific. He was maddeningly brilliant, incisive, aloof, all the characteristics you've heard about, and very brave. Very brave. Working in that environment [with the leading industrialists] was fantastic. That was in the days when the "le plastique," which were the bombs, were going off all over Paris, and Algeria was a big thing. We began to get very good marks, and the result was that suddenly . . . it all happened in a period of a couple of years, it was not only an acceptable thing to retain McKinsey & Co., but boy, it was a very prestigious thing if you could get them to come to work for you. This all happened because we got on the trolley car with the [business] leadership of France.

The same thing applied in Switzerland . . . we somehow got into the establishment. It wasn't a concerted effort. We weren't saying we've got to get into the establishment. We were trying to get to know people . . . which we did. And it just happened that we did extremely good work in Switzerland and in Germany and in Amsterdam.

When we landed in Europe, Europe was waiting for us. We didn't know it, but it soon became evident that they were hungry for the kind of work that Marvin really wanted us to do, which was strategic, top management stuff that really impacted the direction of the company. And, by the way, it also impacted the countries in which we were operating. There is no question, at least in the early days. McKinsey & Co. did as much as any institution to rebuild European productivity. No question. In fact, I don't think anyone even came close to doing as much as we did for the automobile industry, the banking industry, the airline industry, the oil business. Those industries all had a huge benefit from this.

The client list in France was unbelievable. I think it was because they knew that we may not always come up with the right answer, and we might have done dumb things, but there never was one scintilla of a doubt about what was motivating us. And it wasn't money. It was trying to help them. . . . And I think it was the fact that, obviously we had interesting, bright, attractive, convincing people . . . and the ideas were good—but the thing that I think always really worked was the conviction of what our motivation was. And our motivation was really to help.

I think almost all the work we did in Europe, whether it was from Germany, France, or Amsterdam which were the big units, was aimed at trying to help [the clients] figure out what they wanted to do. At Zwanenberg-Organon (a prestigious Dutch firm engaged in pharmaceutical and food manufacturing on an international scale), the issue was, "Are we in the pharmaceutical business or are we in the specialty chemical business? What are we? What do we need to do? And, by the way, what are the pros and cons of these different choices?" Because in almost every one of these companies there was conflict about what they were trying to do. At Rhône-Poulenc they were absolutely beside themselves. "Are we a chemical company, are we a pharmaceutical company, a fine chemical company, and by the way, what's our relationship with the government?" It was all this stuff that, as a psychologist would say, was not together. It was not together.

The people we had, at least in those days, were enormously able convincers. And they should have been. Because they were bright, articulate, and they had done their homework. . . . When you were successful you could just see the results. That's what made consulting fun. It was really powerful stuff. Max Geldens really changed the whole industrial base of Holland. And I think the team in France did the same thing. And Germany with John McDonald. Amazing performance. Of course we had, in many ways, significantly less sophisticated clients. But we had much more sophisticated clients in another way because they were dealing with public policy. And they were also broke after the war.

Marvin would make annual trips and we'd have reviews. I think he was astounded by what happened, absolutely astounded. And the reach of the firm. The influence of the firm. I think Marvin was truly proud, he was impressed, but he was truly proud of the impact that the people in Amsterdam and Paris and Germany—these were in the early days—were making on the lives of the ordinary citizen. That was a big motivator for us.[57]

Although, as John Macomber noted, Marvin would never come out and directly state "I am proud of you," he was nothing less than bursting with pride at how the partnership and the teams took their stellar capabilities abroad, penetrated foreign cultures, and helped a postwar continent rebuild its economic infrastructure.

When all was said and done, McKinsey's global expansion proved to be phenomenally successful, but not at all like the partnership had imagined.

Much to the surprise of all, the opportunities were not with global operations of U.S. companies, but rather with leading European companies.
Thus, in Europe, McKinsey & Co. found itself primarily serving European
companies out of local country offices, rather than the original conception
of dealing with the European subsidiaries of American corporations out of
a small number of regional offices. So, what began, according to Marvin, as
"strategic opportunism" culminated in one of the most powerful outcomes
in the history of management consulting.

Women Managing Studies—1968

In 1964, Marvin had stopped wearing his hat, the firm had six offices in
the United States and two in Europe, the first women were graduated
from the Harvard Business School,[58] and the first women associates were
hired. Within this ostensibly conservative firm environment, a major transition was quietly occurring. Harvey Golub remembers the decision four
years later to have a woman manage a study because he was the catalyst:

> There was a woman associate named Mary Falvey (with McKin-
> sey from 1967 through 1975) who had an economics degree from
> Cornell and an MBA from Harvard . . . and was one of the
> smartest people I've ever met. There were no women partners at
> the time and they were just beginning to hire woman in any kind
> of numbers. Mary worked with me on a study for the Insurance
> Company of North American, which is now part of Cigna. . . .
> They were going to go into a second phase of the study, and I con-
> cluded that she would manage that phase of the study. . . . Dick
> Neuschel was the director in charge of McKinsey's relationship
> with Insurance of North America. I went to talk with him and
> Marvin about this next phase. Dick asked who I thought should
> manage it, and I said Mary. . . . He thought for a minute and said,
> "Are you going to ask the client about it?" I said "No." He asked
> why and I said, "If you ask the client about it they will think that
> it is an issue that they need to think about. They are not equipped
> to tell who the best engagement manager is—I am; that's my
> responsibility, not theirs." Marvin smiled and asked what I was
> going to do and I said, "Well, I already did it, Marvin. I went down

and told them that they are going to have a new engagement manager starting on Monday and that she is the smartest person that I've ever met and that they are going to love her." And he said, "Oh." And that was it.

That was an inflection point on how people think about staff. It's an inflection point in an adjustment to a firm that was as straight an establishment you could ever get. And Marvin and Dick's reaction was simple. They probably wouldn't have done it on their own. . . . But they adapted to the change very well. To a man who might not even know how to think about these things. It's the firm Marvin built. It's guys like Dick Neuschel who would be willing to change a lifetime of habit on a dime.[59]

As Mary Falvey remembers her early time in the firm:

I was totally in awe of Marvin, from the time I heard him speak at training. I was walking down the hall with another associate. Marvin was coming the other way. Marvin said hello to the other associate [an unidentified man] first. Before Marvin had a chance to greet me, I said, "Hello, Marvin." Marvin replied, "Hello, Mary." And I felt that I had been accepted. He knew I was an associate, and he knew my name.[60]

Mary knew that her need to be accepted went beyond the halls of McKinsey:

When I was managing the study, it was a very tricky situation; the client had invested a ton of money over the previous two years in systems that were not delivering what they wanted. We told them to stop investing, it would not work. There were no women in management [at the client]. They accepted me as an adviser. It was a phenomenal feeling.[61]

Marvin may have been somewhat reticent when it came to embracing the notion of women professionals in leadership positions. However, his commitment to providing the best capabilities to the clients outweighed any concerns he may have had that, like hatless heads or argyle socks, a female engagement manager (not an accepted practice at the time) would be a distraction from the matter at hand. As Marvin's experience with female consultants progressed, he came to see them as a definite advantage. In 1999, he said:

> Put women on every team. All-male teams often wind up spinning wheels. Add women, and you're likely to break through problems. It's true that women have more intuition than men. I have observed that when I have worked for some time with an all-male team and then add a woman, the team becomes more imaginative, has more and better ideas, and is more sensitive to what's on the mind of client(s).[62]

As Linda Levinson, the first female partner, remembers the early days of female consultants:

> The men were worrying about how to behave with women in the firm; the women were afraid of making a mistake; and Marvin fostered that McKinsey was a gender-blind meritocracy. Marvin made it possible for women to succeed. He held us to the same standards and made us feel we could meet those standards. Marvin's definition of professionalism has left an indelible impression:
>
> > Speak your mind.
> > Hold to the highest standards of integrity.
> > Deliver more than your clients expect.
>
> It was a very special place because of the values Marvin was setting.[63]

Not Going Public: Selling Stock To Partners—1966

During the late 1960s and early 1970s, there was a definite move for a number of service firms to go public—Arthur D. Little & Co., Booz·Allen & Hamilton—as well as the sale of Cresap, McCormick & Paget to Citicorp. With this trend unfolding around them and evidence of personal fortunes being amassed by the partners in these now public firms, while there was no strong sentiment to go public within the McKinsey partnership, a conscious decision on this matter was called for.

Marvin was convinced that going public would be wrong for the firm, and that the economic performance pressures created by being beholden to stockholders and satisfying the expectations of the market gurus could impair McKinsey's need for independence. He also believed that going public would encourage the acceptance of questionable client engagements for the sake of quarterly revenue reporting, as well as compromise McKinsey's reputation and hence its sustainability. Marvin had many conversations with his peers in other institutions as they pondered this option, and he reflects on this time:

> The three of us had a debate at a meeting of management consultants (see Figure 4.4). Richard M. Paget for his firm, James W. Taylor, the head of Booz, and myself. We argued the pros and cons of having shares owned outside. I maintained that it's better to have all the shares owned inside because then the firm can be more

Consultants Differ on Ownership

Marvin Bower, right, a director of McKinsey & Co., and Richard M. Paget, center, president of Cresap, McCormick & Paget, who had a spirited debate concerning management consultants, talking with James W. Taylor, president of Booz, Allen & Hamilton.

By LEONARD SLOANE

Two leaders of the management-consulting fraternity yesterday, argued — genteelly, of course — as to whether private firms or those owned publicly or by institutions represented the future of their profession.

Marvin Bower, a director of McKinsey & Co., Inc., told the North American Conference of Management Consultants that "the posture of independence is greatest when the firms are owned by individuals associated with it rather than by outsiders."

However, speaking to the same 300 consultants attending the all-day conference at the Plaza Hotel, Richard M. Paget, president of Cresap, McCormick & Paget, said, "The fact of private ownership is no guarantee against malfeasance, as some of us here have seen. Nor is pub-

lic ownership necessarily conducive to malfeasance."

Yesterday's debate was a continuation of the battle that has erupted in recent years over the ownership of consulting firms. During this period, such giants as Booz, Allen & Hamilton and Arthur D. Little have gone public, while Cresap, McCormick; Fry Consultants and William

Continued on Page 46, Column 4

FIGURE 4.4   CONSULTANTS DIFFER ON OWNERSHIP
(*The New York Times*, January 26, 1972 © The New York Times Company)

flexible; we don't have to have compliance with government regulations. Most important of all, we can run the firm the way we want to run it without having to think about earnings for outside shareholders. We can and do take a long-term viewpoint. If we want to take a lot of money to get our practice in China started, for example, we don't have to make profits satisfactory to an owner. In fact, Booz·Allen & Hamilton did sell 15 percent of their shares to the public. That meant that they had to comply with regulations that we didn't have to. They lost some of their flexibility and for one reason or another, they bought the shares back. They borrowed money from a bank and bought them back from the public. I believe that they are now back where they started from. Then there was Cresap, McCormick & Paget which sold their shares to Citicorp and they have bought their shares back from Citicorp. . . .

We never had a serious discussion about going public. If there was any demand for it, it was minimal. The firm was approached by Citicorp in 1966, before they got Cresap. I wasn't the managing director after 1967. Lee Walton was approached and he too turned it down without even referring it to all the partners. He told Citicorp it would be a mistake from their standpoint, which they subsequently found to be the case.[64]

While at the time there was no push to go public at McKinsey, Marvin was not confident that this matter was put to bed forever:

I feel quite sure there will be future push by some partners to sell shares to the public or to some bank or other corporation. Such share prices will be a way to capitalize on the goodwill built by earlier partners. If such a sellout does take place (which is against our policy and which I hope will never happen), there will be quite a few of us spinning in our graves. If it does happen, it will be to satisfy the greed of the partners instead of following our deeply embedded policy of passing along the firm to succeeding generations of partners stronger than those partners received it from their predecessors. That move would violate our founding mission of establishing a firm that would continue in perpetuity.[65]

Despite Marvin's debates with his peers, the mismatch between a service firm and a publicly held firm was less obvious to others who then had to learn the hard way. As the period is described in an internal book *Booz·Allen & Hamilton: Seventy Years of Client Service, 1914–1984:*

> In addition, the talk, as the 1960s drew to a close, was bottom-line talk: Going public. There was a way to realize one's assets in the consulting business. Boom times were making optimists out of almost everyone. Business was good. The market was hot. . . . In its December 20, 1969, issue, *Business Week* told part of the "rich inside story" of Booz·Allen & Hamilton as the firm prepared to sell 500,000 shares of its common stock to the public. Net billings for 1969 were $55 million. They had doubled since 1956. Net income had done better, having risen from $1.5 million in 1964 to over $3.5 million. At the proposed $30 a share, Allen's and Bowen's holdings each were to top $7 million, and those of eight other officer-directors would range from $1.6 million to $4.5 million.
>
> . . . Going public had its own rationale [beyond personal wealth]: to make it easier to acquire other companies, to give stockholders (including officer-owners) some liquidity for their stock, and to be, in Jim Allen's words, "in the spirit of the times."
>
> It turned out to be a bad idea. Booz·Allen & Hamilton stock hit the market at its peak and went down. "Being public was not serving us well," said Allen. "Also, it was not a way to enlarge the firm. The way to do that was to get people, not companies."[66]

Several years later, Booz·Allen & Hamilton bought the shares back and struggled to reposition itself as an objective outsider. And Walter Wriston, president of Citicorp from 1967 to 1984, found that Cresap had not been as profitable a subsidiary as had been expected.[67]

Marvin Bower gave up the opportunity for a personal fortune by not jumping on the bandwagon. This decision provides strong evidence of Marvin's commitment to his personal values and to the values he had established for the firm. He believed that, if management consultants had to answer to shareholders, they would inevitably provide poorer service to clients. It would simply not be possible to be a preferred counselor to a public company while also being a public company.

John Forbis, currently the head of development at Canon and with McKinsey from 1971 to 1983, captures this trade-off between wealth and reputation/values:

When I joined the firm in the early 1970s, we knew we would never be as wealthy as investment bankers, but we would be well off. We also knew we could not be public and be McKinsey—it was not a concept that would work—the values were embedded. The institution was built on integrity. Marvin not taking McKinsey public is like George Washington refusing the title of king—it did not match the founding principles.[68]

Rather than move the firm in a direction that would provide him with a "wealth beyond Caesar's," Marvin went in almost the opposite direction: He adhered to policies he had had the foresight to put in place. He sold his stock back to the partnership at its book value, thereby cementing McKinsey & Co. as an enduring professional management consulting firm with the appropriate financial infrastructure to provide unbiased, independent advice to other businesses.

This action was lauded by the then current partners and won the respect of partners to come. Peter Foy, currently chairman of Whitehead Mann Group P/C, who was with McKinsey from 1968 to 1973, and again from 1974 to 1996, captured this sentiment:

The greatest thing Marvin ever did was to give his shares away. If you look at the demise of other entrepreneurial places like this, you often see the emerging greed of the founder. . . . But our founder Marvin Bower didn't. If there is one thing, it's hopeful if you're an icon to be the beneficiary of longevity. I just made that up but I think it's true. And the fact that he's been around all these years helps the effectiveness of his legacy. And the fact that he bequeathed his wealth in the equity stakes to the firm, rather than squeeze every last drop of the dollar benefit that he could have, was for me an enormous professional gift and role model gesture that all these other guys failed on.[69]

As Henry Strage points out, very few people would forsake their own fortune for the future of an institution:

The thing that always struck me as being quite unbelievable was when he came up with this formula that no partner should own more than 5 percent of the firm. The implications of that were that he had to sell his shares back to the firm at a ridiculous price. Did he have, what, 50 percent or 60 percent? Something like that. It's inconceivable that anybody would have done that today. Can you imagine? To say, "Well, look, I want this firm to continue, so no partner should own more than 5 percent, and by the way, I'm going to sell my shares back. At a huge discount.[70]

Marvin, as was his nature, was a bit more humble about his decision to sell his shares back: he viewed his decision as a natural requirement of his vision to create an enduring institution. The only way the firm would continue would be if all the partners would do the same:

Many people have mentioned the fact that I could have made more money by staying in the job, by selling the firm to somebody else, or by holding out for higher prices for my shares, which were all bought up as part of the regular plan (with no special payments). I did not think of that decision in those terms because my purpose was to establish a firm that would live on after me. Since that was my ambition, I did not look at it as a generous decision.[71]

Insisting on Succession—1967

Marvin believed that old leaders need to get out of the way to make room for new leaders, so that an institution could have a future. So, in October of 1967, at the age of 64, Marvin Bower stepped down as managing director of the firm. With Marvin acting in this position formally for 17 years and effectively for 28 years, there was pressure for him to stay on in this role and concern and uncertainty about what the future would bring without Marvin at the helm. Hugh Parker captures the mood prevailing at the time:

Everybody knew what was coming. He had told us. I remember discussions upon discussions about [the concern that] there was nobody to replace Marvin. Changing over McKinsey from Marvin was like saying get rid of your spouse. It was no simple matter. A lot of people were closely hinged on Marvin Bower.[72]

Mac Stewart remembers that no one thought they could find a good enough replacement for Marvin:

Marvin Bower had established the principle that managing directors of the firm should retire at the age of 65. Well, Marvin Bower, as he approached 65, made it very clear that he intended to do that. But the other partners, I think most of them, wanted him to stay on. They felt that he was doing a superb job and none of them could do as good a job as he did. But he insisted.[73]

Mac Stewart also remembers how the transition was made:

There was a very interesting article about how you put together a team that runs a company. So Marvin decided to create this executive group and he picked the three candidates for his job—Everett Smith, Gilbert Clee, and Richard Neuschel. The executive group went on for a couple of years. Then, I think it was at my second directors' meeting Marvin said, "Is everybody satisfied with the work of the executive group?" I stuck up my hand and said, "No. I'm not and if anybody in the room, except executive group members, feels satisfied stick up your hand." No hand went up.

I was rewarded for this dissent by being made the head of the committee to examine the situation. What we found out was, the executive group wasn't working because Marvin had been such a superb leader. We would have these partner meetings from Friday morning until about noon on Saturday. The next Monday morning, we'd get a blue paper that said, in effect, "This is what we decided, here is who is responsible for making it happen, and here is the deadline for when it should be finished." Bing, bing, bing. When he created this executive group, the three candidates didn't want to look as though they were politicking, so they didn't do anything. So for about a year and a half, maybe two years, nothing was decided and nothing was implemented. So, our committee recommended that Marvin resume the chair for another nine months. Meanwhile, we worked out an election procedure for managing partner that's pretty much still the same today. It got gussied up a bit. And Gilbert Clee was elected.[74]

In a 1968 *International Management* article by Geraldine Hinds, entitled "Step Down and Let Younger Men Lead," Marvin explained his philosophy about succession:

"If a man has imagination, initiative and the will to be a good chief executive, he will usually plan his own retirement. He won't necessarily stop working," says Bower, who still logs a 65-hour work week and an international travel schedule, "but he will certainly plan to do other things than manage.

"I do not believe a retired chief executive should even be on the board. I'll offend a lot of people with that comment." Accordingly, Bower has dropped off McKinsey's managing committee, the equivalent to a board of directors.

"In a business operating in today's environment, any chief executive over 65 is likely to get out of touch without realizing it; is likely to make his decisions on experience that is out of date. Too often he doesn't know his mind isn't open. And people just won't tell him.

"Right now I'm agonizing with a client who doesn't have to retire until 70. He's just 65. It's very traumatic because it's an easy thing for him to rationalize that he should stay on. He's done an outstanding job. There is no pressure from the board for him to quit. He has done an excellent job of developing a successor. But it would be good for the man and the company for him to retire. I think he will.

"A chief executive ought to have at least 10 years—seven at a minimum—at his job. If one executive holds on too long, his successor doesn't have a chance to put his own individual stamp on the business.

"Even if you have a successor who is less able than the executive he replaces, he will still probably do a better job because of his fresh ideas. Change is good for an enterprise. And much of its value comes in the realignment of existing relationships. I've seen firms just blow up. In the last five years, four management consulting firms have disintegrated, been bought up, or split up . . . all because the major influence hung on." Bower readily admits that the decision to retire can be painful. But he thinks a chief executive must face up to its inevitability, the sooner the better. "I began to think about retirement in 1955 because it takes a good length of time."

Bower still holds the title of a director and "may remain on McKinsey premises," as he puts it, until he is 70 years old. But after the age of 65, he must be affirmatively re-elected each year. This is a policy safeguard which Bower engineered.

"It is not realistic in the typical situation to deal with retirement on anything other than a calendar basis. As soon as you put it on a judgmental basis, the decision for when a man must retire falls to the directors. Then the problems start. When you pass 65, the directors lose the leverage of calendar age. The next psychological calendar age is 70. So directors face the problem of possibly having to tell a friend at some point between 65 and 70 that he should step down because he is no longer effective in handling the business.

"A lot of executives who come upon retirement suddenly ask 'what do I do now?' They've been working 70 to 80 hours a week, and they come up to the last day on the job and don't know what to do. My answer to this: they should have thought of that several years before. This is one of the advantages of having a precise retirement date.

"If you are going to have a dynamic economy, don't let the elderly run the enterprises of the economy."[75]

Jeffery Sonnenfeld's 1998 book *The Hero's Farewell*, cites Marvin's retirement as an example of a graceful, positive exit:

> The ambassadors [Marvin Bower, Thomas J. Watson Jr., and Albert Gordon] expressed the greatest career contentment on leaving a firm and greeted their retirement with feelings of pride and pleasure. . . . While they had a strong affinity for their firms, their identity did not hinge on their role as the leader. Their firms tended to be larger firms with moderate performance across the financial indices. Their accomplishments may have been no more modest than those of the monarchs or generals, but their attitudes were.[76]

Although Marvin Bower stepped down in 1967, he continued to be viewed as the grand old master of consulting throughout his life. Fourteen years later, in 1981, when Reg Jones, the chairman of GE, was playing golf with Ron Daniel, the managing director of McKinsey since 1976, he asked Ron, "How is the boss treating you?"[77]

In an interview with BBC television in 1988, when asked why he was still working after stepping down as McKinsey's managing director, Marvin replied:

> I'll wait until they throw me out, you see. Because I like the work. I like to work at this. And, as long as they let me stay, why, I'll be there. Except as I feel that I am not being productive myself then I'll step out. That's of course a biased decision but that's the way I look at it.

In 1992, Marvin did formally retire. He moved to Florida and began his first postretirement project: writing a new book, *The Will To Lead.* Marvin passionately explained his rationale for this book: while American business has evolved dynamically in recent decades, we still lack the courage and the will to address a core issue constraining our success—excessive hierarchy. A combined Chairman and CEO concentrates too much power is subjected to too little review, and shields CEOs from invaluable insights inside their own organizations by the deference inherent in a command and control agenda. "This will only change when executives understand the much greater power of leadership." So, upon reflection, he added, "I mislabeled my first book when what we need is leaders." Although he retired from McKinsey, Marvin did not retire from his battle against hierarchy.

Objecting to a Joint Venture with DLJ—1969

When Marvin did step down in 1967, he consciously and conspicuously would not get involved in firm issues. Inside the firm, 1967 through 1972 were termed Marvin's dark years. He changed his day-to-day behavior overnight, although McKinsey & Co. was no less important to him when he stepped down as managing director. He never wrote a memorandum, cornered people, or got involved in a discussion about firm direction or decisions. In that five-year period, there was one exception.

Following the sudden death of Marvin's successor, Gilbert Clee, the McKinsey leadership was assumed by Lee Walton. During Lee's early years in this role—perhaps as part of the aftermath of having two new leaders within the span of a year after 28 years of Marvin at the helm—many partners were eager to pursue new opportunities. Lee Walton commissioned six projects investigating new ways McKinsey could work with top management (serving small entrepreneurial companies, serving government, serving universities, serving venture capitalists, and pursuing a joint venture with a technology company). In particular, a joint venture with DLJ was one that was discussed a great deal. Warren Cannon, McKinsey's chief administrative partner at the time, describes what was happening:

> I think there were two things going on. One is that there was a lot of pent-up energy in the firm as a result of this five years of succession, jockeying, and no clear leadership in the firm. That was part of it. The second thing was that we had a lot of young, energetic people in the firm who had ideas about how they could make their mark, not necessarily using Gil as a model, but certainly influenced by the example of adding a major new dimension [going global] to the firm. I think it was all of this that Lee [the new managing director] was reacting to. It was also Lee's style to let it all hang out. Those things came together.[81]

Although Marvin was no longer managing director, his wisdom and values and the tremendous respect he had garnered over the years ensured that he would continue to be a very strong influence on the firm, as the DLJ case confirms. Warren goes on to explain what occurred:

> We had several opportunistic situations that emerged in 1969. Most of them sort of dwindled away. One of Lee's projects was about venture capital that was headed by Jack Crowley (with McKinsey from 1952 to 1977, and subsequently EVP of Xerox). The DLJ joint venture did go so far as the famous confrontation in Madrid . . . and reared its lovely head. We had a lot of associations with the DLJ people. They were Harvard Business School people, there were personal relationships with DLJ, people knew Donaldson, they knew Lufkin. I don't think we, at that time, had many personal contacts with Jenrette. We knew Hexter and some other people in DLJ, and they were doing very well, indeed. They or we got the idea that they could identify companies that were turn-around candidates and, by the way, Booz·Allen & Hamilton was trying to do a little bit of this on its own. They [DLJ] would identify companies that were turnaround candidates . . . and handle

all the financial and other aspects of acquisition. We would provide turnaround management talent, and then when the company was turned around and profitable, they would sell it off and DLJ and McKinsey would profit. In some ways DLJ and McKinsey would own the company. Those details were never spelled out in final detail.

I don't know who came up with the idea originally, but Jack [Crowley] headed a small project team that looked into this. They came back with a recommendation that we try it. There were three reasons for doing it. It provided some excitement in the firm, a moving out, doing something different from what we had been doing. Second, it would provide, we thought, very useful experience for some of our people to have the actual operating responsibility for turning around a company that had been poorly managed but had real potential, and third, it looked like an opportunity to make a lot of money. Crowley discussed it with a number of people and proposed it to the managing committee of the firm. The managing committee, in the end, unanimously approved the proposal that we proceed with DLJ to create such a joint venture.

The management group was meeting in Madrid and there was a meeting of the directors, the managing committee . . . probably Crowley himself, since Crowley was part of the managing committee . . . presented the unanimous recommendation of the committee to the full directorate that we do this. Marvin broke out of his cage and got up and made a speech against the idea. He apologized for breaking his vow of silence, but he felt that the whole character of the firm was at stake. He explained why. He explained why it was so important that he had to speak out. He gave his reasons for being so deeply opposed to it. The most important one was that it distracted us altogether from the achievement of our real goal and our opportunity there was vastly greater than the opportunity to make a quick buck working for, obviously, second-rate or third- or fourth- or fifth-rate companies. We were no longer professional people when we did this, but we were operating businessmen. We probably weren't even good at that.

I don't remember all his arguments, but whatever they were, they were so persuasive that despite the unanimous recommendation of the managing committee, the discussion ended. That was the only time I know that he really stepped out. Then he went back into his cage. People used to talk about his rattling the bars, that was a common phrase, but he really didn't.

Despite the fact that a large part of the leadership of the firm was disposed to pursue this joint venture, the esteem in which he was held guaranteed that when Marvin Bower spoke, everyone listened—and fully appreciated the wisdom in his advice. It took only a few minutes for Marvin to persuade the firm to avoid taking a step that would have inevitably undermined its mission.

From the moment of starting the journey in 1933 to his formal retirement in 1992, Marvin's leadership and influence was a living model on how to make and execute decisions. To this day, every person interviewed, including myself, asks, "What would Marvin do?" John Macomber is only one of many who continues to be influenced by Marvin:

> I think Marvin had a profound effect on me, but also on everybody. Certainly everybody who stayed with the firm, and I suspect that he had a profound effect on those who left the firm as well.
>
> The first [reason] is that Marvin had some very simple, straightforward ideas about not only what a firm should be but about individual behavior. . . . And he was consistent. . . . A few simple concepts and sticking to them and harping on them. . . . And then [second], he had a great gift of surrounding himself with talent, never feeling threatened, glomming on to very good ideas and integrating them into his concepts. Marvin was not necessarily an original thinker, but . . . [his] collection of ideas was absolutely original.[83]

PART II

A Leader's Leader

The moral order is not something static, it is not something enshrined in historic documents, or stowed away like the family silver, or lodged in the minds of pious and somewhat elderly moralists. It is an attribute of a functioning social system. As such it is a living, changing thing, likely to decay and disintegration as well as to revitalizing and reinforcement, and never any better than the generation that holds it in trust.

—John W. Gardner, 1963[1]

All leaders have three responsibilities: instill self-confidence and self-esteem in constituents and make them feel good about themselves; keep up constituents' spirits and morale; and develop constituents by helping them learn their responsibilities and grow and develop as individuals.

—Marvin Bower, 1996[2]

CHAPTER 5

The Bower Reach

The final test of a leader is that he leaves behind in other men the conviction and the will to carry on.

—Walter Lippmann

To understand the power and reach of Marvin Bower's leadership, one only needs to consider the history of courageous changes at Marvin's client companies and the subsequent accomplishments of people at client companies who were members of Marvin's teams and of McKinsey & Co. alumni. Looking at both groups—the client team members and the consultants—from a quantitative perspective, the evidence of leadership success is astounding. Client members of Marvin's teams were 20 times more likely to rise to a senior management level (president or CEO) than were their peers. During Marvin's 17 years as managing director of McKinsey, more than 50 of the consultants evolved into CEOs of leading global companies.[1] This remarkable record of success is no coincidence.

Marvin Bower was directly responsible for this rich legacy of leadership because he lived the attributes he believed were critical to good leadership and encouraged those he worked with to reach a new level of consciousness and behavior incorporating these qualities. When distilled to their essence, these attributes are:

- *Integrity/trustworthiness:* Marvin's insight into people's thoughts and feelings, augmented by his remarkable integrity, bred a unique trust among his colleagues and clients. "There is nothing subtle or complicated about Marvin as far as I can recall. Underneath it all was his integrity. Marvin radiated integrity. People trusted him."[2]
- *Fact-based visioning and a pragmatic "Monday morning" path to turn vision into reality:* The ability to conceptualize at the grandest level, to articulate that concept simply and clearly, and to translate that into something actionable was pure Marvin. He employed a no-nonsense approach.
- *Adherence to principles/values:* Marvin insisted that people he worked with stick to core principles while he actively sought out problems that tested those guiding principles.
- *Humility and unassuming respect for others:* "His generosity in praising others in public and in private and his readiness to give credit to others while playing down his own role—both done sincerely—built Marvin a following of people who were eager to serve in any way he suggested."[3]
- *Strong communications/personal persuasiveness:* Marvin was known for his ability to communicate clearly and efficiently. He knew that others needed to fully understand and engage in the what, why, and the how—and he was an equally tenacious listener.[4]
- *Personal involvement/demonstrated commitment:* Marvin's commitment did not stop with the launch or ending of a study, the execution of a management decision, or the welcoming of new employees at a mass gathering. He was a hands-on, highly visible presence whose caring and concern was ongoing.

With this set of attributes comes courage, and it is the presence of courage that enables every person to excel and any organization to far exceed the sum of its parts and to become something extraordinary. "One man with courage makes a majority."[5]

Perhaps what is particularly telling about this list is what is not on it. It makes no mention of brilliance, charisma, monetary gain, personal power, or command and control maintained through fear. Rather this list is about respecting, building, and empowering the people who are the heart of and, hence, constitute the front line for, the success of an organization.

In bringing his business acumen and leadership model to his consultants, his client team members, and the boardrooms of the United States (and ultimately, of other continents), Marvin Bower carried with him the early lessons of his middle-class Midwestern upbringing and his educational years.

Marvin first came to value integrity and the respect it garnered at home. As he recalled:

> My father was a person of great integrity. He never told even white lies—and he didn't tell us lies of any sort. He was strict in that sense. As I look back, I realize he gave us character training in countless little ways of great value. . . . I saw the respect people had for my father. Everybody respected him and that respect was very powerful. Respect was something he had earned. . . . The greatest was his own example—his high standards of truthfulness and ethics. Those I know he got from his father, the MD from McGill. I frequently visited my grandfather in Waddington, Canada. He was a great person to people in Waddington. He took things like potatoes [as payment] for delivering a baby. I always . . . felt Grandpa's integrity and the respect he commanded. . . . When he died, and they shut the whole town down, it was very impressive and inspiring to think I had some of his blood.[6]

Marvin came to see respect as the key to empowerment of those around him, and throughout his life he held respect and integrity in the highest regard. In 1979, while describing what sort of place he would choose to work, he said, "A place where I respect people who respect me, and that fits with the rest of my life."[7] When asked whether respect was more important to him than money, location, or a particular profession, he answered, "Yes!" without hesitation. Terry Williams, with McKinsey from 1959 through 1997, recalls the respect with which he treated clients:

> He had a great deal of respect for the clients. I worked with him at Texaco, where Gus Long was a titan in American industry. Marvin treated him with great courtesy. And yet he would disagree with him in a polite, but convincing, manner.
>
> Marvin recognized that Gus had built the company. A lot of the good things about the company came from the current

management, but the way Texaco managed was rather Nean-
derthal-like. What Marvin was trying to do for them was get
them to adopt more modern techniques of management—everything from strategic planning to organizational development,
manpower development, respect for each other. He was trying to
break up the incredible hierarchy that Gus had going under him.
When I saw Marvin with Gus, he would explain in some pragmatic way why it would be better to manage differently. He
wasn't criticizing what Gus had done, but he was adding additional ideas that would make it even better and would leverage
the way Gus ran the company. He was teaching almost more than
problem solving. In dealing with organization matters, Marvin
was trying to get these clients to change their nature. And it was
tough.

I saw him do the same thing with the chairman of Geigy
Chemical Company in Ardsley, New York, a guy named Charles
Suter who was a classic Swiss, before we started working with their
headquarters in Switzerland and before they became Ciba Geigy.
Mr. Suter wanted some work done on computers. Marvin knew
very little about it. McKinsey was just really beginning on computers, and Marvin took the classic approach of saying to Mr. Suter,
"Your company seems to be successful, and you are building computers, introducing computers and information technology into
the company in the '60s, but we have to be sure that it suits and fits
with your strategy, and your business. So, we've got to look at more
than the electric plugs of where we are going to put this equipment
to work." And he got Mr. Suter to agree that we would do a general survey of the whole company. And it led to a lot of teaching
going on by Marvin and by our team. Because Marvin was able to
interact with this guy, as a peer, and to explain to him how, if Mr.
Suter was going to leave a bigger and better company behind him,
he had to leverage the management, get away from the Swiss principles of dominant hierarchy and giving orders, and begin to use
foreign nationals, like Americans, in the United States. And it was
quite an education for Mr. Suter, who had extraordinary regard for
Marvin Bower and being Swiss and being very polite, he was
awfully nice to the rest of us on the team as well.

Marvin never talked down to anybody whether you were an associate or the chairman of Texaco.[8]

Marvin also learned at a young age the importance of paying attention to the opinions and ideas of others from all walks of life, and, hence, the importance of cultivating good listening skills. As Marvin learned, when you take the time to listen, you discover there is valuable information to be gleaned from frontline employees:

> When I was in high school, Dad got me a job as a grinding machine operator at Warner & Swasey. I ran a Brown & Sharpe grinder there. I met a man working at the next bench who was a very fine person and who gave me good advice. He knew a lot about how the company operated and what was important.[9]

Fifty-six years later, when Chuck Ames, chairman of Acme Machine Tool company (the company that had acquired Warner & Swasey), was speaking at an all-company meeting, an employee who knew that Chuck had been with McKinsey & Co., came up to him and told him that his father had helped Marvin Bower work the grinding machine.[10]

While an undergraduate student at Brown University, Marvin had the opportunity to benefit from his strong listening skills:

> One of the professors who had special influence on me was the psychology professor who was very good in dealing with people. He was the one who said, "Why don't you apply for this *Class of 1888* prize? You could write a paper and win that." It was a prize that had been going on for a long time. It only paid $50, but that was a lot of money for me in those days, and I needed even small sums, so it was a good incentive. That professor interested me in researching and discovering what people thought—what they really thought versus what they said. So I applied for the prize, worked hard at gaining it, and won it!
>
> I kept wondering why I had won, and I finally decided it was because I had . . . listened well. And because of that prize, even though small, I've always remembered the importance of imagination and listening.[11]

As a young adult, Marvin also used his listening skills to test and collect data on his sometimes radical ideas. After completing his first year at

Harvard Business School, he felt that he had learned all that he could from his graduate studies, and was considering not pursuing a second year at Harvard. Despite his youthful impatience, he remembered the value of getting others' opinions—and, after all, what opinions could be more valuable than those of Harvard Business School alumni? So Marvin went off to the library, reviewed the list of alumni, and selected three to talk to. As Marvin remembered, the advice he received from the first of these three was so compelling that there was no need to visit the other two:

> Helen and I made a trip to New York, and while there I . . . interviewed a Morgan partner named Arthur Marvin Anderson . . . about the second year [at Harvard Business School]. I went up to the guard at 23 Wall Street and said, "I'd like to see Mr. Anderson." He said, "What do you want to see him about?" I said, "I'm a Harvard Business School student and want to ask him about Harvard Business School." He came back and said, "Mr. Anderson will be glad to see you."
>
> I sat down by his desk and said, "Mr. Anderson, I've finished one year at the Harvard Business School and done well. I want to practice law and don't know that it's worthwhile spending that extra year and extra money to get that second year." "Well," he said, "young man, if you don't finish that year, you'll spend the rest of your life explaining that you didn't flunk out." I said, "Mr. Anderson, that's such great common sense I'm going to call off my survey and go back to the school."[12]

In addition to good advice, Marvin also received a job offer:

> I got up to go and he [Mr. Anderson] said, "What are you going to do this summer?" I said, "I'm supposed to find a job and I need a job." He said, "How would you like to work for our law firm?" That law firm is now called Davis, Polk & Wardwell. I told him I'd like to do that. He had a direct phone on his desk, and arranged for me to go right up. So I went up, had four interviews, and came down with a job. [In] the summer of 1929 I worked at Davis Polk, and in the fall I returned for my second year at Harvard Business School.[13]

Marvin's early observations coupled with his later experience dealing with bankrupt companies as a lawyer at Jones, Day culminated in a passionate, lifelong fight against hierarchical organizations. By their very design, hierarchies precluded widespread respect for and critical empowerment of the people assets of the organization; isolated the top from the valuable information and insight that could be gleaned from the middle and bottom tiers of employees; and placed top managers on an untouchable pedestal, exposing them to only limited ongoing scrutiny or integrity checking. To Marvin's mind, none of this squared with the fundamental role of management—namely that of making an integrated set of meaningful and actionable decisions and guiding and supporting people throughout the organization in their execution. Everyone from the line operator to the clerical worker to the chief executive has a management role to play. Thus, the effectiveness of the business can only be enhanced by helping and empowering each member to make better decisions and execute well.

In his zeal to bring his philosophy into the boardrooms of America, the young Marvin Bower still had to learn how to temper his passion when dealing with clients, many of whom were old enough to be his father. As Marvin remembers, this was not easy but certainly necessary if he was to have the opportunity to share his wisdom with clients:

> This is the story of how I made a terrible mistake and spent two weeks of my life locked in my hotel thinking about what I would do after consulting.
>
> The company was Commercial Solvents. [Here Marvin raised an eyebrow and added, "they are no longer solvent."] Commercial Solvents was a fairly sizable chemical company in those days, run by Benjamin Tichnor, an autocratic CEO. The issue at hand was that their marketing efforts were failing.
>
> Mac [James O. McKinsey] came down and started [the study], introduced me to Mr. Tichnor, outlined for me how I should carry on until his next visit, and [told me to] call on him when needed. I had a couple of other associates working on the study. It quickly became apparent that prices were not being properly set. That impeded their sales effectiveness. The marketing director was held accountable for profits but the president set the prices. So the poor marketing director was a victim of poor pricing, which was done by the president.

Now we come to a very important point. . . . The truth as I saw it was that the problems of marketing rested with the president because he set the prices which controlled volume and profits. I went in to see Mr. Tichnor and told him the problem as I saw it. He said, "Young man, I did not bring your firm in here to make an examination of me. I brought you in to make an examination of our marketing. You have no right to talk to me the way you are. And I'm going to call Mr. McKinsey and tell him to take you off this study." I said, "Mr. Tichnor, I'm telling you what I believe is the truth. Of course you can call Mr. McKinsey and I'm sure he'll take me off but I don't think he'll change the firm's position because I believe I can convince him that [your company's pricing policy] is your problem." He said, "Well, we'll see about that." So he called McKinsey.

I went back to my hotel and waited. I received a call from James O. McKinsey. He would be coming to New York—by train—and I was to wait for his arrival. As I said, I spent two weeks talking to Helen about what might be an appropriate new career for me.

McKinsey came and said to Mr. Tichnor, "Well, this young man is right. He shouldn't have talked to you that way. He should have talked to me first. I agree with his assessment but we'll take him off."

That was a learning experience. Mac didn't berate me. He said, "Your conclusions were right, but you made two mistakes— *age and judgment.* Time will take care of age and I can only hope it will take care of judgment too. You used poor judgment in going to a man who is old enough to be your father and talking to him that way without even talking with me. You should have called me down here. I would have told him the same thing and he would have accepted it without a fuss." Mac didn't fire me. And over time, with Mac's urging, the CEO, who wouldn't take it from me, began to let the head of marketing do his job.

From then on, I tried always to ask myself what the other person would think about my contemplated action, how it would look to him, how it would affect his position. I learned then and later that weighing the other person's probable reactions is essential to reaching a sound judgment.[14]

Almost 70 years later, when asked what aspect of leadership character-istics he had to work hardest at, Marvin replied, "Judgment. I came to learn that virtually no decision can't wait overnight, but judgment gets much better."[15]

At the risk of being prescriptive, it is worthwhile to include the contents of a memorandum written by Marvin (May 19, 1950) titled "Steps in Mak-ing and Executing Decisions."[16] As Marvin acknowledges, this advice is not meant to imply that there are no other or better approaches, but rather that here is one approach that is grounded in a successful track record:

> Management decisions differ from personal decisions. They in-volve, or should involve, a logical process—a deliberate choice of means to ends. Making decisions and getting them executed are important parts of executive know-how.
>
> This memorandum outlines an approach to reaching and exe-cuting decisions. The steps outlined here, which have been com-piled from the experiences of successful executives, are offered simply as one suggested approach.
>
> ### Step 1: Decide Whether to Decide
> 1. Is the question pertinent now—does it fit in with man-agement objectives, plans, and stream of events?
> 2. Can the decision be made now? Will it disrupt present plans? Are subordinates capable of carrying it out? Is enough information available to decide?
> 3. Have you the responsibility and the authority to decide?
> 4. Should higher authority decide? Should a subordinate decide? Should some other executive decide?
> 5. If the decision is not to decide now, let those concerned know—and the reasons why.
>
> ### Step 2: Size Up the Situation
> 1. Get all available facts bearing on problem or question—what, why, when, where, how and who.
> 2. Get opinions and judgments of persons concerned with questions or problems—if at all feasible.
> 3. Go to heart of the matter. Determine which factor or fac-tors limit or prevent achievement of the purpose with which decision is concerned. Subordinate parts to the whole.

4. Reject from consideration all events, objects, details, and circumstances not pertinent to *action now* with *means now available*. "Keep [your] eye on ball."

Step 3: Think the Problem Through
1. Develop alternative solutions.
2. Test alternative solutions for advantages and disadvantages from standpoint of:
   a. Underlying purpose—for example, more profits in long run through better service to customers
   b. Immediate objectives and policies
   c. Cost
   d. Effect on personnel
   e. Moral codes—rightness and reasonableness in light of own and store's codes of square shooting.

Step 4: Determine Procedures for Carrying Out Decisions
1. Break required action into simple parts, putting first things first.
2. Get ideas from those concerned, especially subordinates. "Millions are lost through discouraging subordinates from expressing ideas." Use "consultative management." Admit things you don't know and mistakes made.
3. Set a completion time or date and work backwards to get starting dates and proper timing.

Step 5: Fix Responsibilities
1. See that every individual understands what he is to do and *why* and that he is capable of doing it.
2. Establish reasonable criteria for satisfactory performance.

Step 6: Follow Up
1. Follow up to eliminate difficulties and see that the decision is carried out.
2. Review performance with subordinates concerned, so they will know how well they did. Be sure to emphasize points that will be helpful guides for their *future* action. (This is on-the-job training—one of every executive's most important responsibilities.)

Throughout his life, Marvin held firm to his belief that, because a business organization is run by people, a business in a democratic, capitalistic system with a competitive, global marketplace is most likely to succeed and prosper when all members work together effectively, efficiently, harmoniously, and even enthusiastically to achieve the purpose(s) of the business.

Such a work environment is in direct contradiction to a command and control situation, and Marvin continued to fight the good fight against hierarchy. While he had much success in influencing others to adopt a nonhierarchical philosophy, as he noted in 1992 while discussing his book, *The Will To Lead*, the battle persists, in a large part because the concepts of position, power, and elevation over others feed into the human ego:

> Despite proliferating changes, the basic way most American businesses are run has changed very little over 60 years. The all-powerful CEO sits atop the hierarchy and issues orders to carry out the plans he or she has fashioned. If you still think I exaggerate, let me tell you why that is: it's because people want to "get ahead" (i.e., move up in the hierarchy) so they can boss others. Then they can go home, tell their friends and even read their names in the papers.
>
> . . . Of course, there have also been thousands of incremental changes in administrative methods. And growth in the use of teams . . . falls somewhere between major and incremental change. Currently, change of all kinds is a hot topic in managing. But chief executives who report to the board still have full authority over corporate agendas which give them command and control over the people who execute their agendas.
>
> The authority that each superior has over subordinates imposes these constraints on subordinates: (1) reluctance to disagree with the boss, (2) reluctance to provide information or offer opinions unless asked for and (3) unwillingness to take independent initiatives.
>
> However, good bosses will develop relationships with subordinates that virtually eliminate these constraints.[17]

One can only hope that today's and tomorrow's generations of leaders will continue Marvin Bower's battle against hierarchy and learn how to lead in an empowering manner that helps all involved exceed their assumed potential and feel pride in their collective accomplishments.

CHAPTER 6

Inspiring Organizational Courage

*Success is based on a few simple things. The challenge is
that you have to do them.*

—Marvin Bower, 1979

*Whenever you see a successful business, someone once made a
courageous decision.*

—Peter Drucker, 1999

In working with his clients, Marvin Bower would challenge them as
leaders to give the people in their organizations courage. He would
coach them to take the initiative and to stand up to the boss, to listen to
others, and to let go of hierarchical controls and conventions.

In doing so, Marvin led by example. He was not reckless, but he was
fearless. His teams and his clients bore witness to his many acts of courage
over the years:

- Taking on challenging engagements and telling it like it was
- Imagining what could be even if that meant flying in the face of
  industry convention or trends
- Letting others own his vision and take credit for successful implementation of that vision

Not all clients were willing or able to muster the courage required to
make bold moves; others were put off by Marvin's bluntness. Ron Daniel

and Everett Smith, a McKinsey director who retired in 1972, remember one such instance at Continental Can. In Ron's words:

> I was a relatively new principal working with Marvin at Continental Can on a strategy study for the folding carton division—a small division of a big company. The chairman of Continental Can asked us while we were there on our folding carton engagement to give him any observations we might develop on the overall organization. We were told to be blunt, and if we saw things outside of the division we were working on, we shouldn't shy from giving [the chairman] feedback.
>
> As we began spending time with [the chairman], it became increasingly clear that he was not a good leader. He was egocentric and arrogant. I wrote a memo that stated those points and suggested some changes he might make to be more effective. Marvin reviewed it and said "Good job. Let's send it." I did, and the chairman kicked us out of Continental Can.[1]

Everett Smith had vivid memories of Marvin's horror at the outcome:

> He came in [to my office], and he said, "Have you got a minute?" I said, "Sure." So we went back to his office. I could see he was terribly upset, which is unlike him. He said, "I've got to tell somebody, I've got to talk to a partner." He said, "I've got to talk to you." I said, "What's the matter, Marvin?" He said, "I've hurt the firm." You couldn't say anything that would hurt him more than if he thought he'd hurt the firm. I said, "What's happened?"
>
> He and Ron Daniel had gone down to see [Continental Can], and they had written the chairman a memo, and I guess it was enough to take the skin right off the chairman's back, and he sat them down and gave them hell. "You goddamned well can't write us letters like that. What do you mean by this kind of stuff?" He said, "We don't want any of your people around here ever again."
>
> I said, "Oh, hell, Marvin, we all make mistakes. For heaven's sake, let's assume that you made a mistake. You shouldn't have written the letter, so what. It's not a very good client, anyway." He didn't like that particularly, but he just couldn't get over that he had hurt his firm.[2]

However, as Everett goes on to point out, no permanent damage was done because "[Continental Can] is now a client of ours again. Those people are gone, and [Marvin] didn't hurt the firm."[3]

Encounters such as the one with Continental Can became learning experiences that were vital for refining communications skills and approaches. Ron Daniel recalls that he and Marvin spent hours afterwards discussing what they should have done differently. They concluded that they should have spent some time with the senior team at Continental Can getting their advice on how to pitch the message, and building support for their observations before they delivered them.[4]

Such "failures" did not weaken Marvin's resolve or courage. He continued to say what needed to be said, all in the pursuit of solutions that strengthened his clients, while developing and refining his own communications skills and strategies over the years.

For the many who embraced Marvin's challenge, they and their organizations experienced firsthand how courage translated into successful and sustainable solutions to critical management issues. General Electric was one of those clients. Fred Searby, with McKinsey from 1962 to 1982, had vivid memories of the GE assignment—the first study he worked on with Marvin.[5] The year was 1962 and the issue at hand was how and where General Electric should invest its research dollars. As Fred recalled it:

> At the time, product life cycle was a novel concept being written about in *The Harvard Business Review*.[6] Marvin sat in on a team meeting in which the team spent several hours discussing the refrigerator. The team concluded that, given its age and market saturation, the refrigerator was at a mature point in its product life cycle; hence, GE should not spend significant research dollars on this product. Marvin was quiet until the meeting was almost over. Then he said, "I do not believe that the refrigerator is a mature product. It may be old, but it is so complicated and so essential to human needs that I do not believe that the refrigerator will ever be a mature product."[7]

Now, four decades later, the refrigerator continues to evolve (e.g., ice and water services in the door, side-by-side doors, sub-zeros) and GE is the only brand that has maintained its market position. History has certainly borne out Marvin's message to the team and the client back in 1962.

Finding and putting in place solutions to critical issues is good leadership and often requires: courage to embrace the collective wisdom (versus making decisions in hierarchical isolation); courage to think out of the box (versus automatically following the conventions of the time); courage to empower, equip, and trust others to execute and own the solution (versus blindly following a mandate); and courage to let others take credit for successes (versus having the need to feed a bottomless-pit ego). It is in this approach that real power and leadership resides.

Time and time again, Marvin demonstrated his own courage and inspired courage in others. Three examples are detailed in this chapter: the Royal Dutch Shell Group, Price Waterhouse, and the Harvard Business School. In two cases, it was courage to take fundamentally different organizational paths (Shell and Price Waterhouse); in the third, it was courage to reconfirm but refine its role in corporate America at an especially turbulent time (Harvard Business School).

Royal Dutch Shell, 1956: Challenging the Organizational Heritage of an Established Global Leader

In 1956, John Loudon, one of the managing directors of the Royal Dutch Shell Group, came to the realization that the organization in place was reaching the end of its effective life. A truly multinational and complex business, Royal Dutch Shell presented a significant organizational challenge. Growing out of a 1907 alliance between Royal Dutch Petroleum Company and the Shell Transport and Trading Company, Limited, Royal Dutch Shell was still operating with its original organizational structure a half-century later. The organization relied on centralized control for decision making and a strong, embedded culture for commonality in execution. While this structure had clearly facilitated the company's ability to operate internationally well before other industrial companies, by 1956 it had become expensive, and more important, its decision-making speed was slow relative to that of competitors.

Loudon knew that something had to change, but he also recognized that the existing organization represented a strong heritage and that a convincing, compelling argument needed to be presented before any restructuring was undertaken. In light of this situation, he felt it was important that outside management consultants help him and his team think through the issues. In seeking an outsider's perspective, Loudon was looking for confirmation of his belief that the organization as it had evolved over time was no longer sustainable. He believed that he could find a way to position the company to be more competitive in its business arena. His decision to bring in McKinsey was in part the result of the need to tread carefully within his own company:

> I couldn't have a Dutch [consultant] because the British wouldn't like it, and I couldn't have a Britisher because the Dutch wouldn't like it. I was always very pro-American, having spent so much time working in the U.S. Gus Long, chairman of Texaco, recommended McKinsey & Co. and Marvin Bower in particular.[8]

The Organization and Culture in 1956

The Royal Dutch Shell Group consisted of over 400 national operating companies, which were the basic building blocks of the group. The smallest was in Costa Rica, where Shell had one filling station, and the largest were the truly national companies (e.g., France, Germany, Holland). All of the companies formally reported either to The Hague or to London, although in certain matters they reported to both. Shell did not have the same degree of close line control over these operating companies as its American counterparts, in part because Shell was far more international than any other oil company at this time. By 1956 Royal Dutch Shell was operating comfortably and effectively all over the world. When starting a business in a new location (say, Borneo), they were able to staff that operation with people who were so indoctrinated with the Shell philosophy that they could be relied on to do whatever was necessary without much instruction or reference back to the head office.

Shell employees were highly flexible and accustomed to accepting many different assignments to different sites. If a man (it was men only in 1956) was working in Jakarta and was told to take his family and move to Berlin, he accepted that as part of his life with the company. Some people had moved three or four or a dozen times in the course of their careers at Shell. On reaching retirement age, their reward for long and tough service was a job in London or The Hague (the two head offices). By 1956, this policy resulted in something like 10,000 people staffing each head office. Because of the cultural imperative to check things out with the managers in the two head offices, decisions were made slowly and, arguably, in less than optimal fashion.

The culture of the Royal Dutch Shell Group was multinational and multilingual—relatively rare in 1956. Because it was an Anglo-Dutch organization, all of the key personnel in the head offices in London and The Hague were highly educated and primarily Dutch or English. Only a small number of American employees, managers or frontline, were in the mix. Given the educational backgrounds of the Dutch and the British personnel, the office in The Hague tended to direct the technological groups (exploration, production, and refining) whereas the London office tended to oversee the nontechnical functions, such as marketing, personnel, finance, and shipping.

Royal Dutch Shell had seven managing directors—four Dutchmen and three Englishmen—reflecting the balance of shareholding between the Dutch and the English (60/40). John Loudon was one of those seven and was due to become chairman of the Committee of Managing Directors in the next 12 to 18 months. The managing directors were at the very top of this sophisticated company.

By 1956, available communications and infrastructure were no longer suited to some of Royal Dutch Shell's practices and needs. This was especially problematic because the international oil business was a very complex logistical network of exploration, drilling, tankers, pipelines, and refineries that had to be carefully balanced. No part of the Royal Dutch Shell Group was independent in reality because there was always an imbalance between the oil found and produced and that refined and sold. Rather, the group was an international network that had to be coordinated, with the supply and distribution function critical in that regard. For example, of the oil lifted in Venezuela, that portion refined into heavy fuel might go up to New England in the wintertime and the lighter fractions sold in Europe after being refined in Aruba. With this type of logistics replicated all over the world, the international oil business was an extremely complex operation.

Venezuela—The Testing Ground

John Loudon knew that organizational change was required to address the Shell Group's complex, worldwide operational needs, but where and how to start in such a large, global company? He did not want to take any rash action and risk undermining the operations of a successful company. He decided to begin in Venezuela at Compañía Shell de Venezuela (CSV), where the organizational redesign would be a meaningful pilot test for change. He chose Venezuela because he had worked there himself and knew that CSV's operations included all five elements of the oil industry (exploration, production, refining, shipping, and marketing). CSV was an organizational and cultural microcosm of the Royal Dutch Shell Group. Loudon's intention was to let McKinsey & Co. and Royal Dutch Shell familiarize themselves with one another (in terms of both institutions and key personnel) during the study of operations in Venezuela before moving on to tackle the whole organizational structure once he became chairman of the Committee of Managing Directors.

The effort in Venezuela was the first major study that McKinsey had undertaken outside the continental United States, thus constituting a new experience for everyone on the McKinsey team, including Marvin.

When the effort began, Shell had just combined 13 separate companies in CSV. The management positions in Venezuela were apportioned by nationality (between the Dutch and English) and by function. For example, from among the five oil industry activities performed at CSV, refining typically was Dutch and marketing typically was English. With this split of activities and management positions, managers could find themselves overwhelmed by the requests from both The Hague and the London head office. The McKinsey team (four associates led by Marvin) witnessed this tugging and pulling along with the extraordinary power and economic clout of the Royal Dutch Shell Group in heavily influencing the politics of the countries in which they operated. True to Loudon's expectation, CSV was a realistic proxy for the Royal Dutch Shell Group as a whole.

The study began, as did all of Marvin's studies, with fact finding. Accordingly, the team's initial charter was to "live with the organization" and track decision-making processes, which was a key area of concern for John Loudon and, in Marvin's view, represented the essence of management. In tracking decision making, the team was to focus on who made decisions, what were the key points of decision making, how decisions were made, how long they took, and what issues and/or barriers got in the way of effective, streamlined decision making. This effort, in conjunction with management interviews, would elicit the team's first set of facts.

During the first three weeks of the study, Marvin worked closely with the four associates. He would talk to executives throughout the course of the day and compare notes with his team in the evening, continually refining hypotheses and advising the team on how best to move forward. During these first three weeks, Marvin often invited management to join the team in the evening for dinner in order to solicit management's perspectives in a less formal setting.

Hugh Parker, the McKinsey engagement manager on the effort, remembers how one of the Royal Dutch Shell managers viewed Marvin:

> One of the Shell team members said, "Marvin Bower really is a very simple person with ideas and total integrity." I responded, "Well, I don't think he's simple . . . but I do think he is uncomplicated." The Shell team member said, "uncomplicated and with total integrity—he really wants to do the best thing for us."[9]

Living with the organization meant being on site at CSV's western division located on the shore of Lake Maracaibo and in the surrounding oil camps, as well as the refining division located in Cardon. The geography of CSV's operations was challenging in 1956. Lee Walton, one of the associates and later a managing director of McKinsey, never forgot the novelty of this experience for the team:

> The study began at the grass roots level where they were drilling and producing the wells. So I visited all of the camps around the lake: Bachaquero and Lagunillas Mene Grande. There was one camp that was particularly notable called Casigua. . . . The entire camp was surrounded by the Montelone Indians, a totally untamed tribe. They had interesting bows that they shot with their feet.
>
> . . . To go up the river you had to ride a boat that was roofed over with hardware cloth. Frequently you couldn't see the Indians but you could see the arrows come whistling out and bounce off the hardware cloth into the river. It was great sport. In the oil field, Shell would build a cyclone fence about 200 yards from each well because these Indian bows could carry about 100 yards. The Indians would come up at night and sit on the outside of the fence. The rigs were lit up at night. The Indians would shoot their arrows at

the drilling rig but they'd only carry about halfway. The next morning the drillers would go out and pick the arrows up and take them into Maracaibo to sell them to the tourists. Some of the arrows were extraordinarily long, like four or five feet. I remember graphically one picture of a farmer who was shot near the Shell camp in Casigua. This fellow was sitting on his tractor with an arrow sticking about one foot out of his chest and about one foot out of his back. He was, of course, dead. That gave you pause, to think about these Indians.[10]

After getting the fact gathering under way, Marvin came down about one week every month. Loudon was apparently monitoring the CSV effort all along. He visited Venezuela several times and spoke on the phone with Marvin often.

The first major meeting on the team's preliminary recommendations for a modified organizational structure for CSV came after the facts were collected, compiled, and analyzed. The recommendations were to be presented to John Loudon and the CSV management group. Marvin arrived well in advance of the meeting and as the team was still assembling its reports. Marvin was, as always, a stickler for well-written presentations, which was quite understandable in view of the fact that this was McKinsey & Co.'s first major study outside the continental United States and a challenging organizational effort at that.

While Marvin's input was always invaluable, it also more often than not meant additional work for the team. This was the case on the CSV study, as Lee Walton recollected:

Marvin always managed to stir up a lot of dust while he was there. I was in great awe of Marvin and was very attentive to him. When he had something to offer, it was not trivial and it was something you should listen to and at least contemplate. I always relished Marvin's visits but they sometimes brought with them a lot of headaches.

We'd written reports on each segment of the Shell organization—about a dozen reports. Hugh [Parker, the team manager] and I split them. For example, I had written the refinery report and Hugh wrote the government relations report. But there was one report that had to do with the western division that we wrote jointly since we both had spent so much time down there. Hugh wrote his portion in Caracas and I wrote mine in Maracaibo. Our intention was to get together in Caracas and put these two pieces together into one report. . . . We didn't have time to do this. Marvin had arrived and wanted to see the reports. We were going to hold the western division report and work on it, but somehow it got in the stack, and, worse than that, it was right on top of the stack.

Marvin breezed into our office and said, "I'm going to take some of these reports and read through them." We were still busy editing the last one or two of them so we just nodded and off he went. What in fact he took was the western division report.

He was gone for about an hour when the door slammed open and there was Marvin holding this thing in one hand. He said, "This is the worst report I have ever read." And he said, "If all of them are like this, this is a disaster." He pointed to me and he said, "You come with me. You're coming to my office and I'm going to dictate this report. You're going to listen to me dictate this report and learn how to write reports." I didn't know what to do. Hugh didn't know what to do. So I got up and dutifully went upstairs to Marvin's office. Sure enough he brought a secretary in, sat back in his chair glaring at me all the time and started to dictate.

Well, it soon dawned on me that he had picked up the one report that we had never had a chance to work on and to integrate, and the one he knew the least about. Although Marvin had played a big role in a lot of the problem solving in various segments of the organization, he had not spent that much time out in the western division.

I finally got enough courage up after about 15 minutes and I said, "Marvin, could I have a word with you privately, please." He glared at me because I'd interrupted him and he wasn't too happy with me to start with. He sent the secretary out and I said, "Look, I don't think you can write this report. I don't think you know enough about this particular subject to do that. This is the one . . . we never got a chance to edit so I would suggest that you give me the report and we will get it edited for you . . Frankly, my stomach is tied into a knot over this whole thing. I don't know whether I've got a career left or not because you seem to be very angry about this but I can't just sit here. So I'm going to leave." There was a pregnant, as they say, silence while Marvin fumed and considered this. Finally he said, "All right, take it." And he gave me the report.

So I took the report and went down to work with Hugh. Marvin came barreling in shortly after me, picked up two other reports off the stack and went back to his office without saying a word to Hugh or me. I explained to Hugh what had gone on and what I'd done. . . . So we both started to prepare for my funeral while working on the report, trying to get it married together, which we did in an afternoon.

But lo and behold, to give Marvin his full marks, about two or three hours later he blew back into our office. Of course my heart stopped and Hugh's did, too. Waving a report, Marvin said, "This is the best report I have ever seen." It turned out to be my report on the Cardon refinery. At first I thought he was just being nice but the atmosphere was totally different. He was very positive. He said, "Maybe I've made a mistake with the first report and I'm anxious to see what you guys are going to do with it, but these reports, this and the other one are just excellent. If the rest of them are as good as these, why we're home and dry."

I later learned that Marvin really did think that was a great report. It got included in the firm's Report Writing Guide as an exemplary report.[11]

The team's focus and reports were on organizing the internal structure of CSV, as well as developing an optimal framework for collectively interacting with The Hague and London from the Venezuelan viewpoint. The recommended internal structure entailed creating an operating company, combining some of the 13 independent businesses into six businesses with clear authority and accountability, and creating a CSV management team and enhancing the flow of statistical and financial information (and, hence, communications) to ensure the businesses were well linked.

These recommendations were adopted, and the operating company philosophy proved to work well in Venezuela, paving the way for a study of the headquarters organization. Loudon had known that a headquarters study was required. The CSV effort only confirmed this need: The recommendations on how CSV should interact with The Hague and London were not complete and could not be fully realized in Shell's status quo world.

From Venezuela to the Royal Dutch Shell Headquarters

Immediately following his appointment as chairman of the managing directors in 1957, John Loudon called Marvin and said, "Now I want a study done of the headquarters organization of the Royal Dutch Shell Group."[12] Loudon had already told Marvin that as soon as he assumed the chairmanship, he planned on asking McKinsey & Co. to undertake a full-scale study of the central organization of the Royal Dutch Shell Group.

Up front, Loudon told the McKinsey team what he was looking for in this engagement:

> We want this thing to be a really fundamental search, not a cost-cutting exercise or a superficial thing. We want it to fundamentally look at the way this company is organized and we welcome recommendations that may change it. But you may find that there are some things you cannot change.
>
> For example, you might think it makes sense to combine these two offices, one in London and one in The Hague, and maybe have another office in Nice. Forget it. That is not going to happen. But apart from that, anything you recommend will be listened to and debated.[13]

Loudon's involvement did not end with his initial advice and directive to the team. Although the Committee of Managing Directors had collective authority and the committee's chairman did not have any supervening authority, Loudon did, in fact, have a great deal of power. Once described by a Norwegian ship owner as "the iron fist in a velvet glove," Loudon was an urbane, sophisticated man who spoke seven languages. Underneath his aristocratic exterior, however, he was a tough operator who both helped and pushed the team, staying on top of their effort throughout the engagement. He did so in a relaxed way, drawing on his charm and dry sense of humor. Marvin, by contrast, was described by a client once as the Cleveland Plain

Dealer, but even with this difference in personality, the two men appeared to hit it off in all their interactions. Although there was a regular schedule of formal meetings, John always made sure that the atmosphere was not stiff or stuffy. Like Marvin, he was insightful and courageous, always listening, inquiring, and open to learning. His influence on the management committee was comparable to Marvin's on McKinsey & Co.

Not surprisingly, there was great mutual respect and trust between John Loudon and Marvin. Absent that respect and trust and the fact-based approach, skills of persuasion, passion, practicality on both sides, and the integrity that Marvin built into the fabric of the McKinsey-Shell working relationship, it is unlikely that the joint team would have arrived at a solution and path that Loudon could promote with conviction.

The Team

Marvin led the effort, and Shell assigned John Berkin, one of the managing directors, to act as the team liaison. In addition, Shell contributed three of its people to work with McKinsey—Tom Greaves, Norman Bain, and Hank Kruisinga.

Lee Walton and Hugh Parker, who had played important roles in the Venezuela effort, continued on McKinsey's Shell team, with two other associates, John Macomber and Ian Wishart, joining the team.

These team members, from both the Shell and McKinsey sides, moved on to senior management positions later in their careers, as did so many of those who worked directly with Marvin. Hank Kruisinga became chairman of Akzo-Nobel, and the other two Shell team members ultimately became managing directors. Lee Walton became managing director of McKinsey 13 years later, Hugh Parker ran McKinsey's U.K. office beginning in 1959, John Macomber became a McKinsey director and then CEO of Celanese, and Ian Wishart became member resident in The Hague.

During the course of the engagement, Marvin spent much of his time in London, focusing on testing ideas and listening to Shell senior management. At various stages in the process, he brought over other partners, including Zip Reilley and Gil Clee, to add perspective on the relatively uncharted waters that characterized the Shell study. Marvin was very generous with the client relationship. He allowed each member of the team to develop his own relationships with the managing directors, something that meant a lot to a young associate and helped create an aligned team.

The Engagement

As Lee Walton recalled, the effort began in a manner similar to the Venezuela engagement—collecting facts and gaining an understanding of the organization by getting under the skin of Shell to discover what made it tick:

> We had offices in the Shell building, which was a typical drafty English building. My first memories of it were the tea ladies who came around at 10 o'clock in the morning and sometime in the afternoon. And everybody's first reaction to English coffee in the morning was one of "Yuck." But after about three weeks we got to like it, which shows you can get used to anything.
>
> We didn't stay in London long. We each were sent to different areas . . . I was living in Abadan [Iran], a strange experience for a start. Abadan was and probably still is nothing but an enormous refinery on the edge of the Persian Gulf, but you know, it's pretty bleak and the minute you leave the precincts, you're out in the desert. God, I remember some extraordinary things. For example, driving up to a place called Masjid i-Suleiman, I believe, which was one of the oil fields. We approached it at night and they were flaring gas. When you produce oil, there is often a gas by-product. Nowadays there are ways of capturing it, compressing it, and all that. In those days, unless you wanted to use the gas right there on the site, there was nothing to do with it except get rid of it, and the way they did that was flaring it. But these flares, of which I recall there were six, and each one of them a pipe two feet in diameter with gas pouring out and flames shooting hundreds of feet into the air, that's a sight that you cannot describe. I mean, six of these things, huge flames like enormous torches, you know, illuminating the landscape for miles. If you think about the waste, it's criminal, really. I mean, that's energy. That's the kind of recollection you have."[14]

Despite encountering some resistance, the team was able to be effective in its fact gathering and recommendations, in part because the Committee of Managing Directors was vocal in its full support of the team's efforts. Furthermore, that the team won the confidence of the operating committee was attributable to its ability to listen and thoughtfully interpret what was being said, as well as its demonstrated sensitivity to the people at Shell.

This sensitivity is reflected in Lee Walton's recollections:

There were emotional issues arising from Shell being a 60/40 company, 60 percent Dutch, 40 percent English. The Dutch really wanted to establish that 60/40 rule right down to the lowest possible organizational position. In other words, for every 10 salesmen, 6 would be Dutch and 4 English. It was seriously impeding the growth and development of the Royal Dutch Shell Group to have these nationalistic traits exemplified and executed in organization structure and job content. We had to break that policy and in so doing we engendered a lot of resistance—particularly from the Dutch.

Another 60/40 issue arose from the fact that Shell was building a brand-new building on the south bank of the Thames and the Dutch were insisting that they build a building of exactly the same size and caliber in Holland. That just didn't make any sense at all.

I got to learn a lot about problems associated with or arising from mores, customs, nationalism, and politics. You see this in any corporation, but it was in bold relief there because of the two different nationalities and the two different locations. We spent a lot of time battering those brick walls down and even though the managing directors were fully supportive, we really injured the sensibilities of a lot of the other people and we had to go back and make amends with them as we proceeded.[15]

In overcoming resistance, gathering and communicating credible facts was paramount, as Hugh Parker recalls:

Among the early recommendations we presented to the whole of the Committee of Managing Directors . . . was that control over things in the field, that is, the operating companies, had been overly centralized. . . . There was a strong tendency among the Dutch to say, "Control for everything really ought to be here in The Hague," and by that they meant those functions for which they were responsible—the technical functions of exploration, refining, production . . . not marketing, the marketing was centered in London.

When we said this to the Committee of Managing Directors, they said, "Well, we don't agree. We think you're mistaken and we would like you to demonstrate much more convincingly that this is in fact so," . . . I mean, if too many things were in fact unnecessarily centralized, it would follow that you would have a lot of people in London and The Hague who didn't have to be there.[16]

In response to the Committee of Managing Directors' challenge, Marvin sent out three task forces to find evidence of the claim that Shell was overly centralized. Each task force focused on a different part of the world (Europe, Asia, Africa, and Venezuela) as they sought proof in the form of anecdotes, correspondence, or any other kind of documentation that would say, "Here it is, this proves that you are trying to control too many things from The Hague or from London."

Some six weeks later, the team was able to report back to the Committee of Managing Directors with 50 case examples of overcentralization in their pocket as a result of the task forces' efforts. Hugh Parker remembers that meeting well:

> As we recounted these [case examples] to the managing directors, there were gales of laughter because some of these things were almost absurd. I'll give you some examples. When I was in Venezuela, I was told that the Venezuelan management wanted to erect an oil depot, a storage farm. You know, these big cylindrical tanks, and they had sent a plan of one of their depots back to The Hague and said, "We intend to put another tank here." The Hague came back and said, "We don't think you should put it here, we think you should put it there." Then the answer to that was, "That's all very well but what you don't see from this plan is that that's on a cliff." It was that sort of nonsense, you know.
>
> There was a classic one that Lee Walton came back with from

the Far East. I think it was Malaysia, where, for some reason, 50 years before the head office had demanded to have tire pressures reported each month for all the trucks in the transportation fleet. It was something to do with the rainy season and the traction of tires in mud and all that, but the point is that they were still reporting monthly the tire pressures from the truck fleet . . .

Then there was their man in Cuba . . . , this was, of course, before Castro . . . who was Cuban and a real businessman who was very much respected in London and The Hague, but The Hague resented his independence, and they said, in effect, "Look, if you build a refinery in Cuba, you're going to build it to our standards. We are the experts on engineering standards, and we don't want any cut corners and shoddy refineries operating." This guy said, "Well, look, if you insist, my economics are going to be bad. It cannot be profitable, so you must let me build the refinery in a way that I think is commercially and economically sound." And there was a big fight about this that lasted over six months. But apparently he won the day and instead of building what he contemptuously called a gold-plated refinery, he built one that he thought was commercially right. . . .

These are examples of the kinds of arguments that went on all over the group all the time. There was a constant struggle going on between the head office and the operating companies as to who should have the authority to do what . . . Now, some of those were trivial and we intended them to be trivial, and these are the ones, of course, that people laughed about. There were other more serious things which we felt should not be as centralized as they were.

. . . The effect of that meeting with all of these case histories was that they said, "All right, we agree. You're right. We probably are trying to control too many things centrally. Therefore, let us change." And so we progressed.[17]

Marvin's role in helping to overcome the cultural resistance went well beyond directing his team to uncover the facts. He was a key presence at all of the team's many presentations to the Committee of Managing Directors (such meetings were held every other month), setting the stage for each interaction by creating a philosophical foundation for the conclusions and recommendations.

Every team member remembers those meetings and describes Marvin Bower as brilliant and at his best as he held the full group of managing directors spellbound. Capturing the undivided attention of this group was no small feat—all seven of the managing directors were stellar business statesmen at the international level. And, as Hugh Parker recalls:

> They listened with respect because what he said was said so well and made so much sense that it was almost irrefutable, his logic. Marvin could put over a presentation with enormous conviction. He had conviction and it came across. In a couple of hours of presentation, with slides or without, he more or less lectured them on what management was all about.[18]

In addition to the cultural resistance, there were legal issues and barriers that needed to be overcome. As the recommendations moved toward a more decentralized form of organization, Shell's legal department became very concerned. There is a Napoleonic law in Venezuela that says that taxation vests at the point of the mind and management of the company. So, for example, if the mind and management of Shell Venezuela were found to be in London and The Hague, then the Venezuelan government could tax all of Shell's worldwide activities. A team of lawyers, management, and consultants worked the issue and constructed a solution by creating service companies based in London and The Hague, much to the relief of the managing directors and much to the relief of McKinsey & Co.

The Recommendations

What resulted from this consulting engagement was a matrix organization (in which managers have both geographic and functional responsibilities) for Royal Dutch Shell—quite an achievement in several regards. First, it was one of the first of such organizational structures in Europe. Second, implementing this new organization would be difficult because it required fundamental changes to the company that seemed to conflict with elements of its culture, which had developed over the previous 150 years. Nonetheless, the Marvin-led team had conducted itself flawlessly, providing Loudon with the ammunition he needed and turning the whole of the

Committee of Managing Directors into a receptive and strong advocate of the recommended changes and path.

In reflecting on the recommendations, John Macomber believes that the reason it worked was they knew that Hugh and I and the rest of the team were absolutely rock solid as far as our integrity was concerned. There was never any question about McKinsey hanging around there for more billings. It was clear that the team's motivation was to help them, not just to get paid. And they knew that.[19]

As pointed out earlier, the Committee of Managing Directors maintained a healthy skepticism and demanded a strong, solid rationale for the recommendations. And although he was chairman, John Loudon ostensibly was no more powerful or influential than any of the other six members. In reality, however, he held tremendous power. Marvin was well aware that Loudon was the client, so Marvin worked hard at convincing Loudon of the merits of the overall matrix organization concept, knowing that once Loudon bought in, he would encourage the rest of the committee to accept the bulk of the recommendations, subject to any necessary revisions that might arise during implementation.

The recommendations were based on the belief that management in each operating company needed to be responsible for the performance and long-term viability of its own operations. In carrying out its responsibility, local management could draw on the experience of the service companies and, through them, that of other operating companies. To enable this would require common practices and disciplines in the areas of accounting, safety, environmental controls, and so on; a common language; and very explicit, clear definitions of authority and responsibility. The managing directors carefully considered the viability of this approach before adopting it. In one meeting, they sat with the team and tested how 100 decisions would be made under this scenario, what issues might arise, and who would own each decision.

When distilled down, there were four key recommendations. The first was that there should be a chief executive officer. Marvin was accustomed to the American style of management, and, at that time, he believed very strongly that there should be a single chief executive officer. This was an alien notion to the Shell culture with its Anglo-Dutch parentage. Finally, and with lingering reluctance, the managing directors agreed to this concept, appointing John Berkin to the position.

However, as the managing directors had predicted, this organizational change did not work out because the role and responsibilities proved to be too much for a single person. So, within six months of effecting that change, the position was eliminated.

This failure became an important learning experience for Marvin. He had entered the Shell study absolutely convinced that without a single chief executive, it would be impossible to have a clear line of decisions. And, indeed, the team pushed that argument right to the limit at Shell. Marvin's view softened considerably because he could see that the Royal Dutch Shell Committee could act effectively as a collective chief executive. At the age of 92, when Marvin wrote *The Will To Lead,* he argued for the benefits of having a group, rather than an individual, at the top.[20]

The second recommendation was for a series of functional and regional coordinators. Shell's functions were exploration, production, refining, transportation, and marketing (the basic oil functions), plus finance. The regional coordinators would be responsible for logical groupings of countries, with the United States treated separately for myriad legal reasons (including that Shell U.S. was not 100 percent owned by Royal Dutch Shell). Five regional and five functional coordinators were appointed. Although a complex concept, this change worked to clarify lines of control.

The third recommendation was to establish service organizations to support, advise, and set standards for the operating companies vis-à-vis finance, health, safety and environment, human resources, legal, public affairs, information, materials planning, and research. Tom Schick, the retired director of Shell R&D, described his service organization:

> R&D at Shell in 1959 was set up like most IT organizations are set up now—with central resources serving the business requirements, and supporting them with new technology as needed. The operating companies were treated with care as a customer. We also maintained a small group for advanced, or longer-range research, about 300. I believe it was the strongest R&D group of any oil company for 25 years.[21]

The fourth recommendation was to continue to nurture the common culture, shared experience, and common objectives of the Royal Dutch Shell Group. Marvin invested much time working with Shell in creating the right training programs to help ensure that all of the staff could understand issues as they arose from both the local and the group perspective, and would be aligned with and oriented by the Group's objectives. These recommendations represented fundamental, massive changes at Shell while preserving the benefits of its strong culture. And, with the previously noted exception of the single chief executive position, the recommended organizational changes have stood the test of time.

Impact on John Loudon

John Loudon described Marvin as one of the "most convincing protagonists of certain principles of sound organization."[22] After the study ended in 1959 and up until Loudon's death 35 years later, John and Marvin spoke a couple of times a year and exchanged ideas. On the occasion of Loudon's 80th birthday, his respect for Marvin was still evident: "I was at a party in New York in October . . . a dinner at "21" for my 80th birthday and they [had] asked me whom I wanted, and I said, 'I want Marvin.' And he came. He was very good, excellent."[23] As George Loudon, John's son, noted, "there was nobody my father trusted more in the business world than Marvin Bower."

Three Decades Later

The matrix organization recommended by Marvin and McKinsey & Co. proved its merits through its impressive longevity. As Hugh Parker recalls:

> We left Shell with the new structure in about 1959. And something like 30 years later, I was invited by a middle management club at Shell to give a presentation to them on the history of the organization. Basically, with some minor changes, the essence of what we had recommended and which they adopted was still in place, to my immense satisfaction. Since then, it has been re-studied and reconstructed. But the organization that we put in place did last for something like 30 years.[24]

In a 1983 Conference Board Report, "Organizing for Global Competitiveness: The Matrix Design," the Shell organization was held up as a model of success:

The Group's organizational formula, based upon a decentralized federation of country-based operating units held together by its management systems and strong Group culture, has created one of the world's most successful business corporations. Moreover, the structure has exhibited the resilience to withstand both political/social upheavals in some of its locations as well as major global business turbulence such as that caused by the oil crises of the mid 1970s and 1980s. . . . In recent years, Shell's matrix has been modified in ways to accommodate system-wide information exchange and implement pooling and common structures across certain sets of countries.[25]

Price Waterhouse, 1979: Consulting to the Consultants

In the late 1970s, public accounting (in particular, the then Big Eight) was expanding its horizons in a search for new and different forms of business, as well as seeking to reevaluate the core audit and accounting business to seek more growth and greater profitability. Familiarity with clients' financial processes, gained during auditing, provided a prospective launchpad for diversification into faster-growing tax and information services work. Like its peers, Price Waterhouse saw opportunity in service realms that edged toward the better-paid arena of management consulting. With some trepidation, Price Waterhouse managing partners approached presumptive competitor McKinsey & Co. about working on strategic positioning of the accounting firm.

The initial call from Price Waterhouse came to Marvin Bower, even though he had stepped down as the firm's leader some years earlier. As Joseph E. Connor, then the senior partner at Price Waterhouse, recalls:

> Marvin had a special standing within McKinsey. He was still considered a thought leader and he would undertake those assignments, as I understand it, that interested him. What interested him about the assignment from Price Waterhouse, he told me, was that it was the first time a professional firm in a relatively competitive environment would ask another professional firm to study its strategy.[26]

Connor had pursued Marvin because of his reputation:

I did not know Marvin before we engaged him; I knew who he was and what he did, but we had no personal relationship other than fleeting contacts.[27]

And despite his reputation:

I must say that I had heard Marvin in other venues talking about how the auditing firms were going about their consulting expansion in the wrong way. This was not particularly complimentary to any of the accounting firms.[28]

On his part, Marvin's decision to accept the engagement came only after careful consideration, according to Connor:

It took Marvin a little time to convince himself, and subsequently us, that client confidentiality would be maintained and that McKinsey would not use any information in a competitive situation.[29]

Marvin had great respect for Price Waterhouse, having witnessed the firm's high level of professionalism, its outstanding client roster, and distinctive partnership since the 1930s. Since Price Waterhouse was a very successful professional firm, Marvin was eager to not only assist them, but also to witness firsthand the factors and characteristics that led to Price Waterhouse's long-term success. Even though serving Price Waterhouse was not viewed favorably by many inside McKinsey, Marvin believed strongly that the insights gained would far outweigh the risks. Marvin was determined to not only serve Price Waterhouse, but to serve them superbly and to help shape their future firm.

The overlap of services between the two firms was determined to be about 5 percent, an acceptable amount. Even more important to Marvin than concerns about competitive integrity was the impossibility of externally imposing a strategy on fellow professionals. He knew that whatever the recommended strategy, it must be crafted and owned in partnership with Price Waterhouse. Accordingly, Marvin assembled a small joint team of McKinsey and Price Waterhouse partners, which he would lead.

As the leader of the joint team, Marvin brought to bear his key principles of leadership, garnering the respect of Connor:

He would try to lead you and convince you that his thought process was pretty good, but he was always receptive, ready to exchange views rather than come out with a mandatory one. Still, he did not kowtow to his clients. He told them what he felt was the best advice he could give them—whether they wanted to hear it or not.[30]

Two Views of the Problem Leading to an Unexpected Solution

The effort began with two different views of the challenge at hand. Price Waterhouse wanted McKinsey & Co. to work on a strategic study to assess the market positioning of the U.S. firm and the directions it should pursue. The internal view of the issues at hand was a need to prioritize new practice areas and identify new areas of expertise to develop (e.g., electronic data processing).

The McKinsey team viewed the key issues as organizational; in particular, the internal struggles associated with distinguishing among the accounting and audit, the consulting, and the tax partners (the three big practice areas). They felt that Price Waterhouse did not have a shared set of values that brought together the different areas.

The team began the study in the summer of 1979 with Marvin's preferred approach as phase 1: seeking facts from the front line by interviewing across the Price Waterhouse partnership. Before the team could interview, Marvin made sure that the interview guide was perfect, putting his associates through roughly 10 drafts before he was satisfied the right questions were phrased in exactly the right way.

The team interviewed over 50 Price Waterhouse partners, nearly 10 percent of the firm, to learn their views of how the firm worked, and its standing and direction. Phase 1 also included external interviews with corporate executives, public officials, and others. Analysis of the interview results became the project's core fact base. Even in an organization study, Marvin was a stickler for fact-based analysis and respectful of frontline testimony, although it wasn't strictly quantitative data.

In phase 2, the team drafted the new strategy built on shared value, and in phase 3 they developed an implementation plan and identified necessary revisions in management processes and organization.

The fundamental recommendation that emerged from the study was that Price Waterhouse make more of what it already was: the Tiffany of accounting firms. McKinsey recommended that Price Waterhouse emphasize a distinctive manner of service delivery that existed within the firm but was not embedded as widely or with as much fervor as Marvin believed it should be. The plan relied on the relationship between the engagement partner and his or her client as the delivery mechanism for rendering the highest level of professional service. McKinsey's recommended strategy was built on the special qualities with which Price Waterhouse had always identified itself, but had never explicitly built into its approach to the market. The bias at Price Waterhouse was that their strategy needed to be focused on building new practice areas and expertise to be sold centrally.

Despite a recommendation that did not directly square with Price Waterhouse's view of the issues at hand, leadership at the accounting firm came around to Marvin's and McKinsey's point of view. In the words of Joe Krovanski, a senior partner at Price Waterhouse:

> He made us see what we had always known in our heart existed, but were afraid to rely on. It was unique and it would give us a distinctive market advantage.[31]

Joe Connor remembers receiving the recommendations:

> I was surprised that Marvin was not looking at the type of service but the way in which we delivered it. He found what we were doing and what was working, that we didn't recognize ourselves. That was not what we thought we were getting. However, when the McKinsey report came out, the engagement partners (who constituted 90 percent of the partners in the firm) were basically extremely supportive. They wanted that change in direction to be articulated and then put in our rulebook. They saw it as a decided change in direction, and I think they were a little bit amazed that the firm's leadership could accept it so readily and implement it so vigorously.
>
> That in fact is what happened. This was not a report that met resistance; this was a report that met acclamation. We began to recognize that we had a golden opportunity with our newly articulated professional reliance on the engagement partner. We could preach the message to audit committees as to why we were different and what they could expect from us because of it.[32]

By helping Price Waterhouse gain the courage to take what was unique at their firm and turn it into their explicit calling card, Marvin was able to arm Price Waterhouse with a differentiated basis for competition as the other then Big Eight accounting firms fought for the same extended markets.

Making Each Manager an Owner

This approach was not without risk. Price Waterhouse had been selling the firm's experience on a project-by-project basis from a central head-quarters. Resting the responsibility on the shoulders of the person in the field—the engagement partner—shifted the emphasis from selling to client service. The operating implications were enormous. First and fore-most, the plan gave tremendous responsibility to the engagement partner: He or she basically made the decisions in relation to clients based on what he or she concluded was the right approach. Second, the role of the national office shifted from control to support—to bring all the resources of the firm together to enhance the advice given by the engagement part-ner to the client. That was a radically different approach from that used by most of the other accounting firms at the time.

Minimizing the risk of this revolutionary approach meant properly empowering, training, and supporting the engagement partners. Marvin felt there was much room for improvement in this area, and he challenged the senior partners on numerous policies regarding treatment of staff. He pointed out inconsistencies between the firm's mission statement and the way it really ran things. His message was emphatic:

> You can't run a professional firm this way. You will fail. You will lose good people. Here are some bedrock principles that you need to consider. And I ask you, from my observations, why you don't follow them.[33]

Marvin's list was long. Practices that he found particularly problematic included the internal transfer, compensation, and training policies. Price Waterhouse, like many accounting firms at the time, had transfer policies that did not really respect the needs of either the client or the partner. Every year, the senior management committee met to look at the firm's geographic needs. If Houston, for example, was growing, they would decide to place six more partners there. This policy was not viewed favor-ably by the affected partners. Unless partners were locked in with strong, producing client relationships or had a protector on the senior management committee to act as their advocate, they were subject to reassignment without consultation. After new partners were elected, most of them were asked to move to a different geography. The good news was that you were elected. The bad news was you were uprooted to a new location, which you may or may not have interest in. Every June, several hundred partners would get a letter from the managing partner saying, "We're pleased to tell you that you have been assigned to [a certain] office, effective August 1." There was no negotiation.

Marvin considered that practice to be counter to his belief that people are one of the most important assets of a company; and, as witnesses recall, while never offensive, he did not mince words: "You cannot run a professional firm with a practice like that," he told the senior partners. There was silence. After a few more seconds, he would continue, "So, I assume, when you see our recommendation to change that policy, you will do so."[34]

Marvin had an equally strong point of view on Price Waterhouse's staff and partner compensation program. He felt it was not sufficiently transparent for people to know where they stood. He criticized the lack of good evaluation and advancement mechanisms within the firm. He was also disappointed in the firm's training. While it was strong in technical areas, he thought it should provide the professionals better insight into the businesses they were serving. He believed that auditing couldn't be done just from knowledge of accounting rules. Auditors needed to understand business in order to assess the health of a business.

People policies became the area of implementation on which Marvin focused. As Joe Connor recalls:

> Courses were added on client relations, client problems, that sort of thing. Before, most of the language had been very technical. Now it came out as how you could persuade people, how you could influence the outcome. And, most important, how you could maintain that distinctiveness. Remember, there were a lot of accounting firms. We were faced with developing a commodity product—the audit—that we had to, in effect, customize and articulate and believe in and carry out. And that was not easy to do in a very crowded marketplace.[35]

The McKinsey recommendations provided an independent appraisal that the firm could point to in getting engagement partners to adjust their behavior. The report's recommendations provided the framework for numerous one-on-one conversations between the engagement partners and firm leadership on how to behave toward clients. Behavior modification was a critical requirement for success of the new organization and a difficult nut to crack, as Connor remembers:

> One of the worst examples was when an engagement partner would write to the technical service component of the national office with a request like, "Give me your preliminary thinking relative to the client problem." That was absolutely going 180 degrees the wrong way. The engagement partner should be the one thinking through the advice he was going to give his client. He should use the national office as a resource to marshal all that the firm knew about a particular subject matter. But it was up to the engagement partner, as the third step on that ladder, to put it in place. To bring that news—good, bad, or indifferent—to the client.
>
> That clearly became a new and required process between the engagement partner and the research partner. But the relationship was always advisory. In other firms—and I think Arthur Andersen was one—it was not voluntary, it was mandatory.[36]

A *Business Week* article from 1983 described Price Waterhouse as "bucking the trend" toward centralization.[37] Other firms were described as responding to the intensifying competitive atmosphere by reining in field partners' power and consolidating decision making (something Arthur Andersen was viewed as long having done). As *Business Week* reported, to the contrary, at Price Waterhouse, "making each manager 'an owner' of the firm, its leaders argue, is a powerful motivational tool and a much more effective means of instituting change than an executive fiat."

Impact on Joe Connor

Joe Connor credits Marvin Bower with "turning my thinking all the way around." Before the McKinsey engagement, Connor recalls, Price Waterhouse was heading toward escalation of the same central control, "double- and triple-check" environment, as its competitors. Marvin's thinking moved the firm away from duplication of others' practices to an innovative approach that was unique to Price Waterhouse. Connor goes on to point out that it was not just his thinking that was turned around, but his actions as well:

> Marvin was seizing the high ground in a way that would give us a distinctive relationship that the other firms had not achieved and may not have been able to achieve. The role of the engagement partner took a leap ahead: We began to focus on the relationship between the engagement partner and the CEO, rather than the CFO. We began to act differently.[38]

For Connor, this meant behaving differently in his relationships with engagement managers. In the past, as managing partner of the CPA firm, Connor had devoted much of his time to meeting with major clients to help solidify and expand relationships. He now had to make changes in how that outcome was achieved:

> I had to take a step back to make sure that the prerogatives of the engagement partner were not being curtailed by rank and status. One of the chairman's main jobs is to stay in touch with the blue chip clients that Price Waterhouse has always had. I needed to make sure I didn't show up at a client meeting with the head of IBM as if I was bringing along a little boy who happened to be called the "engagement partner."
>
> He's got to demonstrate his command of the client's business problems, and how we could provide help in solving those business problems. So, I took a step back in those meetings and let the engagement partner carry the ball. Between the two of us, we would in fact divide the professional and the business aspect of our client relationship. I'd handle one and the engagement partner would handle the other.[39]

Connor shifted the emphasis of his visits from that of being the primary person on the relationship-building end to that of staying abreast of client requirements and soliciting performance feedback:

> As chairman, you visit clients to ask, "What are we doing right for you and what could we be doing better for you?" That inherently has a questioning value relative to the partner and how he is exercising

his responsibility. And sometimes we found that they weren't exercising it properly.[40]

The culmination of Marvin and McKinsey's effort was the Price Waterhouse partners' meeting in the fall of 1983 in Phoenix, when the final McKinsey report and recommended strategy would be shared with all the partners. In preparation for that meeting, Marvin wrote to Connor in August, detailing the speech he would give if he were chairman. The two traded drafts several times, and Marvin helped Connor practice the speech the night before he gave it.

Arriving the day before the meeting, Marvin took advantage of those remaining hours to gauge the pulse of the audience (the Price Waterhouse partners). With his typical formality, he was dressed in a blue suit as he made his way around the pool talking to the golf-shirted partners, still listening and learning even at this late stage of the engagement. That night, he helped Connor practice his speech, and early the next morning, he suggested a few minor adjustments to the speech to better reflect the partners' mood.

Connor recalls that working with Bower on the speech fed his own excitement:

> He was articulating a concept that I knew was there and hadn't [been] found. He opened the floodgates, so that it became acceptable to go in a different direction than the other firms.
>
> Simultaneously, there was a willing and excited audience in the engagement partners. They wanted to be professional service leaders, not just somebody conveying advice from the national office. So, we had a good reception. We could deliver what we said we were going to do, we could act differently from other firms, and all that gave us a competitive advantage.[41]

Connor says he has never forgotten Bower's words: "This can be the reward of unleashing the inherent power of a professional service firm. And you can do it." He remembers Marvin the consultant as "a caring person":

> He wanted the client, at the end of the engagement, to say, "This was the best work we've ever had." He held his own organization— he held himself—to the highest challenges. And I'm sure he didn't miss many of them.
>
> He came across not as a guru of consulting, but as an involved, interested, dedicated professional who was trying to help a client

through whatever problem was on the table. He got down into the trenches and worked very, very hard himself. This was not a consulting assignment where his staff did all the writing. Marvin was in there. You know, I asked myself several times, why does he want to do this? He must have been in his 80s at this point.

It was the challenge—nobody had ever developed a strategy for a professional firm. That's what he got out of it. He not only did our job, but he satisfied himself that there was another practice area for McKinsey.[42]

Two Decades Later

It is not difficult to imagine what Marvin Bower would say about the tarnished reputation of public accounting today. He was a constant critic of the marriage of auditing and consulting, and not because this would raise the prospect of potential competition for his own firm. McKinsey's origin as the first modern management consulting firm rested largely on Marvin's belief in the distinction between the historical, reporting perspective of the accountant, and the unbounded, "what if" view of the consultant. The perils of unbounded "creative" accounting, on the other hand, became all too vivid as the century turned.

Two of Marvin Bower's McKinsey colleagues on the Price Waterhouse team credited him with anticipation of today's issues in the now 20-year-old study. Don Gogel found Marvin's advice to Price Waterhouse particularly prescient:

> There is no question that, if you went back to the study and had Bill Donaldson at the SEC read it as part of his speech on the way accounting firms should work, it would ring absolutely true today.[43]

And Robert O'Block, a retired McKinsey director, who was with the firm from 1969 through 1998, remembers that Marvin

> . . . continually advised Price Waterhouse to avoid conflict of interest potential. He was adamant that consulting and accounting and auditing services did not belong together. He also raised issues of potential conflicts between auditing and tax services 20 years ago.[44]

There is no doubt that Marvin's involvement with Price Waterhouse left a business-values compass in place that remained influential after the firm merged with Coopers & Lybrand and helped restrain the merged entity from engaging in the questionable practices that damaged its peers in the late 1990s. In 2002, PriceWaterhouseCoopers divested its 60,000-person consulting division to IBM, eliminating a potential source of conflicting interests. Although it should be noted that some of the elements of the organization changed over time with growth, acquisitions, and Connor's retirement from Price Waterhouse, in its public communications, the firm continues to stress its dedication to responsibility, honesty, and integrity.

Harvard, 1979: Making the Case for the Case Method

In 1979, Marvin Bower took on a daunting challenge: responding to Harvard University president Derek Bok's criticisms (some might say attack) of the Harvard Business School (HBS). This was a particularly formidable task. If not handled properly, Marvin's close association with HBS (initially as a student, later as a member of several Harvard committees and as an employer of HBS MBA graduates) could give the appearance of bias. To complicate matters, the issues on the table, particularly the use of the "case method," were fundamental to how Marvin believed leaders should be trained. Derek Bok, with a law degree and strong academic orientation, was skilled at controlling the discussion and not easily dissuaded from his beliefs. And finally, while Bok's criticisms may not have been delivered in the most tactful or considerate way, stirring up anger among faculty members and alumni of HBS, many of his concerns were justified and had to be addressed.

What unfolded at HBS shows how one can avoid the appearance of bias by presenting credible facts and persuasive arguments to support an alternative vision and how one can gain the respect of a leader despite differing opinions. It also shows how to design and execute an unemotional communications strategy that will be effective in a university environment; and how to stay committed after the study ended. Marvin's partner on the HBS effort was Albert Gordon, who was the chairman of Kidder Peabody from 1957 to 1986. He describes Marvin's approach:

> He was superior to most of us in that . . . he was much better trained mentally. Much more like Bok. He could put himself in

Bok's shoes. He was a great listener. He was judicial. Marvin was a huge intellect and not assertive. And he was phenomenally meticulous in his communications.[45]

HBS in 1979

In 1979, Derek Bok created a storm of alumni fury by daring to criticize HBS in his annual report to the Harvard Board of Overseers. As was his tradition, each year he would single out one of the Harvard schools and or some major part of the university for scrutiny. By 1979, he had addressed virtually all components of the university except HBS. His overall approach was always the same: act as prosecutor in making his case and then put on his judicial robes to listen to the full case as it was filled in by the defense. From this, he would form a set of working ideas on moving forward. Sometimes it led to picking a new dean, thereby influencing the direction of the school in question.

Ten years prior to Bok's controversial report, Larry Fouraker had been appointed dean of HBS by President Nathan Pusey, Bok's predecessor. Shortly thereafter, Bok became president. When Dean Fouraker took over the helm at HBS, he was faced with an academic institution that was suffering from many of the by-products of rapid, unfettered growth—namely, lack of direction, a fragmented faculty, lack of continuity, and highly problematic economics. He knew he had to rein in growth (not an easy decision given the career implications for the nontenured faculty). While taking a more paced and vigilant approach to growth was an important and courageous step, it was not sufficient. By 1979, competition had increased with over 700 business schools in the United States, and there was much turmoil in terms of what methods were best for management training. The broader political unrest (civil rights and antiwar movements) on campuses across the country made things more difficult. Further, Dean Fouraker's relationship with Bok over an almost 10-year period could not be described as the easiest of associations.

The Bok Report

President Bok's critique of the school was logical in its argument and also productive, as it included many suggestions for improvement. The essence of his critique was that HBS's strict adherence to the case method as the primary means of imparting a business education was possibly outmoded. He also questioned whether the current crop of business graduates was acquiring the knowledge it would need to become successful.

The Bok report was lengthy, but the following extracts capture the heart of the message. Bok began by laying out his sense of the needs of a business school graduate:

> Over the past twenty years, as corporations have grown larger and more complex, the practice of management has become more sophisticated. Society has been making greater demands on companies to serve new interests of public concern. Government agencies and nonprofit institutions are looking to corporations for management methods to improve their operations.
>
> . . . Under these circumstances, management arguably exists not simply to serve shareholders but to exercise leadership in reconciling the needs of stockholders, customers, employees, and suppliers, along with members of the public and their representatives in government.
>
> . . . Every professional school must come to grips with two questions that involve its essential nature and mission. What balance will it attempt to strike between research and teaching? And in its teaching, what roles within the profession will it try to prepare its students to fill? . . . Without neglecting research, the Harvard Business School has consistently maintained that it is, first and foremost, a teaching school and that its teaching is aimed at preparing general managers rather than staff experts or functional specialists. In other words, Harvard seeks to produce top executives for corporations everywhere, and all its principal activities are shaped to support that overriding goal.
>
> . . . The Socratic Method pushes students into active roles in which they must direct their thoughts not as much to the acquisition of knowledge as to the crucial task of making decisions. Vigorous class discussions also help students to learn when to speak, when not to speak, and how to speak—skills essential for encounters with public officials, union leaders, stockholders, and, above all, with management colleagues in the endless parade of meetings where the critical corporate decisions will be made. So important

is this learning process that the School follows the practice—unknown in any other Harvard Faculty—of actually grading students on the quality of their classroom performance.

. . . While retaining its traditional mission, the Business School must make sure that it devotes its energies to the most important issues that have arisen in the wake of the changes that have affected American corporations over the past quarter of a century. . . . These problems . . . will require a wide variety of disciplines and perspectives. Fortunately, the Business faculty is already at work on many of these issues.[46]

After covering the requirements that he believed business schools needed to meet and giving credit to HBS for proactively trying to stay abreast of market needs, Bok moved on to the bad news:

. . . Professional schools have a higher calling that derives from their ability to be thoroughly informed about their profession, yet sufficiently detached to examine dispassionately [their] larger responsibilities to society. To the extent that business schools neglect this responsibility, they become little more than purveyors of technique, indifferent to the ways in which their methods are used or the ends to which they are directed.

. . . Although leading executives often declare that the role of free enterprise in society is the principal issue facing the corporate community, no one would ever guess that this was so by examining the curricula of our major schools of business. Most classroom discussions still proceed on the unexamined assumption that growth and profits are the only serious concerns of the corporate manager. The study of ethics has fared no better . . .

. . . By remaining silent, business schools not only fail to awaken their students to a larger sense of their calling; they neglect their responsibility to their profession and the society to contribute vigorously to a debate of great public importance.

. . . As the problems of business grow more complicated, however, a separation between teaching and research becomes progressively harder to sustain. If the ablest scholars in the School are not centrally involved in teaching, their work may be insufficiently related to the actual problems that executives confront in the conduct of their business. If teachers are not themselves involved in research, they may fail to keep abreast of the conceptual insights and techniques required to penetrate beyond ad hoc, anecdotal encounters with particular problems. Hence, continued progress requires increasing numbers of teacher-scholars who can carry on a constant interplay between the practical problems of the real world and the insights and generalizations derived from research. . . . Insofar as today's practice perpetuates a separation between teaching and scholarship, it deserves reexamination.[47]

Bok then homed in on the major teaching/learning tool at the school (the case method), which, to his mind, was inadequate:

> . . . Despite its virtues, the case method has evident limitations. Although the case is an excellent device for teaching students to apply theory and technique, it does not provide an ideal way of communicating concepts and analytic methods in the first instance. In fact, by concentrating the discussion on detailed factual situations, the case method actually limits the time available for students to master analytic techniques and conceptual material. This extension may have mattered little in an age when the knowledge applicable to business decisions was rudimentary. As the corporate world grows more complex, however, the problem becomes more serious.[48]

News of the Bok report first appeared in a *New York Times* story before Dean Fouraker, or anyone else connected with the school, had seen the report and had an opportunity to discuss it with President Bok. There was a meeting of the Board of Associates of the Harvard Business School the morning the article appeared in the newspaper. Dean Fouraker hadn't yet seen the paper when he entered the room. Sitting there were Marvin, Albert Gordon from Kidder Peabody, William Sneath from Union Carbide, Philip Caldwell from Ford, Charles Brown from AT&T, and Charles Sanders from the Massachusetts General Hospital, among others. The committee members (all involved with Harvard Business School and supporters of Fouraker) were saying "Larry, you have been attacked by your boss, and this is awful."[49] So, they threw out their planned agenda for the day, and they spent hours talking about what they should do. Among other things, they decided to write a report and send it to Bok.

There was a general sense among those present that day and among some alumni that Bok (and the Harvard University administration) had an unstated agenda in unleashing this criticism—namely to rein in HBS from its semi-independent status, a move to be facilitated by bringing in an outsider to be the school's new dean.

Marvin Bower On the Case

At the time, Marvin was formally connected to HBS. He was a member of the Visiting Committee (a university-appointed committee charged with periodically reviewing how well the business school was performing). Al Gordon was also a member. In fact, between 1940 and 1970, Marvin and Al had effectively rotated chairmanship of this committee. Marvin was also a director of the Associates of Harvard Business School—executives of some 100 companies who contributed to HBS's research and case-writing programs. Given the close ties between the associates and the school, it was not surprising that the members' general reaction to the report was one of outrage, particularly at the way Dean Fouraker and his accomplishments were ignored. From their perspective, the relevancy of HBS was being attacked. The committee insisted that there be a formal reply to Bok's criticisms and voted to establish a task force to challenge the credibility of the Bok report. The task force was to be headed by Al Gordon and Marvin Bower.

It was clear that neither Marvin nor Al could be considered an independent outsider when they accepted this challenge: Beyond their services on involved committees, they were HBS role models and undisputed advocates of the school. Zealous in their activities, they were well connected in nonobtrusive ways with the upper echelon of HBS.

In Marvin's case, his close relationship with and advocacy of HBS began the moment he decided to attend the school in 1928 and continued until his death in 2003. He was the first Harvard law graduate to enter HBS and the second person to hold both degrees. His oft-told story of how his decision to pursue a Harvard MBA was received at the time suggested that there was a lack of respect for business within the walls of Harvard University itself.

> Just before graduation [from law school], I was summoned to the office of Roscoe Pound, probably the most famous dean in the

history of Harvard Law School. Instead of a desk, he was seated at the head of a long table. Always brusque, he started right out as I entered the room. "Bower," he said, "I have a job for you with the general counsel's Office of International Paper." "Thank you, Dean," I replied, "but I don't want a job. I'm going to Harvard Business School in the fall."

He stared at me. "My God, Bower, you are about to graduate from the greatest educational institution in the world, and now you're going to *that* place?" He pointed across the Charles River where the Business School is located, picked up a book, and threw it the length of his table. That's what academia thought of business in the twenties. (In fact, the feelings between the Law and Business Schools were so negative that it was several years before the joint program between the two schools could be established, but it did, in time, take place.)[50]

Marvin clearly did not share the dean's feelings about business:

I'd seen so much need for business understanding in law that I knew there was an important body of knowledge to be learned. I felt that it would make me a better lawyer and I would be more attractive to Jones, Day, which was where I wanted to work.[51]

When Marvin entered HBS, the case method had recently been introduced to the business school by Dean Wallace Brett Donham, who, perhaps not so coincidentally, was a prominent Boston attorney. Donham believed that a reality-based case system (as opposed to the public case method used in law education) would facilitate a business education by focusing on the skills required for decision making (the most critical role of leadership according to Marvin).[52] Here, the learning was derived by the "how," not by the "what." In and of itself, a particular answer to a given case was not important: Rather, students were evaluated on their methodology and rationale/supporting logic.

Marvin's postgraduation association with HBS went beyond his previously mentioned committee involvement. He was a major end user of the school's output. Once McKinsey & Co. transitioned from experienced hires to MBA recipients, many a Harvard MBA began his or her career at the consulting firm. Marvin valued and put his trust in the quality of the students coming out of HBS: They were a large part of what differentiated McKinsey. And the relationship was not unreciprocated—Harvard valued Marvin. In 1968, Marvin and Albert Gordon were two of the three recipients of the Distinguished Service Award (Robert McNamara was the third). In bestowing this award, Dean George Baker captured the respect and appreciation the university had for Marvin:

> To Marvin Bower, Harvard LLB '28, MBA '30, conceptual architect in management, constructive critic, and warm friend. Throughout a long and creative career, you have loyally and generously shared your experience, your wisdom, and your insight with the Harvard Business School and effectively imbued generations of talented young people with the will to manage that you personify so ably and articulate so eloquently.[53]

Creating a Powerful, Credible Fact Base

President Bok heard of the plans to respond with a report critiquing him and requested that John McArthur, the subsequent dean of HBS, and at the time an assistant dean, meet with Marvin and Al in New York City to discuss the nature of their report. John met with Al[54] first because he knew him better and recalls:

> In my mind, I wanted to go down and see Marvin with Al. When Al and I went in and suggested that a rebuttal critiquing Bok was not a good idea, Marvin's initial response was that he really felt what Derek had done was wrong. He felt a responsibility to the members of the group who had asked him to do a report and he needed to think about asking them to change direction.[55]
>
> After thoughtful consideration of what the committee's approach should be, the original plan to prepare a direct point-by-point rebuttal of Bok's critique was abandoned. Marvin and Al had decided a more persuasive and useful approach would be to write a strategy report (entitled "The Success of a Strategy"), including a plan for going forward that both embraced the strengths and shored up the weaknesses of the business school. The first challenge would be to diffuse the emotions of the committee and convince them that a positive outcome was more likely from a report that was not

defensive and did not attack Bok or attempt to extract an eye for an eye. Marvin spent many hours on the phone with his committee members (particularly Phil Caldwell and Don Perkins from Jewel) to convince them of the greater value of a fact-based, unemotional approach. His efforts met with success.

In Marvin and Al's report, Bok's issues are thoroughly covered in a fact-based manner that takes into account the historical rationale and freshly collected data that would either modify or support each of Bok's points. Marvin managed to rise above his close relationship with HBS and create a credible, unbiased report that represented an alternative vision for the school.

As the task force got under way, Al Gordon remembers how Marvin crafted a strategy to ensure that their effort would be perceived as fair-minded and communicated in a way that would make Bok receptive:

> I never worked as hard on anything in my life as I did on this. It was all in one summer. Marvin really led the thinking, coordinated, and actively participated in the effort. He felt we needed to write back in the same format Bok had written—it had to have a lawyer's logic to it. He felt we needed to collect all the relevant facts and that the sources needed to be independent, because we were not.[56]

Over the course of the summer of 1979, Marvin and Al drafted hypotheses, planned the report, outlined the fact-finding and analysis on which to base the assessment, did much of the interviewing themselves, and coordinated the overall effort. Marvin had asked his partners at McKinsey for a team to help with fact finding. Richard Cavanagh, currently president and CEO of The Conference Board, was a member of that team:

> Marvin and Al Gordon were organizing a group of business leaders and they were going to do their own analysis of the Harvard Business School and whether or not it worked and what was wrong with it, what was right with it.
>
> I was truly a bit player. They assembled an incredible group of business leaders, including the head of Ford Motor Company, the head of AT&T . . . all the big and successful companies of the day

(the GEs of the time). Everyone on the McKinsey team was given analyses to do.

I think in the end, Marvin did all the work. We were just fact-gatherers trying to come up with information and trying to test hypotheses that Marvin and Al Gordon had created. They came up with a different view from Derek Bok's view.[57]

Steve Walleck, a former McKinsey director and a McKinsey team member, vividly remembers how Marvin helped the team grasp the context of the effort that lay ahead:

I showed up in New York at Marvin's very modest office. It was to be one of the most eye-opening study experiences of my career with the firm.

In our first hour together, Marvin brilliantly dissected President Bok's report. What were his assumptions, his hypotheses, his proofs? What research had he done, what facts had he produced, and what arguments had he made? On what points had he been challenged, either by the business school faculty, the alumni, or by the press? Why were these challenges so acrimonious? What were both sides reacting against? What were they afraid of?

Marvin sent me away with a promise to meet the next day to review my issue analysis and study plan.[58]

As Steve points out, although the nature of the problem was not, at first glance, a conventional McKinsey issue, with Marvin's guidance he was able to bring hard facts to bear on a soft issue:

It was the first time I had tried to apply McKinsey & Co.'s hard problem-solving techniques to so soft a problem, and I wasn't very good at it. But over a week or so Marvin gently brought me along and structured my thinking.

For example, on President Bok's contention that today's business school graduates weren't being trained to be future leaders, I threw up my hands. "How can we get facts to dispute that?" I whined.

"Well," said Marvin with a smile, "we could ask today's leaders what they think of today's graduates, and how they are trained.

You know, it takes one to know one, as they say. Why don't we just call up the CEOs of the top Fortune 500 Companies, and ask them what they think of today's HBS graduates?"

I was aghast at the task being laid out, since I figured I'd have to do the calling. "Marvin, I don't know a lot of CEOs on the Fortune list, but for those I do know their secretaries have secretaries, and those secretaries consider it their first duty to protect their bosses' time. We'd only get through to a few of them, and then how would we protect ourselves from the charge of talking to only friendly CEOs who had nice things to say?"

"You're right, we'd have to talk to them all," Marvin conceded. "So let's just talk to the top 25. Do you think you could get me a list of their telephone numbers?"

Now here was a task I could do.

"I'm having lunch with Ben Shapiro of Dow," said Marvin, "so I'll interview him first. Could you have the rest of the list ready by, say 2:00 P.M.?"

That afternoon, Marvin went right down the list—General Motors, AT&T, IBM, Ford, bang, bang, bang. Every single CEO he called either took the call or was back with him within two hours. Marvin had a polite, carefully structured interview with each, and carefully noted their responses. Some of the interviews took an hour or more, but Marvin wouldn't leave a call until all his questions were answered.

Marvin did the first 10, and then handed the list over to me. "Now you try it," he said. A few we couldn't interview that afternoon, but they called back before the end of the week. Their overall opinion was that the B-school was doing just fine; that they wanted general managers, not functional specialists; and that the business school should keep up the good work.[59]

Steve, like virtually everyone who worked with Bower, came away with an important lesson:

"Now, what did you learn from that, Steve?" Marvin asked as I handed him my write-up of the interviews I had done. I don't remember what I replied, but it was not the answer Marvin wanted.

"But you also learned something else very important, something that will help you in your career every day if you use it," Marvin gently prodded.

"That it's possible to call up the CEOs of the Fortune Top 25 and interview them about HBS?" I guessed.

Marvin beamed. "You got it. CEOs are very lonely people. Most of the time the people who try to talk with them are trying to persuade them of something, or to sell them something. But if you're polite and well prepared and not self-serving, they will talk to you and enjoy it. Never be afraid of calling a CEO. It's the easiest thing in the world."[60]

In addition to interviewing the Fortune Top 25 and many of the directors of the associates of the Harvard Business School on the qualifications they considered necessary for the general manager of the future, the task force examined relevant written material and research reports, interviewed 36 members of the faculty (33 full professors and three administrators), profiled the faculty's background (inside versus outside), interviewed Dean Fouraker, and met on two occasions with President Bok. These activities created a powerful, credible fact base from which to test and refine hypotheses for their alternative vision for the school.

Communicating Effectively to a Tough Audience

The meetings with President Bok were critically important—well deserving of the careful planning that preceded them. Al Gordon remembered how he and Marvin prepared for each meeting:

> Marvin and I had a couple of interviews with . . . President Bok. They were rather stormy interviews. Before we would go into meetings with President Bok, Marvin would review what he thought Bok's logic would be. We would discuss our responses. Marvin could think like Bok, he almost always anticipated his responses. We rehearsed what we were going to do. We had a plan. We executed it.[61]

He also recalled how Marvin was able to avoid confrontation:

Bok is a very persuasive, aggressive lawyer. So, in one of our interviews we realized that we had to get our words in before he started to talk. We got there at 9:00, and before we sat down, by prior arrangement, Marvin immediately went into a story. After he had expostulated for 20 minutes, I rudely interrupted him and grabbed the ball and then went in on my story for another 20 minutes. Bok said, "You two are trying to blackmail me." Marvin did not respond to this affront, but instead blandly replied: "We're just acting on behalf of a mandate we got from our advisory committee."[62]

At Bok's request, Marvin and Al subsequently met with the head of the Board of Overseers, and avoided yet another confrontation by not campaigning for any particular individual to be the next dean of the school.

We anticipated that [the head of the Board of Overseers] would ask who our candidate was to be the next dean. He [Andrew Heiskell] was the chairman of Time Life—a big shot. He warmed us up, then said, "Who's your candidate?" We said, "Our candidate? We haven't got any candidate. It would be presumptuous of us to have a candidate. Forget it." . . . At one stage, he said, "Well, you're not going to get McArthur." We said, "We don't care who we get. We want somebody in the school who would carry on the tradition of the school as we explained in our report." So, that was the end of it.[63]

In fact, Marvin and Al did favor John McArthur as the next dean, and despite Heiskell's assertion, McArthur did replace Fouraker as dean and continued in that role for 16 years.

The Task Force Report

Marvin wrote the report and Al edited it; they both took great care in how they presented their arguments and recommendations. The following extracts from their 80-plus-page report, entitled "The Success of a Strategy," illustrate the flavor of the response. The report began with one of Marvin's favorite quotes:

"The secret of success is constancy to purpose." So said the great British prime minister, Benjamin Disraeli. . . . Harvard Business

School is distinctive in having a clear mission—to be a teaching school dedicated to preparing enlightened general managers for business firms. Constancy to this mission and to its strategy for achieving it is a principal reason for the school's success and leadership position.[64]

Marvin then went on to note the school's overall success as measured along various dimensions:

By quantitative measures, the school's performance is impressive. The demand for the program remains strong. . . . The demand for graduates and the responsible positions and the levels of compensation many of them attain attest to the success of the school's alumni . . . the leadership of the school's alumni in business and non-business institutions throughout the world. The positive evaluation given to the school's executive education programs . . . the school's ability to gain financial support. During the past ten years, . . . the school has been the beneficiary of 16 endowed chairs.[65]

Despite these outward signs of success, Marvin gave credit to President Bok's evaluation of the school and explicitly considered the issues raised in the Bok report, acknowledging their validity and evidencing Marvin's respect for Bok:

A good way to assess the educational strategy and resources of a graduate business school committed to training general managers— and the one chosen by Mr. Bok—is to evaluate the effectiveness of its responses to major forces affecting the corporation and the role of the general manager. During the past several decades, many powerful forces have been operating. Since we could not consider them all, we decided to deal chiefly with those mentioned by Mr. Bok. They are sufficiently representative for our purposes.

Although the survey request assumed that the future manager would have the basic qualities, many directors singled out some for special attention—notably, ethics—a leader must plan for the moral and ethical stance of his corporation. Integrity means that the person does the right thing and represents the company properly under all kinds of circumstances. Leadership—business leadership— requires a personality, a self-confidence, and perhaps a magnetism that give an organization confidence and belief in that leadership, and qualities of the mind. In terms of qualities of mind, the directors broadly agree on the importance of analytical ability. But they cite other qualities of mind that future managers should have.

In his analysis President Bok correctly listed tantalizing problems confronting modern management. Please note these are problems of the present and of the past, and may or may not be the big problems of the future. Even if some of these problems continue unsolved, you can be sure that students today who will be managers tomorrow will face problems now unforeseen. I think the answer lies in preparing to handle the unforecast as well as the predicted problems. . . . The merit of the Business School is that it is providing one way of dealing with the new and the old, with hard and soft information, with cold facts and hot opinions, with poetry and engineering, with pure science and unreasonable human expectations, and with shortages of data, time, and resources.

No one is always right. Therefore, flexibility must be expertly blended with firmness and determination, to find solutions. Above all, a general manager must know how, when, and to what degree to mix toughness and diplomacy (in its best sense).[66]

Then Marvin skillfully argued that the case method was still, in fact, a valid teaching and learning tool given the issues and challenges facing business schools in their mission to help shape future business leaders:

. . . Of the 172 projects referred to in the 1978 report of the Division of Research, 25 are concerned with research on business/government issues. . . . Our assessment of the business/government area shows that the School has devoted increasing attention to course development, culminating in [the newly required] BGIE [Business and Government in the International Environment]. Course development has, in turn, stimulated case development and research on a substantial scale. It is difficult for us to conceive that a graduate business school dedicated to training general managers for business could show a greater sensitivity—and a more effective response—to the impact of government regulation on business strategy, decision making, and the role of the general manager. . . .

A careful examination of the case method convinces us that this distinctive, student-centered learning instrument is superior to the lecture in preparing general managers. This method is especially well suited to teaching decision-making skills, but is not limited to that. Although it is supplemented by other learning instruments—student study groups, lectures and notes on theory, audiovisual materials, and computer games—we urge the school to keep the case method dominant. We also suggest that it make a greater effort to promote understanding of the case method outside the School. Were the method better understood, we believe that its value as a learning instrument would be even more widely recognized.

. . . Although we believe strongly in the current mission of the school, we suggest that it be broadened to include more specific preparation for managerial leadership. This broadened mission would support, not conflict with the present mission. In our survey of the directors of The Associates on general manager qualifications, many respondents mentioned leadership, and one of them put it first.[67]

He concluded by praising both sides—the school for working hard to keep abreast of changing needs in business education and President Bok for identifying and raising awareness of potential vulnerabilities. This evenhandedness was instrumental in helping to diffuse the adversarial environment:

Our general conclusions can be simply stated: The school has been remarkably sensitive to external forces, and its educational responses have usually been timely, effective, and adequate. Although in hindsight some of the responses might have come earlier or been more complete, many have been so forward-looking as to provide leadership for other graduate business schools, and a few have been so substantial as to build knowledge bases that constitute a national resource—for example, in the areas of organizational behavior, the multinational corporation, and energy policy.

At the same time, our appraisal confirms some of the weaknesses noted in Mr. Bok's report. In nearly all cases, we find that the Faculty had previously been aware of the shortcomings and had remedial action under way.[68]

Through their adept handling of the situation, Marvin and Al were able to turn a perceived attack into beneficial actions moving forward. As Marvin noted, the end result was positive in nature:

> Over the subsequent 15 years, McArthur [Dean Fouraker's replacement] addressed a number of the issues that the Bok report outlined—he created a real PhD program, rather than just the DBA program; he connected the school; and he created joint programs with a plethora of other departments at Harvard . . . and he kept the teaching centered around the case method. Anyway, it all worked out, and I believe the business school is better for having appointed McArthur the dean.[69]

While not willing to publicly concede to all of Marvin's arguments as expressed in the task force report, even President Bok begrudgingly gained respect for Marvin.

Marvin's commitment did not end in a published report. He subsequently took proactive steps to address some of the valid issues President Bok had raised. For example, President Bok was concerned about the isolation of the HBS faculty. The Bower fellowship was established to mediate this issue. Ted Levitt, a long-time Harvard Business School professor and thought leader, talked about the fellowship:

> One of the things that impressed me was how little our own faculty was known among the faculty of other schools where we were interested in recruiting. I thought one of the reasons they didn't know us is because our faculty was not interactive . . . I thought it was high time for us to get to be known better by encouraging leading schools elsewhere to see what we do, and Marvin created this idea of a fellowship program for younger faculty. They got regular salary, moving allowance, they could hang around our school, do whatever they wanted, and see what we did, et cetera. And, importantly, we could and did learn from them. So we launched this new program and called it the Bower Fellowships.

They got financed, in part, by contributions from McKinsey partners. Since the first one was appointed, Marvin has sent all of them a letter congratulating them on their appointment.[70]

Impact on Dean McArthur

As noted previously, John McArthur succeeded Dean Fouraker in January 1980. In light of the controversy sparked by the Bok report, Marvin felt that McArthur quickly needed to establish the right working relationship with Bok, as well as help solidify HBS's identity and address certain valid issues raised in the Bok report.

Soon after the appointment, McArthur established a dialogue with Bok that was characterized by give and take and by agreeing to disagree. The fundamental disagreement revolved around the differences between an education in business and an education in the other professional disciplines offered at Harvard. As McArthur remembers:

> Derek [Bok] used to say to me, many times, "I never understand this business education. In medicine, every medical school is the same. The kids have to pass the same board exams at the end. It doesn't matter where they go. And in law schools it's the same thing. The New York Bar exam. The business schools—they teach this way and they teach that way—they teach about this and they teach about that. Some are management science and some are music and poetry. And it doesn't seem to matter in the marketplace. I find it hard to know how to think about your school." I said, "Derek, how you've got to think about it is that it's not clear what is important to study or research today for people like you who, 10 years from now, are going to be running a big university or a big hospital or a big company. We don't know. So, it's a good thing to not have an orthodoxy. . . . It would probably be good there [in medical and law school] too."[71]

Dean McArthur told Bok that business education was not an exact science and would not fit the sort of template that could be applied to other disciplines at the graduate school level. Nevertheless, he worked hard at rebuilding a distinct identity for HBS in the aftermath of the hard questioning from Bok. While the Bower and Gordon report had confirmed the value of the case study method, it had also acknowledged that Bok had raised some real issues that needed to be addressed, and Dean McArthur concurred:

> The [Bok] report itself was good. It forced our generation to come to grips. I was trying to say, "Look, gang, in a lot of different ways, we can fix the things that need fixing." The research wasn't OK. And we weren't open enough to other people's ideas about management and where the important questions were.[72]

At the heart of the matter was the challenge of linking business with theory—the same challenge that Marvin's and other management consulting firms faced. Perhaps taking his cue from the approach used by Al Gordon and Marvin in crafting "The Success of a Strategy," McArthur began his effort from an historical perspective by commissioning a study of the history and intellectual roots of HBS that he termed "A Delicate Experiment." This study reaffirmed HBS's identity by linking it to the history of the school and the associated intellectual focus and the history of and rationale for the use of the case method.

While acknowledging the need for reform, McArthur was careful not to throw out the baby with the bathwater:

> I felt that the core of using the case method was an important idea . . . [as] Marvin saw with his firm [McKinsey]. . . . The role of a person running an organization is fundamentally different than every other person in the organization. Marketing, manufacturing, finance, personnel—all important, but nobody was studying what the world looks like if you're Marvin Bower at McKinsey, or Phil Caldwell at Ford. And that's what we do. It's a delicate experiment and if we lose faith in it and lose sight of it, it will be gone because no one else could understand it. And, further, it's an extremely expensive mission because we have to develop all of our own material, almost all of it. Ninety-five percent of the world's cases are done here at this factory.[73]

As McArthur remembers what "Marvinisms" he consciously replicated in his leadership style, he mentions three: caring, being an "intellectual venture capitalist" (investing in people), and succession.

In describing the caring Marvin, McArthur related a story from 1982 where Marvin went beyond the call of duty to help HBS obtain funding to establish a leadership chair:

It was the Thursday before Labor Day. Marvin called and asked me if I had read in *The Economist* that Mr. Matsushita (the founder of Matsushita Electric Industrial Co., Ltd., with Panasonic the principle brand name in America) had just given $46 million to start a new school in Osaka, Japan—a school conceived to train the next generation of leaders for Japan?" I said, "No." He said, "Well, why don't you take a look at it." Marvin had talked about the need for better leadership training at the Harvard Business School for some time.

So, I read the article and talked with Marvin again and he said, "Maybe we should try to raise some money from him if he's in the business of giving money away right now. Why don't you get Hugo Uyterhoeven (a leading professor) and I'll fly up, and we'll write him a letter." He came up on a Friday, just ahead of the long weekend. And I remember this school was empty. We sat around and gamed the thing out in our minds. He called Kenichi Ohmae (the McKinsey director of the Tokyo office and an influential player in Japan) at some point during our conversation because Ken knew Mr. Matsushita.

We wrote a letter to Mr. Matsushita asking for $5 million. We didn't hear anything for quite a while. Finally, Mr. Matsushita's office called and invited me to come and visit to discuss our idea.

So we had another meeting—Marvin, Hugo, and I. Then Marvin looked at me and said, "Well, someone's going to have to go out and see him. You don't look much like a dean. Why don't we think of someone we can send who looks more like a dean." We batted around some names. We picked Roland Christiansen and Abe Zeleznek. They were from the generation ahead of me, and looked something like Marvin imagined a dean must look like in the eyes of an 86-year-old Japanese guy. They went to see him.

When they got there, things went pretty well. Except there was one translation error. We'd asked for $5 million and it had been translated to $50,000. And the error was discovered just before Mr. Matsushita was to be brought in to the room to give the money. So Zeleznek called me. And he said, "Oh, this is awful. I think we should just take it." I said, "No way." I said, "Just stick with it. You know we asked for what we wanted." In the end, after some months, it was worked out. And we did establish this chair at the school in leadership.

This Marvin-led effort profoundly changed the core mission of the school. When you listen now to the dean and to the faculty and if you look at curriculum in the MBA program and in the other programs, leadership is a central part of what it is we're trying to talk about with our students.

Marvin was somebody who really cared. Lots of people you see in the course of life and say, "You should think about doing such and such." But that isn't what Marvin did. Marvin didn't just encourage me to think about doing this or that. He invariably helped me do it. That's the Marvin Bower I knew. And he always kept coming back for more![74]

When McArthur began to think about retiring, he borrowed directly from the succession model established by Marvin's own retirement:

> I retired the way I did because I saw how he [Marvin] did it. And I saw how other founders of Bain and BCG did it. These were all very successful people . . . each one created their own paradigm and built firms that stand at the forefront of consulting. Marvin basically turned the firm over to the next generation, and others handled this challenging transition differently. Many founders hung on, hung around, and were greedy. But McKinsey made it through from Marvin to the next governance system with relatively few problems.[75]

Three Decades Later

It is worth noting that, over the years, the case method has increasingly been accepted by the general business population and other business schools, and remains a validated teaching tool to this day:

> To the extent that general management can be taught in the classroom or through books, it is best done by looking at case studies.

It's not just that stories are more entertaining, although that is certainly true. It's that cases come closest to capturing the multidimensional nature of the work, the need to understand concepts in a specific context. Nevertheless, examples are the only way to show that the principles apply as much to Henry Ford in 1910 as they will to whoever makes the cover of *Fortune* in 2010.[76]

These case examples are stories of courage. Courage on the part of the Royal Dutch Shell Group to let go of the cultural and organizational heritage that had spurred its growth since its birth in favor of an almost unheard-of organizational structure that could properly support and further its growth. Courage on the part of Price Waterhouse to trust in its strengths and translate them into a successful value proposition as it navigated new markets. And courage on the part of the Harvard Business School administration (in particular, Dean McArthur) to admit to and address problems, while staying true to the fundamentals that constituted the strong identity and stellar reputation of the school. But a prime mover in all these examples is the courage shown by Marvin and his teams.

In the words of Winston Churchill, "Courage is rightly deemed the first of human qualities because it is the quality that guarantees all others."

CHAPTER 7

Educating a Generation of Leaders

The problems differ from generation to generation, but the qualities needed to solve them remain unchanged from world's end to world's end.

—Theodore Roosevelt, 1903[1]

Throughout his life, Marvin Bower held fast to his belief that people are the most important assets of any organization. While at Jones, Day, he had experienced only too painfully the downside of hierarchical organizations that, by their inherent structure, failed to leverage this asset. Furthermore, Marvin knew that no organization was sustainable without a strong foundation of committed people willing to act individually and as a team to ensure the future.

Building and empowering people requires integrity, respect, caring, trust, a willingness to invest time and money in development, and other leaders who believe the same. Marvin designed, built, and led McKinsey & Co. with these beliefs in the forefront of his consciousness. Thus, it is not surprising that Marvin's McKinsey became a veritable spawning ground for a generation of business and public sector leaders, who, after leaving McKinsey & Co., took their wisdom and empowerment to new arenas, in turn empowering thousands of others. Marvin's impact attests to the power of one: He influenced those who had the good fortune to work with him either as consultants or clients, and they influenced others, who influenced others, and on and on.

The list of graduates from the "Marvin School" is long, diverse, and impressive, making the task of choosing examples a daunting one. This alumni association is global: Corporations throughout not just the United States but every industrialized country in the world have benefited from Marvin's legacy.

The following four examples (Harvey Golub, retired chairman of American Express; Gary MacDougal, leader of the Illinois welfare system reform; David Ogilvy, founder and former Chairman of Ogilvy & Mather; and Don Gogel, president and CEO of Clayton, Dubilier & Rice, Inc.) are representative of the caliber and subsequent influence of those who learned directly from Marvin. Each example brings to light from the perspective of that individual how Marvin's influence bore directly on his approach, style, and accomplishments. Each man had very different careers in quite dissimilar organizations.

Harvey Golub

Harvey Golub was with McKinsey & Co. from 1966 through 1973, and from 1977 through 1983, when he left to tackle a turnaround situation at Investors Diversified Services (IDS). He ultimately became chairman and CEO of the parent company, American Express.

While at McKinsey, Harvey worked on many client engagements. However, it was in his role as head of the firm's training program that he regularly experienced Marvin's commitment to his employees—the people asset component of the firm. Harvey's training position afforded him a bird's-eye view of Marvin in action, interacting at McKinsey's various mandatory training programs with every new associate and every new manager. In direct contrast to an isolated command-and-control senior executive, Marvin was a known and frequent presence who worked hard at developing his employees into leaders with the courage to believe in and follow their instincts relying on a clear, unmovable set of business values as their compass.

> *Marvin was probably the best business leader I have ever met.*
> *He built the firm and operated the firm based on a very specific*
> *set of values which were well communicated and well understood*
> *and constantly reinforced. And which operated when the times*

were good or not. Marvin illustrated every day all the behaviors and values of the company. And I can't recall that he acted in a way that was inconsistent with those values. That is a powerful way to build a firm (or business) and unleash the creativity and energy of able people. It worked for McKinsey and it worked for IDS and for American Express. It establishes the basis for a sound legacy and continued good results.

—Harvey Golub[2]

Harvey brought professional values to a financial service firm. He recognized that financial businesses are shot through with the need for trust and hence should be run more like professional firms. Even an insurance company that acquires a security business should run the joint business in that manner to avoid fraud. That is how Harvey Golub achieved success with IDS [and American Express]. He personally connected to thousands of people at American Express. He made a difference.

—Marvin Bower[3]

IDS

After almost 20 years at McKinsey & Co., Harvey left to take on a major turnaround challenge at IDS, a Minneapolis-based mutual fund that sold door-to-door and was a recent acquisition of American Express.

In Harvey's view, the first task of any leader is to define reality (or, as Marvin might have said, get the facts).[4] His early assessment of IDS was as follows:

Strengths	Weaknesses
Very good salespeople	High turnover (subject to poaching by competitors); limited commitment to the firm
Organization pride in history of service orientation	Limited support (databases, training, etc.)
Competitively advantageous access to mid-America	No strategy to leverage market access/no relationship selling/no competitively differentiated value proposition

Furthermore, Harvey felt that the IDS culture was not conducive to leveraging the insights of the frontline salespeople or to creating an invigorated, engaged organization with a strong identity. Harvey describes the cultural challenge he faced at IDS:

> I had to create an open environment in which people raised their points and argued about their points and became less Minnesota polite. And I did that by modeling that kind of behavior, and rewarding that kind of behavior over a period of years.[5]

Based on his reality assessment of IDS, Harvey established his initial tasks, drawing heavily on the lessons he had learned from Marvin:

> We had to work through with the organization to define quickly the mission, the strategy, and the values that we would follow in order to achieve a level of success and it was meshing the strategy with the values that ultimately allowed us to be successful. Values without a strategy, values without an objective are just conceptual and soft. And a strategy without values to support it won't get executed. So you have to have the two working together.[6]

Harvey's strategy was to transition IDS's huge, talented sales force into financial planners by arming them with a set of business values to use as their compass, developing and training them, and supporting them with tools and a diversified menu of investment and insurance products that would enable IDS to provide financial planning services:

> Deciding on a financial planning strategy, and then, in fact, executing it. . . . It was all the details of execution that made it successful. And it was having a common set of measures and objectives for all the senior executives against which we would all be judged and against which we would all be paid.[7]

With Harvey leading IDS, developing people meant more than training. He believed it required his personal involvement:

> There were lots of training programs with regard to, for example, leadership training, and when we put in leadership training, I taught the first course, and then the people that I taught would teach the next course and so on. And once a year or so I would teach a new

course. So that people would understand that part of their job was to teach subordinates how to lead. The fact that we were not expert teachers but we were expert leaders impressed the people in our classes. There was a lot of room to be less than outstanding instructors. In fact, I think we were outstanding instructors because we were real.[8]

Harvey began encouraging his employees to express themselves as soon as he arrived at IDS:

When I first got there, there was a question about how we would set accrual rates on annuities, which was a major values-driven and economic question regarding what benefits would accrue to customers who had bought annuities. And one of the people there thought that I was making this decision in an insufficiently principled way. She was a woman named Kathy Waltheiser who was an actuary. Kathy went to her boss and asked permission to come talk to me. And he asked for an appointment and they both came to talk with me. Very, very nervous about it. And Kathy raised her point of view. We discussed this for about an hour. I listened to her and I explained my thinking and we discussed the pros and cons of it. So that at the end, I didn't change my decision, but she understood the basis of it and became convinced that it was a principled decision, one that was different from what she would have made—maybe at that point. But certainly she no longer had concerns about whether or not I was unethical. I used that example . . . at a number of occasions at IDS, in a number of speeches to indicate the value that I put on people who disagree in an appropriate way and raised issues for consideration, not to be nitpicky but to be supportive and helpful. So, I constantly in a sense reinforced Kathy's value by describing her courage.[9]

Similar to Marvin, Harvey valued the input of and ideas from all employees:

I spent a lot of time with people who did not report to me. So, at the time I joined the company, there were 4,411 field representatives and when I left there were about 9,000. I guess I knew personally about a third of those people. I spent a lot of time with them and with people in the home office as well. And all of that time got multiplied by people telling stories. So, it was not a matter of getting information filtered through channels, it was information directly from employees, representatives, and, in fact, customers. . . . That was very Marvinesque.[10]

Golub also shared Marvin's awareness of the danger of being lulled into a complacent, static mode of operations once having achieved success. Such a sense of security was contraindicated in a fast-changing, competitive environment:

> I guess the most difficult parts related to actions taken when we started to become successful. And as we started to become very successful, I think people began to assume that if we continued to do what we were doing, we'd continue to be successful. I was concerned that we were getting into ruts, that our grooves had become rutted. And the difficulty was to get people to shake out of ruts when we were doing well. I did that mostly through consistently defining new standards of performance, new objectives at the individual level and at the corporate level. Trying to identify the company that could put us out of business and become that company.[11]

Critical to Golub's success at IDS was a set of clear values providing a compass and a rationale for management and employee actions and decisions over time:

> At IDS Financial Services, we have rigorous ethical standards that govern everything we do. And we're absolutely serious about living up to them. There is very little gray area: Something is either right—or wrong. And because our values are clear, we believe it's easier for our people, from the bottom to the top, to make the right decisions about how this company should operate.[12]

Harvey subsequently renamed IDS American Express Financial Advisers.[13] In the 1990s, American Express Financial Advisors provided more than half of the parent company's profits. In 1993, the company had reached $2.9 billion in revenue (having grown 30 percent per year since 1985) with financial planners (not salespeople) serving 1.4 million clients. Economists deemed it "the lone star in Amex's gloomy galaxy."

American Express

In 1992, on the heels of his turnaround success at IDS, Harvey Golub became chairman and CEO of American Express, a firm with a 150-year history during which it had evolved from a pre-Civil War delivery service to a massive financial services provider.

As he had done at IDS, Harvey began by performing a reality assessment of American Express. What he discovered was a fast-eroding brand and a direct link between performance slippage and a troublesome culture:

> American Express was hemorrhaging and the corporate culture was arrogant and inflexible. The brand was eroding, and we had a high probability of becoming a smaller, more marginalized company.
>
> Like IDS, American Express . . . had a long and distinguished history of a service orientation. We were very proud of that. It represented the core of what was American Express. What had happened over a period of time was the company got away from that in terms of its actions and became more political, more internally focused, less consumer oriented, and less open in terms of how people talked to each other and how they communicated.[14]

What he also found was a company that had strayed from its core and had become a mishmash of businesses that did not all necessarily align with its strengths:

> The company put together businesses that were not American Express. So the cultural task and the strategic task [did not] again match. You can't just focus on one without the other. And the fundamental strategic decision made at American Express is that we would be a brand company and our objective would be that we would become the most respected service brand in the world. That was relatively easy to adopt because it matched their own view of what American Express was and could be.[15]

Having established that American Express's goal was to be the "most respected service brand in the world," Harvey set about turning that goal into reality:

> What was more difficult is then saying, if that [i.e., that American Express will be the most respected service brand in the world] is

the case, what then do you do about it? What does that mean? It's not just a slogan. What does it mean? First, it means that you have to get rid of any business that is not American Express, that can't be American Express, that can't hold the brand. Which we did.[16]

Within months of becoming CEO, Harvey put Shearson and First Data Corporation on the block. He did not stop there in bringing the strategy to reality:

> Second, it meant that the company, as a brand company, had to become an operating company, not a holding company, which had profound implications on how we structured the organization, how we made the decisions, and criteria for defining those decisions. It had profound implications on the compensation system. It had profound implications on the performance evaluation system. So, having made that top-level decision, there were then a whole series of things that flowed from it. Part of the task of changing the culture was to get people to understand the behaviors that were inconsistent with that vision had to change. And behaviors that were consistent with that vision had to be celebrated and rewarded.[17]

As Harvey had done at IDS, he took an active role in changing the culture of American Express:

> I tried to model the behavior. I also taught classes. I used presentations as learning experiences with people. I changed the performance evaluation systems. I changed the criteria on which people would be paid and illustrated how we'd do it. I tried to model openness and clarity.
>
> For example, we had a meeting in the boardroom. It was a number of senior executives and a number of junior people in the back of the room. And there was a presentation being made. After the presentation, I did something that had never been done as far as I know in the company: I asked all the people in the back of the room, who had done all the work, what they thought and how committed they were to the recommendation, what options they considered, and what they thought of as the risk. They were shocked at having been asked. But that story apparently bounced around the company very, very quickly.[18]

Training was also an important component of the cultural shift:

> There was lots of substantive training. But I guess the most important training was leadership training. How you decide on a leadership style to apply given the readiness level of an employee to do a particular task and how to effectively apply that leadership style. That was probably the most important.[19]

All of these factors—the alignment of strategy with core strengths, the explicit focus on culture, the CEO as a role model, the involvement of more junior people in decision making, and so on—were pure Marvin. Having experienced the effectiveness and power of these very things during his 20 years at McKinsey, Harvey acted on this knowledge at American Express (and IDS). In doing so, he applied his own style, but the fundamentals remain the same. As Harvey remembers:

> One of the things that Marvin did was that he constantly reinforced the values by writing and speaking about them rooted in actions that had actually taken place so that it was a constant reminder. At American Express, I did not do quite the same thing. Instead of writing memos that stated, I tried to write memos that explained the decision—not just what it was, but why it was, how it came about, how I had thought about it. I changed the name of the company magazine to *Context*. It was designed to provide background, or the context for decisions that were made. So that the people would understand where we were coming from and not just the what. They might still disagree with the decision, but they would understand the logic that led to it.[20]

Knowing that organizational values are not lip service platitudes, Harvey took care in selecting the values or principles at American Express, as he noted in a 1995 letter to Marvin:

> You might be interested in some of the other things we are doing. . . . We're approaching the task of defining our organizational attributes with the same rigor we use in developing business strategies.[21]

The values or principles that Harvey embedded at American Express were simple yet powerful:

We would offer products that provided superior value to customers only. We would operate at world-class economics. And we would enhance the brand—anything that we do must support the brand and be consistent with our client's understanding of the brand. If it is not, we can't do it. All three of those decisions, I just illustrated, flow from those operating principles.[22]

As Harvey pointed out, once the right values or principles had been set, what was critical, as he had learned from Marvin, was to make them real every day through actions and decisions. Furthermore, a clear set of values would facilitate efficient operations by substituting a simple compass for cumbersome procedures:

Marvin actually executed against those principles in a very direct and deliberate way. He took them seriously. They were statements of aspiration, but they were not simply platitudes. They had meaning and substance. It was in putting life to those principles that Marvin made a difference, and that's what I try to do. It made the decisions easy.[23]

The most difficult thing to do at American Express, Harvey found, was to make decisions he felt were right and critical when the organization did not fully support them. But once the guiding values were set, the decisions flowed naturally:

There were times I had to make a decision in which I did not have the full support of the organization. So, for example, when I decided that we would issue cards operated under the American Express network with banks, that was not fully supported in the company. And I made that decision and we went ahead with it. When I made the first decision to reengineer the company and take a billion dollars in cost out, people understood that we had to do that, but there was not much support for doing it. When I made the decision that we would attempt to achieve universal coverage for the American Express card, and not settle for just coverage of travel and entertainment venues, it was a difficult decision. There were those kinds of business decisions that were difficult. But . . . the principles we had were clear, and, therefore, the decisions flowed from those principles.[24]

Another important change that Harvey made to create a "competitive advantage out of our employee base" was to put in place an evenly applied performance evaluation process that tied a portion of each executive's bonus—including Harvey's—to a survey of employee value, where value was not defined solely by financial performance:

> We had a principle . . . relating to . . . the necessity to create competitive advantage out of our employee base. To make that real, 25 percent of every executive's bonus, including mine, depended upon the results of an employee value survey that we took every year. So, we had 360-degree data over time. We translated the results of those surveys on unit level into compensation results. The consequence of that was that we reached world-class levels of satisfaction on virtually all of our employee values. And we eliminated all aggregate differences among ethnic groups and between men and women.
>
> Every year, for example, we would evaluate the performance of each business unit for bonus purposes. And I would send out the complete evaluation to all people in the bonus system. We showed the ratings for every business unit in *Context* magazine for all employees to see. So they would see that unit one got a rating of A and unit two got a rating of C–, with an explanation of why. Thus they could understand how evaluations came about, and why they might differ from what the financial results were.
>
> If people argued, I sought information. I'd ask people to give me their comments. And I'd get those comments to make sure that my thinking was as complete as possible. And, at the end of the day, one can look at an essay and conclude that it's an A– or a B+ and be legitimate. What I wanted people to understand was that if I gave somebody a B+, I was applying the same standard elsewhere.[25]

A standard approach to performance evaluation enabled a perception of fairness and, again, was something Marvin had made a point of instituting early on at McKinsey.

Moving American Express to a new world state of mind was an eight-year process for Harvey, punctuated by some difficult and creative management decisions. Fifteen years after first joining American Express to turn around IDS, he stepped down from the job, and did so very much in a Marvin way. As Harvey described it:

Sometimes the outgoing CEO tries too hard to make his last year the best year rather than making the first year of the successor a better year. Some CEOs won't let the successor expand responsibility very much before the changeover and therefore don't have an opportunity to provide at least some level of guidance. The dynamic of having the old CEO hang around in order to be helpful to the new CEO is almost always nonsense. It can create two problems. The successor may not want to make changes because he doesn't want to hurt the feelings of his predecessor. And the person who is being succeeded may feel resentment if something is changed. The old CEO ought to go away, and if the new CEO has a question, he can call him or have lunch with him.[26]

In the 2000 American Express Annual Report, Kenneth I. Chenault, the current CEO of American Express, describes the impact that Harvey had:

> In a 15-year period, Harvey has had an unparalleled impact on American Express's businesses, its corporate culture, its people, and its share value. Whether at the helm of IDS in the 1980s, Travel Related Services in the early 1990s, or the parent company over the past eight years, he has been a dogged champion of the American Express brand. Further, he harnessed the power of that brand—and American Express's people—to lead the turnaround of this company.
> . . . Harvey leaves us with a legacy that will long outlast his years here. He helped mobilize and motivate a dispirited group of employees—people who now see themselves as winners, and who work for a company that is a revitalized force in the marketplace. He articulated the company's values and made them more concrete and meaningful to our employees around the world. And he has entrusted us with a company for which he clearly—and deeply—cares.[27]

Over his post-McKinsey years, Harvey wrote to Marvin regularly, keeping him abreast of efforts at IDS and American Express and crediting Marvin and his approach in building McKinsey with laying the framework for Harvey's leadership at American Express. The following letter, sent to Marvin in January 2001 after Harvey retired from American Express, captures these sentiments:

> I have often been asked about the people who influenced me in my career. There were only two who had a profound effect on me—my father and you. There have been numerous times when I have told "Marvin stories" to illustrate a point.
>
> Marvin, you built a firm based on establishing principles and then adhering to those principles, even when it was expedient not to. That is a powerful way to build a firm (or business) and unleash the creativity and energy of able people. It worked for McKinsey and it worked for IDS and for American Express. It establishes the basis for a sound legacy and continued good results.
>
> From time to time, I have observed that if I had only one lever to pull to ensure success it would be to attract, develop, and retain better people than my competition. Doing that would ensure the nimbleness and ability of the firm to adapt, adjust, and lead. And, the secret to people development is simple—get the hygiene right (pay, benefits, working conditions), give people interesting, challenging work, and finally provide good leadership.
>
> You did all that. And I am and will always be extremely grateful to you and proud of my association with you.[28]

Gary MacDougal

Gary MacDougal was in the Los Angeles office of McKinsey & Co. from 1963 through 1969. In 1969, he left to become CEO of Mark Controls Corporation, and in 1992 he led the effort to overhaul the Illinois welfare system with remarkable success.

> *One of the most flattering things that happened to me after I left the firm was when Marvin showed up as a stockholder. Each week I would glance through a list of stockholders. And all of a sudden Marvin shows up owning 1,000 shares of Mark Controls stock. It wasn't even NASDAQ. It was over the counter, pink sheet, in those days pretty high-risk stuff. It was as though I had been given a cardinal's cap by the pope—a sort of validation I couldn't even have imagined. That he would invest in me,*

> *in this company that had lost money seven out of nine years, a*
> *valve company in the Midwest. It was wonderful.*
>
> —Gary MacDougal[29]

> *Gary has great imagination. He connects to people very well.*
> *The clients who worked with Gary loved him. I think he made*
> *a difference to the UPS board. . . . There was one point when he*
> *was doing very well at Mark Controls that I thought he might*
> *lose his humility. But he didn't. He is still humble and he knows*
> *how to lead. He has a lot of initiative.*
>
> —Marvin Bower[30]

While at McKinsey, Gary interacted regularly with Marvin, who was managing director when Gary arrived at the firm:

> Marvin and Warren Cannon were the central players in the firm.
> And Marvin's presence was everywhere. The blue memos with the
> Judeo-Christian ethic and the occasional incident that happened
> where Marvin stepped in. . . . There was a backbone in the firm
> that was nonnegotiable when it came to matters of ethics.[31]

During Gary's last year with the firm, he led the financial services practice, and had multiple opportunities to learn about leadership and business from Marvin:

> One of my heroes is most assuredly Marvin Bower. He came
> along when I was fresh out of business school. I didn't know how
> to work the buttons on a button phone; I had been in the Navy
> and I had been in undergraduate engineering and I just didn't
> know anything about business. Marvin came along in my life at a
> time when I was a sponge absorbing leadership models and under-
> standing how business worked. He was a presence that the minute
> you walked in the door at the firm's new consultant training ses-
> sion—day one—you knew it was real. He was real.[32]

Mark Controls Corporation

When Gary left McKinsey & Co. in 1969 to become CEO of Mark Controls Company, he began a 17-year journey to transition this small, unprofitable valve manufacturer into a very profitable Fortune 1000 electronics and process control company. What at first glance appears a Cinderella story was in fact accomplished through a fearless imagination of what could be and a dogged persistence in communicating that vision and the requirements to the 5,000 employees who would need to be part of this transition every step of the way. In short, Gary's "magic wand" was the many lessons he took with him from his years of working with Marvin:

> In my company, I was faced personally for the first time with taking what I believed and spreading it out to 5,000 people. I remember how scary it was thinking that, 24 hours a day, Mark Controls was operating someplace in the world—be it a factory in Singapore or a sales office in Germany—many people could be hurting our firm or helping our firm depending upon how they behaved. I recognized that I couldn't be there to do it all, so I had to imbue what I thought was important in the organization.[33]

Gary quite directly attributes his success in communicating to a large and geographically dispersed employee base to Marvin:

> I learned that you needed to put a lot of things in writing. There's a common mistake that is made by leaders that if you say something orally and you agree with a small group of people that sit around a table that run the organization, that that is somehow going to find itself disseminated throughout the organization. What Marvin did through his blue memos and the training sessions and his personal visits where he was traveling around the world, is he made sure that those values weren't just for the senior partners in New York who sat around and talked about it, but were communicated throughout. So, with my 5,000 [employees], I had beer and pizza sessions everywhere I went. When I would go to a factory in Singapore or Scotland or whatever, I would take a cross section from the factory, from sales, from management, and we'd go out and have beer and pizza and we'd talk about the company and I would answer questions. I would follow every visit with notes to the people with whom I had spent time, so that there was never any "they." I'm they, or we're they. Don't say "they think this." "What do you think? Is it good? Is it not so good? What are your concerns?" Try to open up the dialogue.[34]

The conversation had to be two-way in order to fully engage employees and develop this people asset base:

[We conducted] attitude surveys, which included ethics, and they were anonymous. We did everything we could to make people feel that they could express their actual feelings and top management would listen.[35]

Gary recognized that the reputation of Mark Controls and its ability to be perceived as something greater than a valve or control manufacturer rested, to a large degree, with the employees:

You really needed to be vigilant all the time. The people that you have representing you carried with them the values. And that included hard work and doing a good job for the customer.[36]

Providing the right role model was an essential element of crafting the sought-after culture at Mark Controls:

Some amount of humbleness [was also needed]. I used to give a session on leadership at Mark Controls management conferences, where we would have 200 people from around the world. I would talk about everything from when somebody comes in your office getting out from behind your desk and sitting with them so you're not presiding, the value of listening, the value of the example when it comes time to turn down bonus and pay raises on bad years, which I did on numerous bad years, of which there were many, too many.[37]

Ensuring his organization adopted the values (working hard, doing a good job for the customer, listening to and respecting others, etc.) and demonstrating his own commitment to the company was a full-time job for Gary. As Gary notes, the preceding points are just some examples of how he accomplished this: "There are lots of ways to communicate what you believe to an organization. I learned a lot of them from Marvin."[38]

Gary's persistence and hard work paid off. Seventeen years after he took over the leadership at Mark Controls, it was clear that Gary had achieved what for others might have been unthinkable: "In 1987, the various divisions of Mark Controls were, in total, worth almost three times what the company's stock sold for on the New York Stock Exchange."[39]

In fact, Gary was so successful that he worked himself out of a job:

> I decided I should break it up by selling the pieces before some Wall Street raider decided to do it for me—our longtime investors deserved those gains. A *Chicago Tribune* headline said, "Firm Beating Raiders to the Punch, CEO Manages Himself out of a Job." The overall strategy worked well, with the stock becoming worth $160 per share, compared with $10 per share when I became CEO.[40]

The Illinois Welfare System

After Mark Controls, Gary took his time searching for a place where he could make a difference. This time, that place was in the public sector, the Illinois welfare system, and here the people assets were the government agency employees and the providers along with the clients (the human services recipients). The success of the system could only be measured by the success of the recipients—the notion being to have fewer "customers" over time, rather than more.

Gary's association with this human services system began in 1992, when he proactively created a role for himself:

> This is the story of a from-the-bottom discovery of what is wrong with the current system nationwide, anchored by the views of actual welfare recipients, not ideologues or academics . . . I persuaded the governor to set up a task force on human services reform and name me to chair it . . . champions for change emerged within the huge bureaucracies . . . the initiatives began to change people's lives— mostly by using existing taxpayer dollars better.[41]

Unlike Mark Controls, the output here was not pieces of equipment, but rather a fundamental improvement in people's lives and their ability to be economically self-sufficient. Against this output, Gary adopted a Marvinesque way of problem solving, going directly to the front line (welfare recipients, state employees, and providers, in this case) to gather the facts necessary to reform the current system into an effective, reality-based system. He spent time with "the ladies in the backyard," the men in prison, the agency employees, and the supervisors.

This fact-finding mission provided Gary with the ammunition to create a different logic for the Illinois welfare system, one grounded in some very practical realities about the recipients and one that took a "what if" mind-set to the governmental, bureaucratic side of the equation.

Gary's experiences while chairing the governor-created task force on human services reform in Illinois are captured in his 2000 book, *Make a Difference*.[42] The following excerpts illustrate how he took his fact-finding mission to the end users (the "ladies in the backyard") and the providers (e.g., the government employees and legislators).

"The Ladies in the Backyard"

The Reverend B. Herbert Martin had set up a meeting for me with a group of African-American women that . . . [we] came to call "the ladies in the backyard" . . . [A] group of welfare recipients . . . who gathered most afternoons in the small backyard of his apartment building. "The bottom line," he [Reverend Martin] said, "is unless we can reach this group and do things that will result in a change in their behavior, we won't have succeeded in our reform efforts."

I knew that you don't really understand until you've spent meaningful time face-to-face with the "customers."

I was headed for an afternoon discussion with . . . Maxine, a dour twenty-year old felon and mother recently released from prison, and Lavon, a vivacious mid-twenties mother and prostitute, among others.

I leaped in. "What would you do if you were governor?"

[Maxine responded] "I'd get me a job. I apply for jobs, but they always wantin' work experience. How'm I gonna get work experience if I can't get no job?"

Yet she was sitting in this living room facing a world that she knew did not want to hire her—a felon with no work experience, two kids, and like all but one of the women in the room, a high school drop-out [in the ninth grade to take care of her son].

"Have you thought about getting a GED?" I asked.

Maxine looked thoughtful, and replied, "The only GED course is at night up at Dawson [Community College] and it ain't safe. They rapes us up there."

Kathy, in her mid-thirties, unlike the others, had some work experience, both domestic work, and for a brief period, work in an office. I asked why the office job didn't work out. "The job was out in the suburbs. A friend helped me get it. To get there I had to take a bus up into the Loop and then wait for a train for Des Plaines. Then I had to arrange to be picked up or take a cab from the train to the office building. It took me over two hours each way, and it was expensive. With a car I could have done it in about an hour, but I can't afford a car. Traveling close to five hours a day, and with three kids, I just couldn't do it."[43]

Gary held extensive interviews with the welfare recipients, bringing a face (or many faces) and clear needs to that side of the equation:

The stories these women and men on welfare and in poverty told gave me a richer understanding of the clients and circumstances encountered in the welfare and human services systems. My meetings with the ladies in the backyard and other close-up exposures as "the only white guy in the room" always remind me that there is a wide range of individual differences among the welfare population, just as in any other large group. One-size-fits-all thinking is usually a mistake.[44]

And, like most people, they wanted an opportunity to do their best:

At the heart of all this are real people, people whom most of us, including policymakers, rarely get to know. I contend that the great majority of the individuals on welfare share the same desire to work and have the same personal aspirations for themselves and their families that most Americans hold. We need to create a ladder of opportunity for those willing to climb it.[45]

The Government Employees

Gary's fact finding also included visiting the plethora of involved government agencies learning how time was spent, what the results were, and where people saw opportunity to do things better.

An important baseline for Gary's investigation was the creation of a chart of the organization and the processes of how decisions and dollars were flowing from each involved department, and, as he called it, a "Rube Goldberg can of snakes." What he found was a system characterized by excessive rules and procedures and not tied to meaningful measures of success:

> Much of what I saw seemed poorly managed or on the edge of being out of control. I was determined to learn what was really going on.
>
> The people at the top, especially those who wrote the regulations, were evaluated on reducing the agency's legal risk to an absolute minimum, satisfying the federal inspectors, and avoiding embarrassment to the governor. Since real outcomes in the form of helping people change their lives and become self-sufficient are rarely measured, micromanagement and the pile of rules grow unrestrained.
>
> I arranged to see a program called Project Chance. I asked one of the attendees why he was there. "Got to do this to get my check; this is my second time."
>
> "Do you think you'll be able to get a job?" I queried.
>
> "Ain't no jobs 'round here no how," was the response.[46]

Gary found that those running the program were as aware as the welfare recipients of its shortcomings but, as in other overbureaucratized organizations, people's ideas were unlikely to get acted on (or even heard). In response to Gary's question on what he would do if this were his own money, Fred Collins, the program administrator, had a ready, practical answer:

> "Heck, that's easy, I'd use the money to run a van from the Robert Taylor Homes where many of these people live out to Elk Grove Village where the jobs are." On to the list went "outcome measurement." Imagine spending millions and not knowing what you are getting in return other than employment for instructors and MSWs. Also on to the list went "local flexibility." How could we try out his van idea?[47]

However, adopting Fred's good idea was not actionable under the program's then current interpretation of its mission: "We're human services, we don't do transportation."

The Results

Gary created test sites in five areas. In the new world to be tested, the processes began at the front line, decisions would be integrated and aligned, the orientation would be around getting people back to work in a viable way (that fit with their daily realities), and a new, meaningful measurement system would be implemented. This meant locating the center near where the people lived, and collaboration among government organizations.

The five test sites proved successful. The governor signed into law on July 3, 1996, what he termed "the biggest reorganization the State of Illinois has seen since the turn of the century." Most of six separate departments were combined into a single unified department of human services. In the legislation creating the department, it was specified that services be integrated, that they be connected to the communities in which they serve, and that outcomes be measured for all state human service expenditures. The results were not measured on Wall Street, but they were as powerful as what Gary had achieved at Mark Controls—an 82 percent reduction in the number of welfare recipients in Illinois as of September of 2002, by far, the best record of any state since 1996 with more than 25,000 welfare recipients.[48] Donna Shalala called Illinois "the first state with a very big city that has done very well."[49] As Gary shows in his book, most important behind the numbers were a vast number of people with new economic self-sufficiency and a new level of self-esteem:

> Janice McCrae, the chronically unemployed welfare recipient, was able to move into meaningful work, despite having spent thirteen years on welfare. Janice happens to live in the Grand Boulevard community of the south side of Chicago, an area some have called the most disadvantaged urban area in the country. As a result of the Illinois effort, Janice has now worked part-time with full benefits sorting packages at a United Parcel Service hub for over two years, and is being considered for promotion to full-time work. She is thirty-one years old, has sons nine and fourteen, and a twelve-year-old daughter. She lives in the notorious Robert Taylor Homes housing project, a half-hour bus ride from her job.[50]

These results continue.[51] In 2003, President Bush came to UPS on the south side of Chicago to celebrate the success of people who had moved off welfare.[52] On the stage with Mayor Daley; Mike Eskew, the CEO of UPS; and President Bush was Vivian Kimmons. As the fourth speaker, she related her story—on welfare for nine years, mother of nine children, and now a three-year employee, manager, and stockholder of UPS. There were tears in many people's eyes.

Over his lifetime, Marvin Bower had stressed the need to give back to the community. With his role in helping reshape the Illinois welfare system into an effective provider of human resource services, Gary MacDougal was able to apply his business acumen and skills to the benefit of the community and to the creation of a priceless product—people's self-worth and pride.

As Marvin noted in 2002, "Gary has made an important difference." MacDougal's respect for Marvin continues to this day: "He was one of those people who was absolutely unwavering in his integrity and commitment to other people."[53]

David Ogilvy

David Ogilvy, founder of Ogilvy & Mather and one of the legendary giants of advertising, had a long relationship with Marvin Bower. Like Marvin, he had a background that ideally qualified him for his leadership role. He started out as a salesman (he sold Aga stoves and did so well that he was assigned to write the salesman's handbook),[54] worked for George Gallup (and never forgot the importance of hard, scientific data on opinion and preference), worked a farm in Amish country, and served in British intelligence in the Second World War (where the importance of understanding the front line and using facts was driven home). Ogilvy and Marvin were among the last survivors of people who contributed to the Industrial Revolution. Ogilvy and Marvin also contributed to the leadership culture of today.

> *I have learned from my own mistakes, from the counsel of my partners, from the literature, from George Gallup, Raymond Rubicam, and Marvin Bower.*[55]
>
> *My admiration for Marvin amounts to hero-worship. My partners are sick to death of hearing me exhort them to conduct our business the way McKinsey conducts theirs.*[56]
>
> *The great leaders I have known have been curiously complicated men. Howard Johnson, the former President of MIT,*

has described it as "a visceral form of spiritual energy which pro-
vides the element of mystery in leadership." I have seen this mys-
terious energy in Marvin Bower of McKinsey.

—David Ogilvy[57]

David Ogilvy was a great leader. He fundamentally changed
how people viewed advertising.
  He understood and appreciated the requirements of build-
ing an institution.
  We were never close socially, but I viewed David as a very
close friend.

—Marvin Bower[58]

The Bonds of Shared Values

In the 1950s, four men were independently trying to build professional ser-
vice firms linking theory with practicality—Marvin Bower, David Ogilvy of
Ogilvy & Mather (O&M), Leonard Spacek of Arthur Andersen, and Gus
Levy of Goldman Sachs. They would frequently lunch at the University
Club and compare notes on their common ambition. Marvin often commented to his partners on how Andersen had one door around the country—
every office had its door carved exactly the same way—and, on occasion, how
Goldman invested in training and tools to support consistent services. Marvin Bower and David Ogilvy were particularly close. They shared a number
of philosophies and basic characteristics, which makes it difficult to isolate
the many and different ways in which they influenced and supported each
other. Yet it is clear that each of them often spoke or wrote of the other person as a role model, and they frequently discussed key decisions. They
encouraged each other in breaking new ground and redefining the great service company.

Above all, they shared an unremitting drive to achieve excellence in
everything they did. And both men were grounded in nothing but the
truth. Anything less than excellent was not good enough. Anything other
than the truth was not tolerated. The key to that pursuit of excellence was,
as both Ogilvy and Bower said on separate occasions, to hire people who
were better than you.[59] And to keep them. Both of their firms were often
on lists of best companies to work for. In 1965, Ogilvy & Mather and
McKinsey & Co. had two of the most generous retirement programs in
America, which had David's and Marvin's signatures on them.

Inside both McKinsey and O&M, everybody from the boardroom to the mailroom knew and understood what the firms' values were, what the mission was, and "the way things are done here." In both cases every employee had an obligation to dissent.

As Ken Roman, the former chairman of O&M, describes the O&M culture: "The Ogilvy philosophy rested on four pillars: Research. Results. Creative brilliance. Professional discipline. Ogilvy believed in studying precedents and codifying experience into principles—treating advertising as a profession with a body of knowledge."[60]

Research

David Ogilvy's rigorous training during his years with Gallup taught him to always do the same things that Marvin urged his associates to do: find out the facts first and respect the front line. It was David's belief that working at Gallup and interviewing a vast range of Americans accounts for much of his success in this country. And he respected the consumer and consistently preached "the consumer is not a moron."[61]

Results

Ogilvy, like Marvin, believed serving clients well led to results. As Ogilvy wrote in his autobiography:

> The most priceless asset we have is the respect of our clients. . . .
> When a client hires Ogilvy & Mather—or McKinsey—he expects the best. If you don't make sure that he gets it, you shortchange him—and he won't come back for more.[62]

Creative Brilliance

"Encourage ferment and innovation. In advertising, the beginning of success is to be different, the beginning of failure is to be the same."[63]

"Brains? It doesn't necessarily mean a high IQ. It means curiosity, common sense, wisdom, imagination, and literacy."[64]

Professional Discipline

Much of David Ogilvy's professional discipline mirrored Marvin's, in orientation and in his own involvement and commitment. As David writes:

> Superior service to our clients depends on making the most of our people. Give them challenging opportunities, recognition for achievement, job enrichment, and the maximum responsibility. Treat them as grown-ups—and they will grow up. Help them when they are in difficulty. Be affectionate and human.
>
> Encourage your staff to be candid with you. Ask their advice—and listen to it. Ogilvy & Mather offices should not be structured like an army, with over-privileged officers and underprivileged subordinates. Top bananas have no monopoly on ideas.
>
> I see all the campaigns created by our fifty-five offices, praising the good ones and damning the bad.
>
> It does a company no good when its leader refuses to share his leadership functions with his lieutenants. The more centers of leadership you find in a company, the stronger it will become. That is how Ogilvy & Mather became strong.[65]

As David Ogilvy led Ogilvy & Mather, he made a number of decisions like Marvin, for instance, setting up international offices, putting in strict antinepotism policies, and opening up the leadership ranks to women. He frequently referenced Marvin both formally

> . . . There is no one that had greater influence on how I led Ogilvy & Mather than Marvin Bower. He helped me and continually reminded me to articulate my convictions so an organization could operate by them. No one better defines what it takes to create and be an excellent service firm, no . . . any firm.[66]

and informally:

> It is said that if you send an engraved wedding-invitation to my friend Marvin Bower, the great man of McKinsey, he will return it to you—with revisions.[67]

As Ogilvy frequently referenced Marvin as a role model, Marvin pointed to David Ogilvy as an example for McKinsey on many occasions.

For example, in 1961, one of Marvin's blue memos quoted some Ogilvy wisdom:

> Before I turn to the future, I would like to preach my perennial sermon on the subject of <u>behavior</u>. I want the newcomers to know what kind of behavior we admire, and what kind of behavior we deplore:
>
> 1. First, we admire people who work hard. We dislike passengers who don't pull their weight in the boat.
> 2. We admire people with first-class brains, because you cannot run a great advertising agency without brainy people.
> 3. We admire people who <u>avoid politics</u>—office politics, I mean.
> 4. We despise toadies who suck up to their bosses; they are generally the same people who bully their subordinates.
> 5. We admire the great professionals, the craftsmen who do their jobs with superlative excellence. We notice that these people always respect the professional expertise of their colleagues in other departments.
> 6. We admire people who hire subordinates who are good enough to succeed them. We pity people who are so insecure that they feel compelled to hire inferior specimens as their subordinates.
> 7. We admire people who build up and develop their subordinates, because this is the only way we can promote from within the ranks. We detest having to go outside to fill important jobs, and I look forward to the day when that will never be necessary.
> 8. We admire people who practice delegation. The more you delegate, the more responsibility will be loaded upon you.
> 9. We admire kindly people with gentle manners who treat other people as human beings—particularly the people who sell things to us. We abhor <u>quarrelsome</u> people. We abhor people who wage paper warfare. We abhor buck-passers and people who don't tell the truth.
> 10. We admire well-organized people who keep their offices ship-shape, and deliver their work on time.

11. We admire people who are good citizens in their communities—people who work for their local hospitals, their church, the PTA, the Community Chest, and so on. In this connection, I am proud of the example set by some of my colleagues during the year.[68]

Don Gogel

Don Gogel was with McKinsey & Co. in New York from 1976 through 1985. Marvin was still a very active force in the firm during these years, and Don had the opportunity to work with Marvin on several client assignments. In 1985, Don moved on to Kidder Peabody where he worked with Al Gordon for the next 12 years in mergers and acquisitions. In 1989, Don joined the investment firm of Clayton, Dubilier & Rice, Inc. and became CEO in 1999. This firm was a good fit because Marvin's philosophy was well embedded in the institution. Martin Dubilier, one of the founders, and many of the subsequent partners had all graduated from the Marvin school of leadership. Don frequently references Marvin, Al Gordon, and Joe Rice in influencing the type of firm he joined, his values-based style of leadership, and key leadership decisions he has made.

> *I think probably most people have these Marvin vignettes, because they are just so memorable. I can't remember as many things about anyone else that I've encountered over the years. So he really is a larger-than-life presence.*
>
> *For several years in the late 1980s . . . I used to see Marvin on the train platform at the Bronxville station going into Manhattan, which was always a treat, if I could get up early enough in the morning to catch a train as early as Marvin.*
>
> —Don Gogel[69]

> *Don and Georgia moved to Bronxville. When Don missed his early train, we would ride in together. I always enjoyed getting Don's thoughts on current issues. He wasn't constrained to what he read. He really thought about the implication of his responses.*
>
> —Marvin Bower[70]

As Don notes, his decision to join Clayton, Dubilier & Rice was a direct offshoot of Marvin's influence:

The book Marvin told me to read—we were talking about leadership . . . —was John Gardner's *The Leader As Servant*. And that was very influential. I think my management style reflects a lot of that. There are a lot of leadership styles. But one of them is more consensus building, more listening, more a definition that says leadership is providing opportunities for other people to succeed. I think that's really what Marvin tried to do. His leadership was providing opportunities for other people to succeed. I think that affects how I operate here and it also affected my career path. I was really not interested in command and control.

I really wasn't interested in running a big business. That's what led me to a smaller firm like this where my job really is to motivate and lead a group of very strong partners. This is a firm of 14 partners and 10 associates. So it's a firm of leaders. It's a natural outgrowth of what I learned from Marvin.[71]

Strong, explicit values and a disciplined adherence to those values are critical elements of Clayton, Dubilier & Rice, Inc., and Don acknowledges Marvin's impact in this regard:

It certainly resonates with me from Marvin, but also from Joe Rice, who, not coincidentally, was trained as a lawyer, and [who] established this firm with principles similar to the ones Marvin did. . . . Joe brought some of the same standards of professionalism that Marvin incorporated in the code of ethics in establishing this firm. And, we're probably the only private equity firm that has a formal policy manual with a code of ethics. . . . We are a value-driven organization, and I think that the firm had that at its roots . . . Chuck Ames [a partner with Clayton, Dubilier & Rice, Inc. and with McKinsey & Co. from 1957 to 1972] and I, with Marvin's deep impact on us, have made that far more explicit here. . . . There is no doubt that Chuck's and my training at McKinsey led us to try to shape the firm to be more formally value driven.[72]

Common values enabled Don to effect a leadership style whereby all partners were equally engaged:

In terms of creating opportunities for others, this business really works when individual partners find investment opportunities that they really like, understand, and work. So, my job is really to encourage each of the partners to reach for investment opportunities that they like and develop, and not to hog it myself. I've turned out to be, to my surprise, a pretty good deal person. So, for the first eight or nine years that I was here, I did the deals. I mean I did the negotiation, I met the CEO, I negotiated the price. And I love to do that. But you don't build an organization by having me do that and not have the other partners do that. So, I've had to, when I formally took on the leadership role here which is now six years ago, step back and encourage people to do that and not do it myself, which is hard sometimes.[73]

Although delegation can be difficult, Don recognized that a one-person show that did not provide equal opportunities and potential rewards for other partners would not translate into a sustainable company. Some of the key decisions that were made to ensure the sustainability of Clayton, Dubilier & Rice, Inc., can be directly linked to Marvin's role-modeling behavior at McKinsey:

But there is no question that that's how you build an institution. It's in that regard that I often think about Marvin because Joe Rice is very much like Marvin in wanting the firm to outlast his personality or mine. He wants to build an ongoing institution. Because it's value based, we think it really has value. Not only the people that work here, but we think we do a good thing in transforming tired businesses into businesses that otherwise wouldn't succeed, and making them work and creating employment and wealth and a lot of other good things.

But to institutionalize . . . that isn't easy. To date, investment firms haven't proven they can be institutionalized . . . because they are only 25 years old and they haven't had to outlast their founders. But we're at the stage of doing it. We're doing a lot of things to try and institutionalize that.

In Joe's mind, the most important first thing was transition. And, very interestingly, Joe looked at transition in some ways similar[ly] to Marvin because Joe and Marty [Dubilier] gave up a lot of their economic interest in the firm to the next generation. Not when pushed out the door, but early on. They said that's a better way to run the firm.

Joe did it as soon as he brought in partners. . . . The compensation here is very simple. You come in as a one-point partner and then if you are here and you make it you're a two-point partner. Joe is a two-point partner. I came in as a one-point partner, and I proved myself and now I'm a two-point partner the same as Joe and Marty. Joe and Marty did not keep the entrepreneur's premium, so to speak. All of the senior people have the same level of compensation. That clearly was helpful.

This contrasts, by the way, with how most of the other firms like Henry Kravits or John Hicks and Muse operate: The founders keep half for themselves and then they split the rest even if they have 15 partners. With us, it just was never that way. I think that was pretty remarkable.

I think of Marvin when thinking of building an institution, as does Joe. When Marvin gave up a lot of his shares, I said it's amazing. I can't imagine someone doing that. Then when I came here and saw Joe do it I thought it was pretty amazing.[74]

Like Marvin and Joe Rice, Don was willing to forgo personal gain to ensure that his firm would be an enduring institution:

. . . This is sort of a compressed history of the firm, but we had a billion-dollar fund that I helped raise when I came here and then we raised a billion-five fund. Then, about three years ago, we raised a $3.5 billion fund. We really had to increase the size of the partnership. The structure at the time . . . was the sort of two-to-one structure, [and] Joe and I and Chuck Ames were the only two-point partners at the time. The three of us concluded that we needed to change the structure and give up half of that premium. So the structure of the partnership is now 1.5 to 1 for partners because that seemed a better way of building a partnership without creating tensions.

Ironically, after having been amazed twice at people voluntarily doing this, I found myself doing it . . . and it just seemed like the most natural thing to do in the world. I know of no other cases where it's happened. And I'm not saying that because I'm such a great guy. It's natural to do if you're really as interested in building an institution as Marvin was. That's what you do. I'm not sure it would have been natural for me had I not thought about Marvin and that experience.[75]

Don also points out the similarities between the working style/philosophy at Clayton, Dubilier & Rice, Inc., and that of Marvin's McKinsey:

The ability to both conceptualize at the grandest level hence the strategy practice, and yet to translate that into something that is actionable is Marvin. I think it really reflects a habit of mind. It's very important as you institutionalize a culture. Marvin developed this habit of mind. Looking at big problems and then pushing them down to what you do tomorrow morning. That's pure Marvin and that's still the essence of McKinsey.

That's the style of investing here. I've never quite articulated it this way but it is parallel—the investment decision that we make is the early, McKinsey, fact-finding analysis, deductive or reductive logic, but we have to reach a conclusion that there is an investment thesis that we can support and [that] it's a smart thing to do to put all this money to work. Unlike other firms, though, we're very activist. We're interventionist in the extreme. One of our partners is always the chairman of the board of the company and it's not a nonexecutive role. It's a very in-your-face kind of role. So that when we make an investment we know we are going to have to do five or six things. And, when we do them, the investment is a success, and if we don't do them, we're not successful. And, of course, things change and by the time we are into year five, two of the things that were on our initial list of things that we have to do have changed, and there are two more things. So, it's interactive that way. But very much the investment thesis is the McKinsey analysis and then the question, now that we have this investment, how do we execute the strategy?[76]

Don tells the story of an acquisition from Kraft to exemplify Clayton, Dubilier & Rice's action-oriented approach:

We bought . . . an institutional food service distribution company that serves hospitals and restaurants from Kraft [Phillip Morris]. The cost structure was crazy for a business with 18 percent gross margins. So, part of our investment thesis was you have to run this like an 18 percent gross margins business, not the 70 percent Kraft was used to. In the Kraft business, when you have those gross margins, you drive sales and you don't pay a lot of attention to cost. In an 18 percent business you don't want to forgo sales, but you can't chase sales without much greater attention to cost.

When we bought the business, it was growing at 17 percent a year on the top line and was losing more money as it grew. It was a sales-oriented place. Having recognized that, we realized we had to change that orientation to make the business a lot more profitable. Then we spent five years changing it. We started by changing sales compensation: Instead of having people paid on a sales line we ended up paying on gross margin only. So, salespeople now understood that this was possible. It turned out that gross margin wasn't sensitive enough because our below gross margin cost varied so much. We didn't even know that until we started studying some classic McKinsey customer segment profitability analysis. Once we saw that, we had to change the compensation system again, so it was really based on true customer profitability because food service distribution is a huge logistics chain, and it's very easy to end up chasing the wrong volume.[77]

Don remains president and CEO of Clayton, Dubilier & Rice, Inc., today and continues to hold Marvin's accomplishments in the highest regard, recognizing that Marvin's methods continue to be very relevant for all leaders:

If we could bottle it, it would be worth a lot wouldn't it? First, he led by example. He was so successful, and he had done it for such a long time, and he was so consistent. I came to the altar, so to speak, inclined to listen carefully because I knew of his success. It wasn't pontificating, and it wasn't, "Of course, this doesn't apply to me, but I think you should do it." Because he was all of one piece. He was wholly consistent, he had done it for such a long time, it was so successful. So, the consistency in living in his life and living by his own principles I think certainly had an impact.[78]

McKinsey mafia

The international management consultant does more than provide advice: its old boys wield power in boardrooms all over the world. But, say **Rufus Olins** and **Matthew Lynn**, the going is getting tougher

BETWEEN Downing Street, the Bank of England, the Confederation of British Industry and many powerful FT-SE 100 companies runs an invisible thread. It can be traced back to 1 Jermyn Street, in the heart of London's clubland.

The marbled atrium on the corner belongs to the British headquarters of McKinsey & Co, the American firm that has cultivated a reputation as the Rolls-Royce of management consultants. It is from here that a network of power and influence has emerged, a network that has come to rival the great Oxbridge colleges and ancient public schools.

For the McKinsey mafia, as it is sometimes called, this has been a year of unusually high achievement in Britain. In February, Norman Blackwell was headhunted from the business to run the prime minister's policy unit, a position from which he will oversee the formation of government policy as well as the next Conservative election manifesto.

Earlier this year William Hague became the youngest member of the cabinet when he was promoted to succeed John Redwood as secretary of state for Wales. He also has McKinsey on his CV.

Howard Davies, a McKinsey high-flyer from 1982 to 1987, recently left his job as director-general of the CBI to become deputy governor of the Bank of England.

Adir Turner, his successor at the CBI, was another man plucked from McKinsey. Turner is the third McKinsey man in a row to head the organisation. The man before Davies was Sir John Banham, who now chairs Tarmac and Westcountry TV.

These appointments place McKinsey men at the heart of political, economic and industrial policymaking. They join a long list of people who first made their mark in Jermyn Street and went on to occupy positions of power within many leading British companies.

The top executives at Asda, Inchcape and Burmah Castrol are all former McKinsey men. So too is Don Cruickshank,

McKinsey graduates: Asda's Archie Norman, top, and Bank of England's Howard Davies

company Groupe Bull, and Lukas Mühlemann, who runs the insurance giant Swiss Re, are McKinsey graduates.

In America, the grip of the alumni on the industrial establishment is formidable; the corporate titans running IBM, American Express, Westinghouse, Levi Strauss, TCI, Duracell and even Ben & Jerry's ice cream all cut their teeth at The Firm.

Though other networks may be more powerful within national boundaries, few have the same influence internationally. And few have been so assiduously cultivated over nearly eight decades. "They are very helpful to each other," says

ing person who has worked for the consultancy, where they are now, and what they are doing. Titles, home addresses and the dates of their McKinsey careers are given. Across the pale blue cover runs the warning: "This directory is to be used exclusively by alumni of the firm."

McKinsey, which refused any interviews for this article, is reluctant even to acknowledge the existence of this book. "The pretence of diffidence is part of their carefully cultivated mystique," says one rival. "It's a subtle way of attracting attention and makes people feel they are dealing with an elite."

The book is the glue that holds the network together. On a recent trip to America, Archie Norman, Asda's chief executive, wanted to talk to local retailers. He dipped into the book to see who he could tap and found Julian Day, chief financial officer at Safeway. "That's what you call a commercial network. It is not a social club," says Norman.

As well as receiving the book, every year former staffers are invited to an event at one of the offices — either a discussion on a commercial topic or a cocktail party — enabling old friendships to be renewed and different generations of McKinseyites to become acquainted.

"They manage their alumni quite actively," says London Transport's Ford, who worked for the firm in the 1960s at the same time as Lou Gerstner, now chief executive of IBM. In the 1960s, the alumni evenings were black-tie affairs with two dozen people. Now the numbers can run to hundreds.

The weaving of the web comes not just from McKinsey's 67 offices in 35 countries, or from its 3,300 consultants, but from the alumni themselves, many of whom are anxious to exploit their background. "It is as much the McKinsey people parlaying their experience, as McKinsey seeking to infiltrate the world. But McKinsey would be daft not to take advantage of it," says Peter Wallis, co-founder of the management consultancy SRU. "I feel perfectly happy

into a company boardroom. One in five continues in consulting, and the rest scatter into different fields. Paul Henderson, for example, now runs the luxury Gidleigh Park hotel, and one Japanese partner recent

Headquarters of a mutual admiration society: even

The moulding within the firm is "It is a very in ence," says Ford. work punishing h also get to tackle issues

The graduates of the Marvin Bower school described in this chapter all evince leadership characteristics that Marvin cherished: the courage to imagine what could be and to follow that imagination; a penchant for getting the facts; respect for and proactive involvement of the people-asset base; humility and an ability to listen to others; adherence to a clear set of values; and readiness to always seek improvements in a rapidly changing world, rather than just sitting on the laurels of their initial successes.

Among the many others from Marvin's McKinsey (See Figure 7.1) who went on to take their leadership abilities and knowledge to new arenas are the following.

Chuck Ames
Retired chairman, Acme Cleveland;
Partner, Clayton, Dubilier & Rice, Inc.

"You have to give up something you want, something that you would like to have, if you are going to stick to your values. And you had better stick to them or they don't mean much. And that's what I always got from Marvin."[79]

Sir John Banham
Chairman, Whitbread PLC

"I joined McKinsey in 1969, and was there until 1983. Nobody who was part of the firm at that time could not have been influenced by Marvin and the way he thought about the nature of management consulting as a profession, the importance of putting the client's interests first, and his whole set of values, which, I must say, have influenced me throughout my professional life. And it didn't take long to experience Marvin's influence. If I spent two hours in total with Marvin that would have been a lot. And yet, in those two hours, he could impress upon you what he believed, what was important, what you should think was important, the kinds of questions you should be asking about yourself and your clients. Marvin's concerns and interests are still with me. And that was a very long time ago.

"Most notably, Marvin's influence directed me when I was setting up the English equivalent of the Congressional Budget Office—called the Audit Commission. The Audit Commission, which was modeled very closely on the firm, has oversight over virtually all of what you would call state and local government expenditure, and the national health service. The commission reviews and reports on all of these key areas. It's very roughly 20 percent of the GNP. It has been one of the most successful examples of public administration in Britain in basically the second half of the twentieth century and is still going strong 20 years later. In structuring the commission, I applied the disciplines and principles that Marvin had been preaching for as long as anyone can remember; in this case, treating the British public as the client. Despite considerable pressure (bureaucrating and political) over the years, the commission has held fast to its principles in providing oversight on behalf of the millions of citizens whose welfare it looks out for.

"In 1994, I wrote a book about the Audit Commission and sent a copy to Marvin. At the age of 91, Marvin responded with an eight-page critique. 'I agree with this. I don't agree with that.' I think it was absolutely astounding. The time he took to read and evaluate my history of this important commission underscored his unwavering support and commitment to his beliefs. And I'm quite sure that, even though I was only one of 40 directors at the time that I left the firm, and I had been gone from the firm 10 years at this point, he knew exactly what I had been up to, and for all the best of reasons. He was a great influence on me and I think on absolutely everybody that had anything to do with the firm. In fact, I believe that the firm and people Marvin touched in Europe are even more influential than those on your side of the Atlantic.

"There is absolutely no doubt that Marvin's approach to leadership and the notion that leadership is all about serving, not ordering, was a huge influence on me personally. And I'm absolutely convinced that anything I've been able to do since owes a great deal to Marvin."[80]

Sir Roderick Carnegie
Retired Chairman, TRA

"What I learned from Marvin: Number one—don't think that simply making money is a good focus for your life. Number two—in whatever you do, have a vision about where you want to be in 10 years' time and why will that make you feel good about what you've done with that 10 years of your life. Number three— keep your mind open to new possibilities which you hadn't thought of before. Number four—remember the world is changing and you better keep yourself trained and educated and alert because the new possibility, or the new thought, might be the one you need. If you're not open-minded, you'll forget it or you'll miss it.

"When I went back to Australia and ran a large mining company, I had a clear view about what had to be done in 10 years' time. I wanted the business to be seen as a responsible mining company. Therefore, I wanted us to discover enough new resources so that we weren't simply using up the resources of the world as we mined. It was important to articulate this vision in a convincing manner because being a responsible mining company sometimes meant you had to spend money, which was awkward to find, on exploration with attendant risks.

"We had to define how to mine wisely and responsibly. That meant not wasting—on average, a lot of what is mined is wasted, and that mode of operations would be unacceptable in our company; adding maximum value; rebalancing our activities and being countercyclical (e.g., taking advantage of good prospecting prices); and keeping a constant eye on safety—in mining, there are always chances that a rock could fall. It was critical to constantly reinforce that we not do anything that would reduce safety.

"We had to use human beings as wisely as possible. That meant trusting human beings to maximize their potential in a way that was satisfying to them.

"We had to be commercially viable—not maximizing profit but ensuring we were solid economically.

"And finally, we had to communicate. To turn our vision of being a responsible mining company into a publicly viewed reality, we had to get all of our people on board with and speaking and living that vision, on both the decision-making and execution ends."[81]

Richard Cavanagh
President and CEO of The Conference Board

"To me he was a father figure. I knew nothing about how to navigate in the world when I joined McKinsey. He cared about the organization he was building and leading. I think he really did see it as an extended family. He was a wonderful teacher. He cared enough to spend time teaching me. And he would go out of his way to do kindnesses. He got me appointed to the Brookings Board when he retired from it. As a great teacher and leader, he changed the world."[82]

Ron Daniel
Retired Managing Director of McKinsey

"What did I learn from Marvin:

"1. The immense power of shared values.
"2. How critical it is for a leader to communicate to the troops.
"3. The power of recognition/acknowledgement of others' ideas and successes."[83]

George Dively, Deceased
Chairman, Harris Graphics (1939 to 1972)

"I could not make a major decision without checking with Marvin."[84]

Roger Ferguson
Vice Chairman of the Federal Reserve

"I give a speech here to our up-and-coming leaders where I talk about leadership and the great leaders I have known, and Marvin is one of the few people I always talk about. Marvin remains high on my list for many reasons:

"• His obvious ability to shape the culture of McKinsey.

"• His obvious self-sacrifice in a financial sense to keep McKinsey a private organization.

"• His combination of astuteness and modesty to not name the firm after him when he had a chance to do so early on.

"• The way that he, until the last I assume, and certainly until the last piece of correspondence that I got, always used every moment as a teachable opportunity to reinforce the values of the firm and bring those values to our attention, even to those of us who were no longer in the firm. There was a strong sense that he was watching and trying to reinforce in all of us the kinds of things he thought were so important, and proved to be so important, about the success of McKinsey.

"The Federal Reserve is a superb organization in terms of its strong culture and its strong sense of values that go hand in hand with public service. I have explicitly tried to encourage in the Fed that we add to our values the obligation to dissent. We don't quite call it that, but the obligation to have an independent point of view based on analysis, and to bring that to the forefront.

"I also hope that I leave people here with an impression that I really do care about how they're doing: How they are doing their jobs, how the Fed is treating them, how they are treating the Fed, whether or not they think we are living up to our mission as a public service institution. But, in a very real, more personal sense, I hope I am doing this in the way that Marvin would do it. I'm not as good as I'd like to be at writing those little notes that he would write to people, reminding them of the right way to do things. But, I hope

I'm at least as good as he was at recognizing when people do extraordinary things and making an effort to notice the human side.

"Another thing I'm doing is trying to introduce the concept that it's actually okay to call the most senior people in this institution by their first names, which was very much a Marvin concept. It doesn't work nearly as well here because we all have titles. It's not the first name in and of itself that matters obviously. It's what a first-name environment reflects about a lack of hierarchy in a cultural sense. There is obviously a hierarchy in this institution, and there is obviously a hierarchy in McKinsey. But there is no hierarchy when it comes to McKinsey problem solving. And I think calling people by their first name is emblematic of that. And, frankly, I think there should be no hierarchy when it comes to the Federal Reserve addressing the challenges that confront our nation. It is with this mind-set that I encourage the most junior person that I happen to work with on any of the initiatives and projects I have under way to call me by my first name. It's not something I would have thought of doing were it not for Marvin. By signaling that it's okay to be called by one's first name, you are giving a clear message that you're not trying to use the hierarchy in a way that's inappropriate. In fact, you are inviting others to come in and criticize you—at least your ideas—to help you get to a better solution.[85]

Michael Fleischer
President, Bogen Communications

"Although I never met Marvin, he had a profound impact on me. When I went to West Point, they taught us that a general feeds the troops before he eats himself. In that setting, it was straightforward and a matter of survival. When I saw those same values, take care of others first, evident at McKinsey and always attributed to 'Well, that's what Marvin Bower did,' I paused. I tried to take that same perspective when I led companies, and I found that decisions were easier and, more importantly, that the ability to create a motivated, effective, and ethical organization was greatly facilitated. That is the mark Marvin Bower had on me."[86]

Lou Gerstner
Retired Chairman, IBM
Chairman, Carlyle Group

On business: "I believe that I learned from [Marvin] the importance of articulating a set of principles that drive people's behavior and actions. And that's a much more powerful leadership tool than a bunch of procedures and guidelines—particularly in a knowledge-based enterprise like consulting. Principles connect people to a sense of rightness, and for this reason people follow them and follow leaders who adhere to them. I learned this from Marvin and I've carried it forward to every company I've operated in. IBM has been the most important place for me to apply these learnings, because it is, in a sense, a knowledge company just as McKinsey is."[87]

On community: "I remember Marvin marching into my office one day 35 years ago. 'What are you going to do to give something back?' he asked. 'Come with me.' We went together to a meeting on public-school reform, something I'm still involved in."[88]

Albert Gordon
Partner, Kidder Peabody (1931–1957)
Chairman, Kidder Peabody (1957–1986)
Honorary Chairman, Kidder Peabody (1986–1994)

"Marvin will be remembered with Alfred Sloan as a great business leader. We all learned from Marvin. The only thing I beat Marvin on was longevity."[89]

Bruce Henderson, Deceased
Founder, The Boston Consulting Group

"Marvin Bower precipitated the initial decision that eventually led to my book [*Henderson on Corporate Strategy*]."[90]

Herbert Henzler
Vice Chairman, Credit Suisse

"I am trying to bring Marvin's definition of professionalism to Credit Suisse."[91]

Jon Katzenbach
President of Katzenbach and Associates

"Mother and Marvin."[92]

Steve Kaufman
Retired Chairman, Arrow Electronics
Professor, Harvard Business School

"Marvin Bower, fabled builder and leader of McKinsey, could greet me and my wife, by name, when I was at McKinsey. When I was a three-year associate, Marvin sent me a simple, three-sentence note telling me how pleased he was with the work I had done for client X. I took that note home and showed it to my wife Sharon, to my son Jeremy, who was all of three months old at the time, and then I pinned it to my wall, where it stayed until we moved, eight years later. Marvin's note, and his remembering my name and how it made me feel, was a major lesson for me.

"I worked hard at trying to replicate for others [at Arrow] Marvin's personal impact on me. I consciously developed some memory tricks to remember names . . . or at least appear to remember names, by having a little 3×5 card in my pocket. So, I'd be ready to greet and mention something personally.

"I also religiously spent (my assistant made sure to schedule in this time) 30 minutes each month in my office, writing short notes to five or ten junior people congratulating them for some accomplishment or thanking them for some extra contribution I had heard about.

"Toward the end of my Arrow career in the late 90s, I was profiled in the New York Times. The Wednesday after that profile appeared, I received a letter from Marvin. Inside the letter was a clipping of the article, with certain sections underlined. The note said:

> 'The New York Times got it wrong in describing you as an effective manager. For what they were describing was an effective leader, something much more rare and valuable. And I am proud to have known you at McKinsey.'

"After I read the note, I let out a whoop, called Sharon, and taped it to the wall in my office at Arrow. Here I was, approaching 60, a big shot CEO at the peak of his career, and that letter turned me into Jell-o.[93]

"My objective at Arrow Electronics was to create the pride of association that Marvin had created at McKinsey. That was the power and legacy of Marvin Bower."[94]

Linda Fayne Levinson
Senior Partner, GRP Partners

"I'm a member of several boards. Over the last year, the values I learned from Marvin helped me navigate through all sorts of professional and corporate governance issues that many peers had trouble with in difficult times."[95]

John Macomber
Retired Chairman, Celanese
Retired Head, Import/Export Bank

"I think Marvin had a profound effect on me and on everybody. I started at McKinsey & Co. when I was 26 years old. I'm almost 75 years old now, and I can still tell you, almost verbatim, what Marvin meant by the top management approach. And he was consistent. He never wavered from the concepts of one firm, and the clients' interests always being first. He was absolutely predictable. There was never a surprise."[96]

Leo F. Mullin
Chairman and CEO of Delta Air Lines

"Ralph Waldo Emerson said, 'Great institutions are the reflection of one man,' and that is absolutely true in the case of McKinsey and Marvin Bower."[97]

Andrall Pearson
Retired President, Pepsico
Founding Chairman, Yum! Brands

"Well, I learned a hell of a lot from Marvin. First, and foremost was the impact that a leader can have on the work environment of a firm or a company. Although I graduated from business school back in the early 1900s, they didn't really teach anything about what I call the work environment or the culture and what goes on in the business. Marvin understood the importance of the culture and elevated it to an explicit dimension of a successful firm. At McKinsey, he worked hard to create an environment that would attract, motivate, and retain high-talent people and that was aligned with the vision for the firm which was to serve the top managements of the Fortune 500. The McKinsey culture was built on a whole set of values, not the least of which were integrity and putting the client's interests first—not doing studies for the sake of doing studies.

"I guess another thing I learned from him was to be comfortable about delegating a lot of responsibility and authority to quite young people. When I was still in my early 30s, I was the head of McKinsey's global marketing practice. I had relationships with the CEOs of most of the major consumer goods companies and retailers, and Marvin was comfortable with letting that level of responsibility rest on my young shoulders.

"I can remember riding on the train with Marvin from Bronxville, where we both lived, to White Plains, where General Foods was located. I said to Marvin, 'What role would you like to play?' (He was the managing director of the firm so I didn't expect him to do everything.) He said, 'Well, isn't that sort of up to you,

Andy? Whatever you can't do I'll do.' He was true to his word. You didn't feel like he was looking over your shoulder and constantly second-guessing you. If you made a mistake or he discovered you were about to do something stupid, he was willing to point that out. If he praised you, you knew it was praise. If he criticized you, it was . . . you winced at it, but you finally came to realize that he wasn't doing it to embarrass you, he was doing it to improve the breed. The nature of that relationship was that you felt he had confidence in your abilities or he wouldn't have delegated the job to you. That's helped me a lot through the years. When I left Pepsico, there were people in their thirties running big, multi-hundred-million-dollar businesses representing billions of dollars in decisions and revenue."[98]

John Sawhill, Deceased
President and CEO, The Nature Conservancy

"Marvin convinced me that the power of cooperative effort cannot be underestimated. At the Nature Conservancy, our philosophy is to never approach an issue with an adversarial stance, but to find solutions for all interested parties.[99]

"Marvin's major influence on me was in the arena of emphasizing the importance of organizational values. I always thought that it was very important for the head of an organization to communicate clearly with other people in the organization about what values the organization endorsed and stood for."[100]

Frederick Schieffer, Deceased
Chairman of the Board of Management, The Allianz AG

"Marvin's influence meant McKinsey had a tremendous capability to meld or to develop cosmopolitan characters through the work, the transfers, through exchange at large, through practice groups, through committees, you name it. People behaved differently, they talked differently, they argued differently. That's what I tried to replicate at Allianz."[101]

Klaus Zumwinkel,
Chairman of the Management Board, Deutsche Post AG

"When I came to Deutsche 14 years ago, my main message was to deliver quality to everyone. What I learned from Marvin was the power of values, consistency, and communication. When I talk to our top 500 executives about the importance of our corporate culture (which I will do in a few weeks), I talk about our core values, which are:

1. To deliver excellent quality—I think Marvin would have said this
2. To make customers more successful—customers at McKinsey were clients and I remember learning that value from Marvin
3. To foster openness—at McKinsey, Marvin called it the obligation to dissent; in fact, young associates, when doing problem-solving, had the same tenure as a director
4. To always act in the context of our priorities— Marvin called it 'how things are done around here'
5. To act as entrepreneurs—Marvin said 'every partner is a leader'
6. To act with integrity, inside and outside—Marvin called it professionalism
7. To accept social responsibility—Marvin called it being part of the community"[102]

Believing as I do that every citizen of the world has a duty to do what he or she can to help increase the strength, productivity, and character-building contributions of our private-enterprise system, I feel some obligation to make the distillate of my experience available to others.

—Marvin Bower, 1966[103]

Author's Note

I first heard of Marvin Bower in 1962. I was eight years old. My father, a mathematician and provost at Purdue University who was working with Marvin at the time on a project for General Motors Institute, spoke of Marvin with the same respect he gave to John von Neumann. That got my attention. Two years later, as a 10-year-old with a precocious interest in how things were manufactured, I had occasion to meet Marvin, and came away knowing that business could be a respectable and rewarding pursuit even though I had grown up in an environment where scholarship was considered a higher calling than business.

Some 14 years later, I was in my graduate school office at MIT when Marvin phoned me to welcome me to my new job as an associate at McKinsey & Co. and to talk about what I had been doing at MIT. When I realized it was Marvin on the line, I immediately stood up. My adviser, who happened to be in my office when the call came in, asked with whom I was speaking. When I told him, he said, "I'm glad you're standing up; Marvin Bower deserves your respect."

For my first assignment with McKinsey, I had the good fortune to be on one of Marvin's teams. When encouraged to go beyond the project's base information gathering and analytical functions, my mind quickly opened to new dimensions—namely, the power that comes from respecting an organization and its people. I felt personally powerful after every conversation with Marvin, and I watched him use this power to transform a machine tool company in Detroit, positively changing the fundamental orientation and character of the company.

237

Some years later, when I left McKinsey to start my own business, I found myself applying the "What would Marvin do?" gauge to every challenging decision I had to make and, when necessary, asking Marvin for guidance. He was always available and insightful.

When I was 48, and Marvin was 98, I had the courage to begin writing this book. I called Marvin and asked him if we could work on his biography together. I explained that it was something I felt was important and had been thinking about for almost 20 years. Marvin was initially hesitant because, as it turned out, he was working on his memoirs and felt that it would be difficult for him to handle both projects at the same time. Nonetheless, he invited me down to Florida to discuss the possibility of a biography.

On the flight down, I was both scared and exhilarated at the prospect of writing a book (up until that point, I had only written articles) and bringing to a wider audience Marvin Bower's valuable wisdom and insight. I was wrestling with conflicting thoughts. I felt it was very important that young people hear Marvin's stories and have the opportunity to meet Marvin through these stories as he was a compelling role model of professionalism and character. On the other hand, I did not want to impair Marvin's efforts to document his personal memoirs for his family. (Marvin was already 98 years old.) Throughout the flight, I took deep breaths and found comfort in the thought that Marvin would know what to do. But my comfort was short-lived as I began to worry that perhaps his memory was failing. Would he even remember me? It had been a dozen years since we had last seen each other.

After landing, I went to meet Marvin in his office, which was located across the street from his apartment. When I walked in, as always, Marvin was impeccably dressed and we connected in our personal space, when he looked directly at me. It was not his age or posture that captured my attention, and that surprised me. Rather, it was his familiar gaze and the absolute sparkle in his eye. On the wall hung his favorite painting, *Forces in Motion*. He saw me looking at it and smiled, reminding me that he had bought it in London in the 1950s for $57 because he had liked the title.

We sat down at his desk. I asked him about his current project, and he explained to me that before Cleo, his second wife, had passed away, he had promised her that he would complete his memoirs. We looked through his manuscripts and talked about what was required to finish them.

We then discussed the possible biography. I explained that the first step would be to interview people Marvin had influenced and hear their "Marvin stories." The challenge would be to weave those stories together so that more than just providing isolated anecdotes, they would comprise a compelling and robust lesson in integrity-based business values for the reader. I gave Marvin a copy of some of the stories I had already begun to collect.

Marvin looked through a few of the stories, underlining with his blue-green pen, and then told me that it was time to have lunch. He grabbed his walker, and we went outside and crossed the street to his apartment. He showed me around, crediting Cleo for everything in the apartment. Marvin's love for and pride in his second wife was evident. He then took me on a tour of the apartment complex, providing detailed commentary about the landscape that I hadn't even noticed myself.

During lunch, several people stopped by and introduced themselves. Juliette Dively, George Dively's widow, came over to our table and kidded Marvin about not having seen him for a while. Marvin introduced me and explained that I was writing his biography. (He had not given me a definitive yes or no while we were discussing the project earlier in his office, so I was both surprised and pleased by how he chose to introduce me.) He then asked me if I knew who George and Juliette Dively were. I proudly responded, "Of course, George was chairman of Harris Intertype that he turned into Harris Graphics and the man you checked with before you joined McKinsey; and Juliette is a very important person for me to interview and in getting this book started." Marvin chuckled—a familiar sound even though it had been years since I had heard it.

After lunch, we returned to his apartment and agreed to meet two weeks later to discuss the two books. And so our journey began, with

Marvin actively participating in and giving his blessing to the biography, and me helping Marvin to complete his memoirs.

I was able to work closely with Marvin for most of 2002. Once again, he inspired and impressed me. He was characteristically modest ("I can't believe people have time to talk to you about me") and precise ("The year was 1967, *not* 1966") . He was energetic and determined to use his time efficiently ("I get up at seven because there is so much to do").

As I continued collecting and compiling Marvin Bower lore (as told by him and others), I discovered that an extraordinary number of today's leaders credit Marvin with helping them understand what really matters—the power of values. They, like me, continue to apply the "What would Marvin do?" gauge when making major decisions.

From April through September 2002, I conducted the bulk of my interviewing, with 92 individuals who had worked with Marvin either at McKinsey or at a client, to gain firsthand insights on people's experiences and how Marvin had influenced them. Throughout the time period, I met with Marvin often, and we would discuss what I was hearing and who I was interviewing. Marvin would share with me his correspondence and files on each person before I would conduct the interview and he would read through my subsequent interview notes. In the end, over 100 senior executives and business leaders took an hour—or, in some cases, a day—out of their busy schedules to spend time with me. On each visit, we would also spend time on his memoirs.

From September through December 2002, Marvin was reading, underlining, and on occasion correcting the drafts of Part I of the book. We also spent some time talking about the stories in Part II, and he indicated what he thought was key in the client case studies and in the success of the leaders he influenced.

I spent the last two weeks of December with Marvin in the hospital, and at his home observing his visitors and reading him his letters (somewhat of a "who's who" in the business world). As it turned out, these two weeks were our opportunity to say good-bye. In one of my last visits with Marvin, he sat up from his hospital bed, holding the draft of the book in his hand, looked at me, and said, "It has to be original and important." I briefly felt this great weight on my shoulders—

would I let Marvin down? I thought for a moment and looked back at Marvin, and the weight lifted. I said, "It's about you, Marvin; it will be original and important." He smiled and closed his eyes.

From the view of the many individuals he influenced, Marvin radiated insights. The continuing relevance of business values, integrity, and respect for people will live on in those of us who have had the good fortune to know him. For the business leaders of tomorrow who did not have the opportunity to meet Marvin directly, this book provides firsthand lessons from those leaders who worked closely with Marvin, as well as from interviews with Marvin and his writings and speeches. I hope I have managed to convey some of Marvin Bower's timeless wisdom and insights.

Timeline

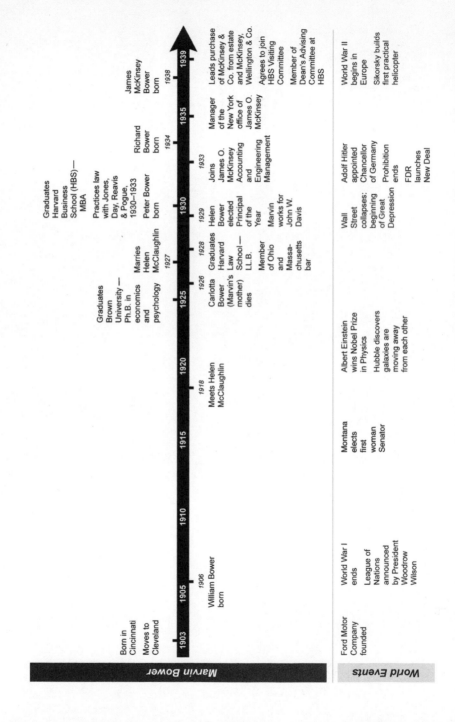

Marvin Bower

| 1903 | 1905 | 1910 | 1915 | 1920 | 1925 | 1926 | 1927 | 1928 | 1929 | 1930 | 1933 | 1934 | 1935 | 1938 | 1939 |

Born in Cincinnati

Moves to Cleveland

1906 William Bower born

Meets Helen McClaughlin

Graduates Brown University — Ph.B. in economics and psychology

Graduates Harvard Business School (HBS)— MBA

1926 Carlotta Bower (Marvin's mother) dies

Marries Helen McClaughlin

1928 Graduates Harvard Law School— LL.B.

Member of Ohio and Massachusetts bar

Practices law with Jones, Day, Reavis & Pogue, 1930–1933

Peter Bower born

1929 Helen Bower elected Principal of the Year

Marvin works for John W. Davis

Joins James O. McKinsey Accounting and Engineering Management

Richard Bower born

Manager of the New York office of James O. McKinsey

James McKinsey Bower born

Leads purchase of McKinsey & Co. from estate and McKinsey, Wellington & Co.

Agrees to join HBS Visiting Committee

Member of Dean's Advising Committee at HBS

World Events

Ford Motor Company founded

World War I ends

League of Nations announced by President Woodrow Wilson

Montana elects first woman Senator

Albert Einstein wins Nobel Prize in Physics

Hubble discovers galaxies are moving away from each other

Wall Street collapses: beginning of Great Depression

Adolf Hitler appointed Chancellor of Germany

Prohibition ends

FDR launches New Deal

World War II begins in Europe

Sikorsky builds first practical helicopter

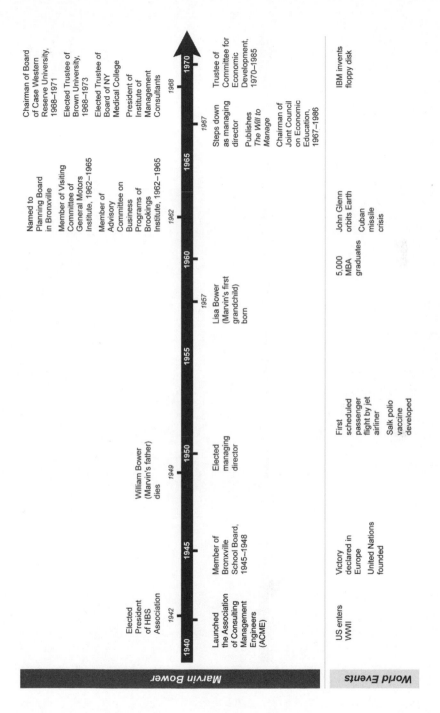

Marvin Bower

1940

Elected President of HBS Association

Launched the Association of Consulting Management Engineers (ACME)

1942

1945

Member of Bronxville School Board, 1945–1948

1949

William Bower (Marvin's father) dies

1950

Elected managing director

1955

1957

Lisa Bower (Marvin's first grandchild) born

1960

1965

1962

Named to Planning Board in Bronxville

Member of Visiting Committee of General Motors Institute, 1962–1965

Member of Advisory Committee on Business Programs of Brookings Institute, 1962–1965

1967

Steps down as managing director

Publishes *The Will to Manage*

Chairman of Joint Council on Economic Education, 1967–1986

1968

Chairman of Board of Case Western Reserve University, 1968–1971

Elected Trustee of Brown University, 1968–1973

Elected Trustee of Board of NY Medical College

President of Institute of Management Consultants

Trustee of Committee for Economic Development, 1970–1985

1970

World Events

US enters WWII

Victory declared in Europe

United Nations founded

First scheduled passenger flight by jet airliner

Salk polio vaccine developed

5,000 MBA graduates

John Glenn orbits Earth

Cuban missile crisis

IBM invents floppy disk

245

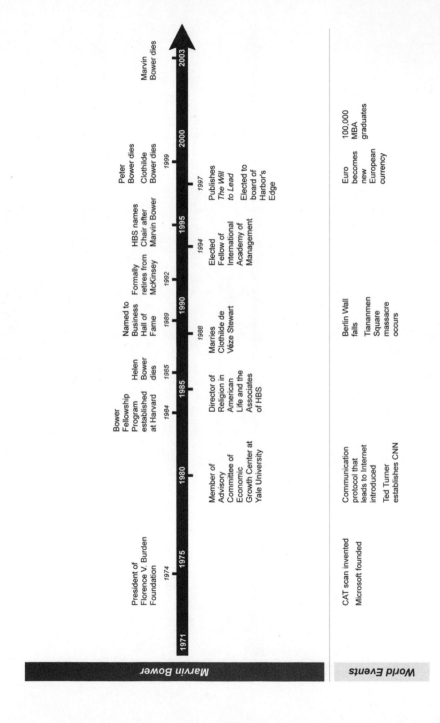

Marvin Bower

1971 · 1974 · 1975 · 1980 · 1984 · 1985 · 1985 · 1988 · 1989 · 1990 · 1992 · 1994 · 1995 · 1997 · 1999 · 2000 · 2003

1974 President of Florence V. Burden Foundation

Member of Advisory Committee of Economic Growth Center at Yale University

1984 Bower Fellowship Program established at Harvard

Director of Religion in American Life and the Associates of HBS

1985 Helen Bower dies

1988 Marries Clothilde de Véze Stewart

Named to Business Hall of Fame

1992 Formally retires from McKinsey

1994 Elected Fellow of International Academy of Management

HBS names Chair after Marvin Bower

1997 Publishes *The Will to Lead*

Elected to board of Harbor's Edge

Peter Bower dies

1999 Clothilde Bower dies

Marvin Bower dies

World Events

CAT scan invented

Microsoft founded

Communication protocol that leads to Internet introduced

Ted Turner establishes CNN

Berlin Wall falls

Tiananmen Square massacre occurs

Euro becomes new European currency

100,000 MBA graduates

246

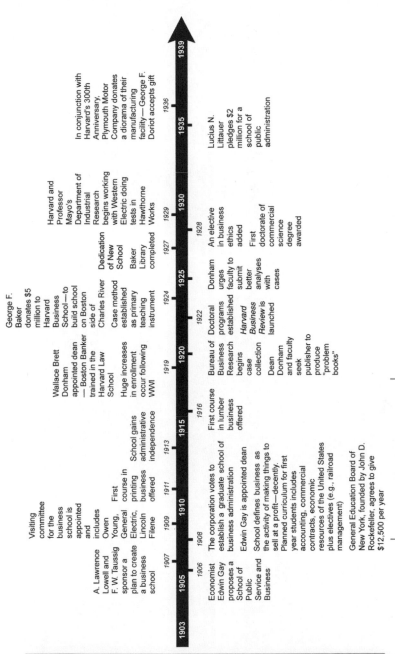

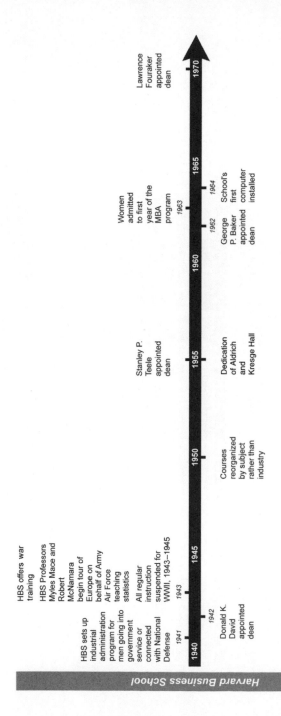

Harvard Business School

1940

1941
HBS sets up industrial administration program for men going into government service or connected with National Defense

Donald K. David appointed dean

1942

1943
HBS offers war training

HBS Professors Myles Mace and Robert McNamara begin tour of Europe on behalf of Army Air Force teaching statistics

All regular instruction suspended for WWII, 1943–1945

1945

1950
Courses reorganized by subject rather than industry

1955
Stanley P. Teele appointed dean

Dedication of Aldrich and Kresge Hall

1960

1962
George P. Baker appointed dean

1963
Women admitted to first year of the MBA program

1964
School's first computer installed

1965

1970
Lawrence Fouraker appointed dean

248

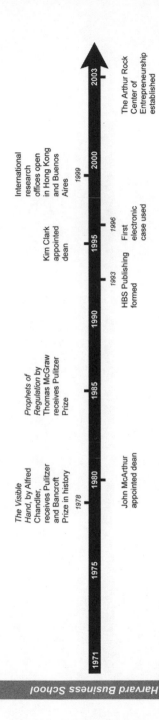

Harvard Business School

1971

1975

The Visible Hand, by Alfred Chandler, receives Pulitzer and Bancroft Prize in history

1978

1980

John McArthur appointed dean

Prophets of Regulation by Thomas McGraw receives Pulitzer Prize

1985

1990

HBS Publishing formed

1993

Kim Clark appointed dean

1995

1996

First electronic case used

International research offices open in Hong Kong and Buenos Aires

1999

2000

2003

The Arthur Rock Center of Entrepreneurship established

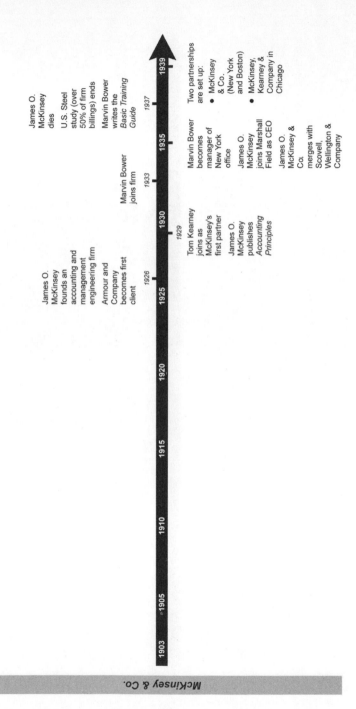

McKinsey & Co.

1903 · 1905 · 1910 · 1915 · 1920 · 1925 1926 1929 1930 · 1933 · 1935 · 1937 · 1939

James O. McKinsey founds an accounting and management engineering firm

Armour and Company becomes first client

Tom Kearney joins as McKinsey's first partner

James O. McKinsey publishes *Accounting Principles*

Marvin Bower joins firm

Marvin Bower becomes manager of New York office

James O. McKinsey joins Marshall Field as CEO

James O. McKinsey & Co. merges with Scovell, Wellington & Company

James O. McKinsey dies

U.S. Steel study (over 50% of firm billings) ends

Marvin Bower writes the *Basic Training Guide*

Two partnerships are set up:
- McKinsey & Co. (New York and Boston)
- McKinsey, Kearney & Company in Chicago

250

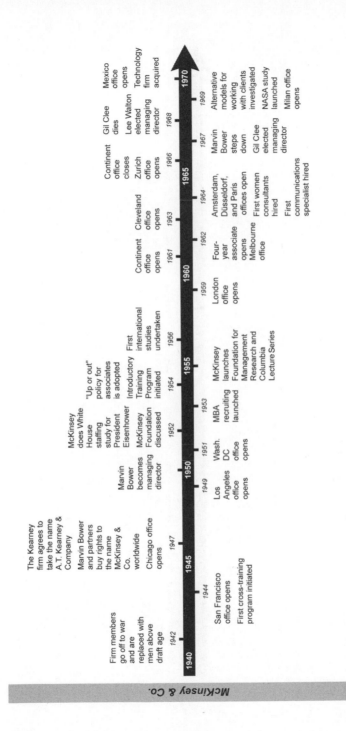

McKinsey & Co.

1940

1942 — Firm members go off to war and are replaced with men above draft age

San Francisco office opens

First cross-training program initiated

1944

1945

1947 — The Kearney firm agrees to take the name A.T. Kearney & Company

Marvin Bower and partners buy rights to the name McKinsey & Co. worldwide

Chicago office opens

1949 — Los Angeles office opens

1950 — Marvin Bower becomes managing director

1951 — Wash. DC office opens

1952 — McKinsey does White House staffing study for President Eisenhower

McKinsey Foundation discussed

1953 — MBA recruiting launched

1954 — "Up or out" policy for associates is adopted

Introductory Training Program initiated

1955 — McKinsey launches Foundation for Management Research and Columbia Lecture Series

1956 — First international studies undertaken

1959 — London office opens

1960 — Continent office opens

1962 — Four-year associate opens

Melbourne office

1963 — Cleveland office opens

1964 — Amsterdam, Düsseldorf, and Paris offices open

First women consultants hired

First communications specialist hired

1965 — Continent office closes

Zurich office opens

1967 — Marvin Bower steps down

Gil Clee elected managing director

1968 — Gil Clee dies

Lee Walton elected managing director

1969 — Alternative models for working with clients investigated

NASA study launched

Milan office opens

1970 — Mexico office opens

Technology firm acquired

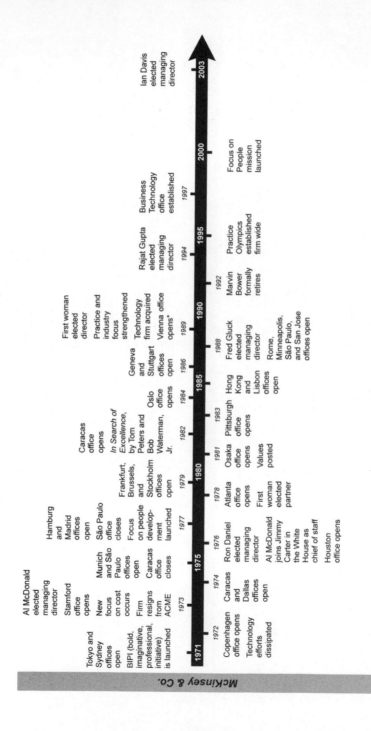

McKinsey & Co.

1971
Tokyo and Sydney offices open
BIPI (bold, imaginative, professional, initiative) is launched

1972
Copenhagen office opens
Technology efforts dissipated

1973
Al McDonald elected managing director
Stamford office opens
New focus on cost occurs
Firm resigns from ACME

1974
Caracas and Dallas offices open

1975
Munich and São Paulo offices open
Caracas office closes
Ron Daniel elected managing director
Al McDonald joins Jimmy Carter in the White House as chief of staff
Houston office opens

1976
Hamburg and Madrid offices open
São Paulo office closes
Focus on people development launched

1977

1978
Atlanta office opens
First woman elected partner

1979
Frankfurt, Brussels, and Stockholm offices open

1980
Caracas office opens
In Search of Excellence, by Tom Peters and Bob Waterman, Jr.
Osaka office opens
Values posted

1981

1982
Pittsburgh office opens

1983

1984
Oslo office opens

1985
Geneva and Stuttgart offices open
Hong Kong and Lisbon offices open

1986
First woman elected director
Practice and industry focus strengthened

1988
Fred Gluck elected managing director
Rome, Minneapolis, São Paulo, and San Jose offices open

1989
Technology firm acquired
Vienna office opens*

1990

1992
Marvin Bower formally retires

1994
Rajat Gupta elected managing director
Practice Olympics established firm wide

1995

1997
Business Technology office established

2000
Focus on People mission launched

2003
Ian Davis elected managing director

* 1990–1999, 35 offices were opened; in 2000–2003, 2 more were opened.

Brief Biography

Born

August 1, 1903, Cincinnati, Ohio

Education

- Brown University, PhB, 1925
- Harvard Law School, LLB, 1928
- Harvard Business School, MBA, 1930

Married Helen M. McLaughlin in 1927. Helen Bower died in January 1985.
Married Clothilde de Vèze Stewart in 1988. Clothilde Bower died in August 1999.

Three children

- Peter Huntington Bower (deceased)
- Richard Hamilton Bower
- James McKinsey Bower

Six grandchildren; 10 great-grandchildren (9 at the time of his death)

Died

January 22, 2003, Delray Beach, Florida

Professional Career

- *1930–1933:* Practiced corporate law with Jones, Day, Reavis & Pogue in Cleveland, Ohio, and was a member of the Ohio and Massachusetts bars.
- *1933:* Hired by James O. McKinsey for his new accounting and engineering management firm, which consisted then of two offices and 15 people. Marvin served as manager of the New York office from 1935 through 1950 and managing director of McKinsey & Co. from 1950 to 1967. At the behest of his partners, he continued to serve clients and the firm until his formal retirement in 1992.

Other Positions/Roles

- Trustee and chairman of the board of Case Western Reserve University (1968–1971)
- Trustee of Brown University (1968–1973)
- Chairman (longest serving) of the Joint Council on Economic Education (1967–1986)
- Committee for Economic Development (trustee/vice chairman and member of the executive committee)
- Member of the Visiting Committee of General Motors Institute (1962–1965)
- Member of the Advisory Committee of the Economic Growth Center at Yale University
- Member of the Bronxville, New York School Board (1945–1948)
- Member of the board of directors of the Associates of Harvard Business School
- Member of the Advisory Committee on Business Programs of the Brookings Institute
- President of the Florence V. Burden Foundation
- Director of Religion in American Life and the Associates of Harvard Business School
- Fellow of the International Academy of Management

- Harvard Business School (member and chairman of the Visiting Committee; chairman of the Dean's Advisory Committee on Administration)

Honors

- Founding member and first president of the U.S. Institute of Management Consultants (1969)
- Elected to *Fortune* magazine's Business Hall of Fame (1989)
- Distinguished Service Award from the Harvard Business School (1968)
- Recipient of a Harvard Medal during the 350th Harvard University anniversary (1986)
- Harvard Business School Marvin Bower Professorship of Leadership Development established (1995)
- His book, *The Will to Manage,* published in 1966, selected in *Business: The Ultimate Resource,* published in 2002, as one of history's 70 most important business books
- Included in Brown University's list of Alumni Who Changed a Century (2000)

Author

- *The Development of Executive Leadership* (Harvard University Press, 1949).
- *The Will to Manage* (McGraw-Hill, 1966). German, French, Swedish, Finnish, Spanish, and Japanese editions.
- *Perspective on McKinsey* (privately printed, McKinsey & Co., 1979).
- *The Will to Lead* (Harvard Business School Press, 1997).
- *Memoirs* (privately printed, 2003).
- Numerous articles on marketing and general management.

McKinsey & Co. Partners' Conference, 1964

Address
by
MARVIN BOWER

Annual Conference
Tarrytown, New York
October 16 and 17, 1964

MR. MARVIN BOWER: Since our last conference, since we last met together in this conference, we have lost by death two directors. Howard Smith, in the sunset of his career, died of cancer and Bob Hall, in the high noon of his career, was snatched out of the sky. These two men have made great contributions to the good things that we have here, and I'd like to pay tribute to them by simply saying that; but more specifically, to illustrate in some of the remarks that I make the contributions that they made so that they would be more real than just words.

In these discussions that I've carried on over the years I've tried to pull together these meetings in terms of a single theme, and that theme is the role of the firm and the individual and what the firm's program means to the individual. As I did that a good many years ago I used to prepare very thoroughly for it: I would write it out and get it thoroughly in mind, and then I found that as the session went on everybody was saying everything I had planned to say. So I got wise to that and I don't prepare any longer. What I do is to make some notes—if I showed you the pack of notes that I've got you'd surely be staggered—and I try to tie the things that have been said into the total theme of the meaning of the firm to the individual, and I found that that works better. Of course some of the figures don't jibe and a few things of that kind, a mechanical problem, but that's what I propose to do today, to try to pull this conference together in that fashion and on that theme.

The first Earl of Beaconsfield, better known as Benjamin Disraeli, one of the great Prime Ministers of Great Britain, said the secret of success is constancy to purpose; and this firm has had that as a guiding light for a long time, constancy to purpose, and my theme then is concerned with how each of the individuals making up our firm can have greater constancy to the purposes of the firm.

The purposes of the firm have been discussed here, of course. It's been quite evident during the last couple of days that we have two purposes: The first one and primary one, of course, is to solve the problems of organizations and to do that in a superior fashion. You notice I don't say corporations and I don't say businesses. Our purposes are broader than that, and just because we have a predominance of corporate clientele doesn't mean that that is our only purpose. John Gallagher pointed out our weaknesses in many respects, and therefore our purpose is not to serve business alone, it's to serve government and other kinds of organizations. The second purpose is to grow in size, stature and profitableness. We think we have to grow in all three respects in order to attract and hold the kind of people that are necessary to achieve our first purpose. So these are two interrelated objectives or purposes, and what we are concerned with is a constancy to those purposes in the words of Disraeli.

Our first speaker talked about the multi-national corporation, and I want to start out with some brief review of the multi-national firm that we are—with six offices in the United States, one in the United Kingdom that you've heard about from the leader of that office, Geneva, Amsterdam, Paris and most recently Düsseldorf. Someone asked me how soon are we going to open the office in Düsseldorf. I said as quickly as they can get the facilities ready; they have a lease and we sent a cable that we've taken up our option, so it's imminent. Paris is being constructed and the people are about ready to move in.

Amsterdam is a jewel of an office—I was in both of those places this summer—and Geneva's being cut back, of course, because the people that were gathered in Geneva have been moved to these other offices and that was, as the old saying goes, according to plan.

Now our multi-national firm has one very remarkable characteristic and that is that it is one firm. It's not only one firm in terms of purposes and attitudes and philosophy; it's one firm in terms of legal entity, and this is quite a surprise to legal and tax experts. They wonder how we did it. Well, we did it because Larry and our lawyers and tax experts in these various countries made it possible, but it has a significance to it: As long as we can, we would like to have a single entity. It may be necessary sometime, as we go into other countries, to have subsidiaries. We hope, however, the subsidiaries will not keep us from being one multi-national firm. We will try to disregard the corporate entity, to refer to the legal language. We don't have to do that yet and we are pleased as a symbol. But more important than the legal setup is the fact that we are one firm in attitude, and I believe this is a very remarkable development and a great element of strength.

If you think back during the course of the last couple of days, I don't believe you will have heard much talk about the profits of our office versus the profits of your office; and what are you doing to us that is hurting our office. And this is an element of great strength in a multi-national firm, and it's something that we want to maintain and that we have to work at. I believe we can take great credit on ourselves for having achieved a singleness of purpose and a unity of the firm. That hasn't come about just by happenstance. A lot of people have worked at it, and Alex Smith was one of the big workers at that. Alex was the manager of the New York office which began shucking off its people to these other offices, and Alex didn't resist it because he could see the value of this in a multi-national firm. As the manager of the office he wasn't worried about the profits of the New York office, and this had a great effect throughout this firm and it's a monument to Alex Smith that it happened.

Now, who are we that are trying to carry out these two basic purposes? Here's where my figures differ—my figures are as recent as last night (laughter) and maybe Bill Watts was the last man aboard, but there are a couple of contenders for that role. My figures tell me that we have a consulting staff of 250 which is up 24 net as of this time; that we have 50 full-time administrators; 263 operations staff—for a total firm personnel of 538. Now those people are scattered all around this world and, more than that, they are multi-national personnel. I only have the nationalities of the consulting staff, but it runs like this: We have 23 Britons, 4 Swiss, 2 French, 3 Australians, 2 Italians, 1 German, 1 Swede, 3 Dutch, 1 New Zealander, 1 Canadian and 1 Yugoslav who's about to become an American. That makes 42 other nationalities, and the balance of the 250 are Americans. So you can see that the proportion is changing rapidly and, as Hugh brought out, it's likely to change with continuing rapidity.

What else can we say about ourselves in terms of the people that are trying to achieve those objectives? I've got some more data here about our educational background. Education isn't important only because of the qualities of mind that it builds in a person; it's an evidence of drive and initiative and ambition and determination and a lot of other things to get all the degrees that this group has gathered and, while I don't have them for the administrative staff and the operations staff, they've got a lot of degrees too. At the university and college level we have 247 degrees—14 PhDs, 9 LLBs, 15 MAs of one kind or another; Masters of Science 23; MBAs from various schools, 148 (laughter)—I'll give you the breakdown: from Columbia, 2; from Wharton, 9; from Stanford, 10; from Harvard, 99; and from others, 28. Of those 99, 39 of them came directly from Harvard Business School and I think about the same proportion—if you can make a statistic out of 2 or 10 or 9—it's about the same, maybe 100 percent for Wharton but I don't think so. I don't have that compiled. Anyway, the people trying to achieve those two objectives have got 461 degrees and that says more than the degrees themselves.

In the achievement of these two objectives, who are we serving currently? Again, I give you the figures as of October 8 in this case. On October 8 we had 147 clients. We've probably got more than that now because this doesn't include Coca-Cola, but we haven't quite started the Coca-Cola study and you can probably think of other ones that are about to start. I'm going to talk only about the clients that we were serving on the 8th of October. I'm not going to go back and talk about the clients we used to serve or the clients we might serve. This is a brief analysis of the clients we are serving in the achievement of those two objectives.

Our largest, most important and perhaps most difficult assignment is for the Air Force Systems Command. It's large because it's a large activity, they have a lot of people on it; it's important because it has to do with the superior Free World and the solvency of the United States government. (Laughter) If we don't keep those missiles in place ready to shoot when the other fellows shoot theirs—and now the Chinese have got one to shoot—then we're in real trouble. And if we don't get those Air Force fellows buying them cheaper, it's going to break us. So between those two things—remember Khrushchev said he was going to bury us economically and now they're burying Khrushchev—but seriously we do have to control the cost at the same time that we are keeping the missiles in place, and that is a great project in which we have an important part.

Our most unusual study is for the International Labor Organization, an organization that includes not only the countries of the Free World but the countries of the Communist World, and we have made an organization study there and it's going on and being implemented. It's a most unusual study and a very prestigious one.

Within the corporate world, we have a number of clients and I've classified them by industry, just to touch on them. Many of them have been already mentioned, but I think it is significant to see for whom we are trying to achieve these objectives. In the oil industry, Texaco, Socony, Shell Mex B.P., Standard of Indiana, Union Tidewater and several others too numerous to mention; in chemicals, Union Carbide, FMC, Celanese, Geigy, Monsanto, Dynamit Nobel and several others; in food, General Foods, Lever and Unilever which are unrelated—that is, one came in one way and the other came in another, and Heinz; in steel, Inland, Wheeling, English, and Stuart & Lloyd; in paper, International, Union Bag, Scott, Goldwater and others; in airlines, American, KLM; in railroads, C&O, B&O, Southern, Reading, Southern Pacific, and the Boston & Maine; in the insurance field, Metropolitan, New York Life, Life Insurance of Virginia, Equitable of Iowa, Allstate, Minnesota,

British Insurance Association and several others; in banking, Morgan Guaranty, First National City, Commerce Union of Nashville, Northwest Bank Corporation, Seattle First National and others. And then these other miscellaneous—listen to some of the miscellaneous companies: IBM (laughter), International Harvester, Massey Ferguson, Dunlop Brothers, Bally Shoe, Volkswagen, Caterpillar Tractor and Johnson & Johnson.

That's a pretty good group of people to be pursuing these two objectives with and we are trying to serve them well, of course.

Now with all of our people and all of those clients scattered around the world, how do we maintain constancy of purpose? First, we have a philosophy and a set of beliefs and strategic concepts, and, second, we have a system of management geared to our philosophy. If the system of management doesn't sometimes seem like a system, it's only because it doesn't look like it. It has been planned and we are trying to program it.

Not long ago you all received—and all of you who have joined the firm recently, I hope have received—a memorandum called "The Strategy for Professional Growth." This is a document that summarizes our concepts, our beliefs and our philosophy, and also gives some thought for the future. This is a document that was prepared under the leadership of the Executive Group; it was processed seven drafts by the Management Group, in all offices; many revisions were made; many contributions went into it from people in various parts of the world. Here in a few pages—let's see, twenty pages—we have a statement of what it is we're trying to do and what are the things that are holding us together in terms of this scattered group of people, serving this scattered group of clients on all of the problems that we are dealing with them. And so I commend this to you as a document of real importance, if we are going to hold this group of people into one firm and make it effective for the client and make it effective for ourselves and make it grow and prosper in size and stature and in profit.

So we start out with that as a set of beliefs, and I'd like to read you a few sentences here now from The McKinsey Foundation Book that Tom Watson of IBM prepared. These are lectures, as you know, delivered in the McKinsey Foundation Lectures at Columbia. He says: "I believe the real difference between success and failure in a corporation can very often be traced to the question of how well the organization brings out the great energies and talents of its people. What does it do to help these people find common cause with each other? How does it keep them pointed in the right direction despite the many rivalries and differences that exist among them? And how can it sustain this common cause and sense of direction through the many changes which take place from one generation to another? These problems are not unique to corporations; they exist in all large organizations, in political and religious institutions. Consider any great organization, one that has lasted over the years, and I think you will find it owes its resiliency not to its form of organization or administrative skill but to the power of what we call the beliefs and the appeal these beliefs have for its people. This, then, is my thesis: I firmly believe that any organization in order to survive and achieve success must have a sound set of beliefs on which it premises all its policies and actions.

Now we have a set of beliefs that's been hammered out over the years and this set of beliefs is contained in this Strategy memorandum. I don't want to go over that memorandum. What I would like to do is to look forward rather than even look at the present but, drawing on our Strategy memorandum, to thread some of the comments on Six Basic Requirements for Continued Growth in the firm, in size, in stature and profit. None of these things that I call requirements is not contained in the Strategy memorandum. I'm simply putting them in a little different order and trying to pull together some of the things that we have talked about in the last couple of days so that this might be in a more cohesive form that we can think about.

When you're tying to carry out strategy, concepts, philosophy and to meet requirements, there are only two ways to do it: One is to inspire that it be done; and the other is to require that it be done. We have over the years depended chiefly on inspiring. I don't mean by inspiring exhortation. I mean leadership and dedication of people, and that comes mostly on the job. It doesn't come very much in the office and it doesn't come very much in gatherings. It comes on the job where we have an inspiration from people who are really dedicated to their work, to do that work well, and this requires people to adhere to common beliefs and to have constancy of purpose.

Now the second thing is requiring. We have insisted that certain standards be met; we have insisted that some discipline be adhered to. This over the years has been a minimum, and so we have hoped that through inspiring rather than requiring people would first become committed to the work of this firm and these objectives, and finally become dedicated. And we hope that by the time they have been promoted to the management group they are dedicated as well as committed. Having been dedicated, they are in a much better position to inspire rather than require.

So now let's take each of these six requirements and look ahead and see what some of the problems are of meeting them and what some of the problems are of inspiring and requiring that people meet these six requirements.

First requirement is to bring beliefs and the ethical values essential for a professional practice and required to attract, hold, and make fully productive the outstanding men and women needed to conduct that practice. And here is a contribution that Alex Smith made in great measure. Alex joined this firm when the management consulting profession was not much of a profession, in fact, it was very new and it was kind of scattered and people wondered if this was an activity carried on by charlatans. Alex joined the firm many years ago and I'm sure that some of you are here, joined the firm, because of Alex's scintillating personality and eminent quality; and I'm sure that some of you stayed because of his leadership and his requiring that you stay because of the inspiration that he gave.

For those of you who didn't know him that may sound a little sticky, but there was nothing about Alex that didn't come through in a very solid fashion.

Now the belief and ethical values is something that comes out of your own training and your family background, and it can only be brought out by other people. Alex did that.

In the adherence to ethical value we have some requiring. Over the years we've had very few problems of people meeting high standards because we have selected them carefully. But we have had to eliminate people rather quickly because they didn't, and we even ushered one man right off the premises without giving him a chance to do anything more than pick up his belongings and get out. This is the other side of the equation; we haven't had to use this very often.

One of the attributes of adhering to high ethical values that is essential in maintaining constancy to purpose is the supportive attitudes that we have to have for each other. If this group doesn't support the group and if the individuals don't support the other individuals, we can fly apart because we're scattered around, we're serving all these clients, we have all these nationalities. Our common denominator must be to support the group and not to downgrade the other fellow and not to pick at him, not to make it more difficult, but to help him succeed in our common purpose. This is an aspect of ethical values.

It always sounds a little bit sticky to talk about ethical values. We expect that in people. They've been trained by the family and the church and the school and the university to have high ethical values. It's one of our strategic concepts, and I'd like to show you how practical this can be. We have in this room a network of people scattered from Australia on one hand and Germany on the other, and if we can have confidence in each other and in the quality of the work and the professional adherence to standards, think of the power that we have to offer to our clients— when the fellow here can make an arrangement for someone else to carry out there and know that he might make some mistakes of judgment, he might be technically unqualified; he might fall on his face for a variety of reasons, but he isn't going to fall on his face because he tries to trim any corners or to depart from ethical values. This is an element of strength of the greatest value to our clients and of the greatest value to the firm, and it must be something to which we constantly adhere.

I've made a study of the history of the professions: The doctor, the lawyer, and all of the other professions adhere to these professional standards for selfish reasons. This is a concept, and here's how it works. Think of the value of the doctor who establishes a reputation that he is never going to operate unless it's necessary, that he is never going to say come back and pay me another visit at another $10, $15, $25, $35 unless it's necessary, and only he can make that decision. It's a subjective decision. But think of the value to him when people recognize that he meets that kind of standard, and they can go to him in confidence and put themselves in his hands. This is the reason for professional standards. It is a selfish thing although it looks unselfish at the outset. And we adhere to it for selfish reasons, if you take away the surface and look at it. So therefore the maintenance of high ethical values in this group by each of the individuals can be looked at, if you will, in a very selfish way: that any of us who departs from the highest ethical values in the professional approach to our work is cutting at the heart of the thing that we stand for and, if you will, he's cutting our stature, he's slowing down our size and he's cutting our profits, because the thing that will cause people to come to us is because, like the doctor, they can put themselves in our hands and know that we are going to treat them in their interest. And this is an asset of great value. This firm has worked hard to achieve that role, and it's the responsibility of each of us as individuals to maintain that constancy of purpose. And here is a place where Alex made the greatest contribution.

Now, our second requirement is high standards and willingness to pay the price for enforcing them. Especially important are: the professional approach, quality standards for client work, standards for caliber and performance of consultants, and professional standards for income development. We've heard a lot about that during the past two days. We've had some excellent discussions and presentations. The M&M boys on problem-solving process were especially good, and I only want to add one thing to the Morrison and McDonald presentation and it's a phrase that I think Hugh gave me, or someone around the firm gave me. They said, "What are the characteristics of our problem-solving process? The way that we do it is that we swarm all over the problem." And it's not a bad thought. We have all kinds of approaches to it and we don't accept the client's statement of what the problem is. When we were doing the Dunlop study we didn't accept the fact that they wanted to have an office layout problem to determine whether they needed more space or not. We swarmed all over that problem, and Roger and Al McDonald have told us how to do it.

The professional approach is something that we've heard a lot about, and I would like to give you a specific example of the value of the professional approach. This is how we were retained by Dynamit Nobel—I hope I have the facts accurately: Dynamit Nobel is a big explosives manufacturer in Germany with a major chemical position;

it's part of a very important German group, one of maybe fifteen of the companies in Germany that would be the best to start with and they heard about our work at Imperial Chemicals Industries Ltd., ICI to those of us who know it. Whether they heard about it through discussion with the people there or whether they read about it in the chemical journals or the general press, I don't know, but in any event they talked with the ICI executives and they told them that they thought that we were doing, had done good work and so they got in touch with us. John McDonald and Peter Hobbins went to see them, and the thing that they started talking about was the clerical cost reduction study.

Here were two people very anxious to build a practice in Germany, offered an opportunity to take on a clerical cost reduction study, a perfectly fine thing to do, but they said, "Are you sure that this is the right place to start?" And they offered to spend three days looking at the situation. And after having spent that three days they then said, "This is not the place to start" because they found that there were some organizational concepts in that company that would make it very difficult, or at least wasteful, to try to reduce the clerical costs when, by organizing it in a different fashion, you could cut out more costs and this would affect the clerical costs. So at the risk of losing the study they came back to them and said it ought to be approached in this way.

Well, this met with the approval of the executives and then they appeared before the board. In appearing before the board they described the approach, they told them about the work that had been done during these three days, and they indicated that they were ready to sign a contract. Well, they had had some unfortunate experience with other consultants and they wanted to be very careful about signing the contract and so our fellows said to them, "You don't have to sign a contract with McKinsey & Company." They were quite surprised about that. They were more surprised about the fee. (Laughter) And Peter, who of course is fluent in German, heard one of the directors turn to another on the side and he said, "I suppose there are fees that high but I didn't know it before." (Laughter)

So they decided that they would put themselves in our hands, and therefore the professional approach had great value. In the first place, they had a study that was much more interesting to us and much more important to them; we had it at a high fee; and we had it without a contract which was much to their liking and to ours, because if we are pursuing a professional approach and they lose confidence in us or we don't think that they're going to act on our recommendations, we'd like to be free to discontinue the work.

Now the third requirement for success in the future, it seems to me, is the perceptive and conceptual thinking that can detect client opportunities and needs and can detect external and internal forces affecting the firm—you saw a diagram on these forces last night—and can capitalize on these factors through developing improved and new services and better firm management methods and program. That's what a lot of this conference has been about, how to do all those things, and we have Warren Cannon to thank for the format of this. I believe that this conference has been very well conceived and every session that I was in was well prepared and well presented; so it has helped us in the development of new services and in the improvement of existing services.

This firm has a set of concepts and beliefs that as Tom Watson says ought to be immutable, but if we get rigid and we feel that everything ought to remain the same, why then we're going to be in trouble. So this requirement says that we must be perceptive to changes going on about us, we must be perceptive to things that are going on in the firm, and we must adjust our services to clients to meet the external factors and we must adjust the policies, procedures and programs in leadership, personnel and everything else to the things that are going on in the firm because we can't serve our clients well unless we have people in the firm who are productive and the right people to do that job.

And we have been sensitive to the external factors and you have heard some client names of the 147 we're serving currently that couldn't have been client names a while back. In the insurance field, you heard a number of names and the figures behind those names are big. This came about because we had leadership in Dick Neuschel and John Garrity to be sensitive to the first insurance study that we had quite by chance and to capitalize on that to apply one after another good pieces of work to the insurance field. Now in the railroad field we have the same thing happening. We were sensitive to the opportunities for work in the railroad field, and Bob Hall had the sensitivity to see the opportunities in the railroad field and he immersed himself in several railroad studies—the Southern, the Reading, the B&O and C&O—and he was providing at the time his career was so abruptly terminated a high degree of leadership in the railroad field. This leadership which Phil Babb shared has been carried on by Phil Babb, but let me give you something that is quite interesting to me about Bob Hall.

This is a memorandum that I received the day after Bob died. It must have been mailed from the airport from the date on it, and it showed his continuing interest in the railroad field. I'd like to read it to you—it's just one small page. It's in longhand, that's why I think he wrote it at the airport. He says, "Marvin, The reaction to the Reading report has been increasingly favorable." (The Reading report was done under Bob Hall's direction and was one of the things that has advanced our railroad practice.) "To date the railroad has distributed about 100 copies and has asked us for an additional supply. We are also planning a mailing of our mass transportation commission report to specific railroads and public agencies. It has been well received already by the Commission members."

So here was a man probably sitting at the airport getting ready to go to another client, thinking about his leadership in a field of our practice, and he attached to it a little printed booklet here called "The Reading Commuter." Apparently the Reading Railroad had digested for their riders the McKinsey study and Bob had underscored the various places—there must have been eight or ten of them—where the McKinsey report is referred to in this little handbook that I suppose they distribute to the commuters on the Reading Railroad because this study had to do with their commuting business. This is one little tangible evidence of the kind of leadership that Bob Hall was providing on that front and on the front of the development of a phase of our practice. No one asked Bob to do it, no one told Bob to do it. He seized the opportunity and he was pursuing it vigorously at the time of his death.

Our fourth requirement for success in the future is continuing attention to maintaining a working atmosphere in the firm that will attract, hold, and make fully productive the high talent men we need to conduct our practice. That sounds kind of wordy to keep repeating "to attract, hold and make fully productive," but that's what we have to do. We have to attract the highest caliber people, which I think you can recognize we're doing. You can't deny it individually. (Laughter) And I think one of the things we all get out of this conference is looking at ourselves collectively and then we begin to believe it. So we have attracted the highest caliber people. Our recruiters had a conference the other day, the day before this conference started, and talked about recruiting and if you think your job is hard just think of the fact that those poor fellows have to interview from 75 to 100 people, some of us do, in order to get one. So this business of attracting is pretty expensive business.

Now, to hold those people and to make them productive we have to create an atmosphere that that kind of a man likes. You must remember that the fellow that is selected from the 75 to 100 against the standards we have is a fellow who can get a job any time that he wants to. We know that, you know it, everybody knows it; we might as well face it as a fact. Therefore, you are going to stay in this work, dedicated to these common causes only so long as you find it interesting, profitable, rewarding in a whole variety of ways; and we know you won't do it if you're living in an atmosphere that is not conducive to doing good work, if you have to watch the other fellow—if you have to think what is the politics of this situation and is someone undercutting me, is he downgrading me—and a whole range of other things that the high talent man does not like to have in the working atmosphere where he is trying to put out as much as this demanding work requires. And so morale for a group of high caliber people is a very intangible thing. It has to be stimulating and it has to be wholesome, and this is something that we not only try to inspire but we also require. It's one of the cohesive things, the glue that will hold us together, and we do have to watch it all of the time. And the cliché at the moment at least is, "Let's show supportive attitudes toward each other," the best way to create that kind of morale for this kind of person.

Our fifth requirement is a progressive, innovating, forward-looking point of view on moving ahead and taking risks in serving clients and managing the firm. Maybe some of you don't think that we're very good risk-takers, but in moving ahead as rapidly as we have in the international field the same time that we've opened an office in the United

States and putting people on the important problems for those important companies that we do, with as limited experience with us as we do, we think is risk-taking. It is risk-taking with our most important asset, our reputation and our standing with our clients.

Innovation we're a little slow at, I think. We didn't get into the Operations Research field as soon as we should, but I think one of the characteristics of this group at least is when we do it, we do it; and those of you who had the stimulation of sitting in on our Operations Research presentations, I'm sure, feel that we are really in it—the one that was a description of what we have done for Johnson & Johnson and the one dealing with the application of Operations Research to top management. We had to go outside to get our leadership in this in Dave Hertz, and we've had that leadership, we're profiting from it, and we have a whole group of fellows who are good at this. We didn't do it as fast as we should have but it's in and it is permeating everything we're doing and it is stimulating a lot of thinking on a great many other fronts. I'm sure those of you who were in those presentations could just think about getting a dozen presidents together and giving them that Johnson & Johnson presentation, they would understand Operations Research. The only trouble with doing it is that we'd have so many requests for assistance that we don't dare do it for a while.

So, we have in this group some inertia. I suppose the inertia comes because we're so analytical and so critical that we're always finding the things that are wrong, finding the things that are difficult to do. So on the one hand we're pretty good risk-takers in many ways, and we're a little slow in other ways. I hope that, as we move ahead, we can be a little faster in innovating than we have been; and yet innovation in minor ways is going on all the time as people are finding new ways of doing things. These are going on, but I'm talking about innovation in the big things where I believe we could speed up if we would all open our minds a little bit more to the fact that this may be a good thing to do.

Our sixth and last requirement for progress, it seems to me, is continuing attention to improving our internal management and leadership. At our present and future size everything we want to do requires effective management and capable leadership. Leadership in a professional firm is a peculiar sort of thing that has to be given by the man on the job, the engagement director, and it's his responsibility to give it. He must make the people not only work well and do a good job for the client; it's part of his job to insure commitment and ultimately dedication to this profession and to this firm as a career.

In the development of our management system, and having heard the description by Russ Aycoff of a system I couldn't help think that maybe our system isn't as bad as it sometimes is reported to be, because we in our management of this firm meet those requirements, I think, fairly well. But we do have some defects and we might as well face them and we ought to overcome them, and one of those is the role of what we call the specialist in our firm. That isn't, perhaps, a good term. I had luncheon with Jim Fischer one time and I took down some notes of his that indicated to me that there is another approach to this and I'm going to try to work that out, because his concept was that this is experience in depth that runs clear across our practice, that that's the kind of specialization that we need. We can't be at this size; we can't have the kinds of clients that those 147 represent, and we can't solve the complex problems without the specialist; and if any of you were in those two sessions on OR you're sure of that now. So here is some inertia. We're going to do this, we are doing it, but we certainly have resistance to the concept that this firm has got to move ahead not just with generalists but with specialists and that we must not destroy our assets by having the specialist inspired to become a generalist, because he then can't be experienced in depth and deal with these complex problems. This is something that if we have common cause, constancy of purpose, we ought to address ourselves to and the way to address ourselves to it is to be sure that we all recognize that value to every one of us in common cause in this firm in going ahead from here.

And so we have the problem finally in meeting those six requirements to be sure that we are convinced of the worthwhileness of all of these requirements, the worthwhileness of what we're doing. I don't believe that if you stop to analyze the things that you are working on that you can question very much their worthwhileness if you would like to be a professional man working in the problem-solving of business, Government, and other kinds of organizations. You must satisfy yourself that the professional approach is valuable to the client and worthwhile to the client and therefore something you want to participate in.

You must satisfy yourself that the addition of what you are doing to that client is valuable, not only valuable to the client because it produces profits but valuable to the economy because it makes things better for people. And Khrushchev was probably dumped because he couldn't do that under their system.

I talked with Dave Morse who's Gil's friend, the head of ILO, and Gil arranged for me to have luncheon with him and he had just come back from behind the Iron Curtain two or three weeks ago, and he said, "I have talked with the people who belong to the ILO behind the Iron Curtain," and he said, "They are in trouble. They admitted that." And he had dinner with Khrushchev—I don't suppose Khrushchev admitted it—but people very close to Khrushchev had told Dave Morse that they were in trouble. This was just a few days before the news came out during this conference that they had changed the command.

So the work that we do is designed to make things better for people, and it's designed to make the government that we're serving better government for people. It seems to me that in making common cause we can first have commitment and later have dedication, and we have had examples here, very brief, but they were of two men who have left us who had dedication in the extreme—Alex, who made the contribution throughout his life of these very deep kinds; Bob Hall who went to Washington to add something to that office, who later took it over, and then provided the leadership for our railroad practice. It is that kind of contribution made by many men and women who are going to give us common cause in the achievement of these objectives.

I want to conclude with a statement by a British economist—I asked two or three of the Britons how to pronounce his name; they weren't sure and I've got two versions and I'm going to use one of those versions—the British economist Walter Badgett, who said, "Strong beliefs win strong men and make them stronger." And my addition to that is that as our own men become stronger in their beliefs and deeper in their dedication, so will we achieve constancy of purpose in the achievement of our two objectives. (Applause)

CHAIRMAN: In just a few minutes I will adjourn this conference and we won't be meeting again, of course, for another two years. Anything that I might add to what Marvin has just said would be anticlimactic and I therefore do not intend to say very much, but I don't think it is inappropriate in closing this conference for me to attempt a tribute to the leadership of Marvin Bower himself.

Now some of you are here for your first annual conference hence-forth to be biennial. I myself am attending my fourteenth. Others are here on their nineteenth, twentieth and other anniversaries. Marvin Bower has just spoken to us—not to me, of course, but to this kind of a conference—for the twenty-seventh time. In the fourteen conferences that I have attended I have seen some good ones, some outstanding, some not so good, and some more or less unmemorable—let's say indifferent—but one common feature in all of them, and I mean this without exception, has been the quality of the closing address always given by Marvin Bower.

It has been a source of wonder to me, quite honestly, how any man could sustain the inspired addresses that he has given over twenty-seven years, and it seems to me that the answer or the explanation for it can be summed up in the one word leadership. (Applause)

MR. BOWER: I should have included this before but I certainly must now. Twenty-seven times here is not the total time that I have been with the firm, and obviously I'm dedicated further. One of the problems about any firm, though, that's had someone at it as long as I have is the problem of getting rid of them, and I want everyone to know that I'm on record with the managing committee that I'm not only ready to take the first step of leaving the succession that I've taken but I'm ready to take all the steps just as rapidly as anyone tells me that they should be taken. This is important to me because it's important to the firm, and I think that everybody ought to know that that is the case because one of the things that has hurt many firms and many busi-nesses that you've seen is that some one person who had a hand in their development keeps his hand in too long, and it's your responsibility to tell the managing committee when you've had enough. (Applause)

Notes

Part I: Translating a Vision into Reality

1. Marvin Bower, personal files ("Protecting the Foundations of Firm Success," draft memo, 1969); Marvin Bower, in discussion with the author, 2001.

Chapter 1: Marvin Bower

1. Marvin Bower, "Living Legends," National Business Hall of Fame interview, sponsored by Junior Achievement and *Fortune* (Hollywood, CA, Strategic Perceptions, Inc., 1988).
2. John Byrne, "Goodbye to an Ethicist," *Business Week,* February 10, 2003.
3. Marvin Bower, *Memoirs* (New York, privately published, 2003).
4. Ibid.
5. Ibid.
6. Ibid.
7. Ibid.
8. Ibid.
9. Ibid; Marvin Bower, in discussion with the author, 2002.
10. Marvin Bower, in discussion with the author, 2001.
11. *Memoirs;* interviews for McKinsey's oral history conducted by Jessica Holland, 1986–1988.
12. Ibid.
13. *Memoirs.*
14. Interviews for McKinsey's oral history, 1986–1988.
15. Marvin Bower, personal files (scrapbook); in discussion with the author, 2002.
16. *The Cleveland News,* August 14, 1927.
17. Marvin Bower, personal files (scrapbooks).
18. Marvin Bower, personal files (1961–1972); in discussion with the author, 2002; interview with Ron Daniel.
19. Marvin Bower, personal files (1930–1946).
20. Marvin Bower, personal files (note from Tom Dill, 1970).
21. *Business: The Ultimate Resource,* (Boston, MA, Perseus Publishing, 2002), p. 955.
22. Interview with John Stewart by author.

23. Marvin Bower, personal files (Bronxville newspaper clippings); in discussion with the author, 2002.

24. Marvin Bower, personal files (Bronxville, New York, *The Reformed Church Bulletin,* April 18, 1971).

25. Interview with Jim Bower by author.

26. Marvin Bower, personal files (family correspondence, 1986).

Chapter 2: The Vision

1. Herbert Simon, *The New Science of Management Decisions* (New York, Harper & Brothers, 1960).

2. John G. Neukom, *McKinsey Memoirs: A Personal Perspective* (privately published, McKinsey & Co., 1975).

3. Albert Borowitz, *Jones, Day, Reavis & Pogue: The First Century* (privately published, Jones, Day, Reavis & Pogue, 1993); Marvin Bower, in discussion with the author, 2002.

4. "Living Legends," National Business Hall of Fame interview, sponsored by Junior Achievement and *Fortune* (Hollywood, CA, Strategic Perceptions, Inc., 1988).

5. Interview with Tom Brown, chairman of TB&Co., 2003 by author.

6. Urwick, Orr & Partners (U.K.) was in forming stages and launched in 1934; interview with Peter Drucker by author.

7. Jim Bowman, *Booz·Allen & Hamilton: Seventy Years of Client Service, 1914–1984* (privately published, Booz·Allen & Hamilton Inc., 1984).

8. Notes from Steve Walleck; interview with Helen Bower, 1983, by author.

9. Ibid.

10. *McKinsey Memoirs,* p. 6 and 7.

11. Marvin Bower, *Perspectives on McKinsey* (privately published, McKinsey & Co., 1979), p. 46.

12. Marvin Bower, *Memoirs* (New York, privately published, 2003).

13. Marvin's title was managing partner beginning in 1950; prior to that he was office manager of the New York office.

14. *Perspectives on McKinsey,* p. 43–49; interviews for McKinsey's oral history, 1986–1988.

15. McKinsey Wellington & Co., management engineers, history, 1936.

16. One of the four original partners, Ewing "Zip" Reilley, from Goldman Sachs, joined Marvin as an investor and an associate rather than partner in title, and therefore did not put his personal assets, beyond the capital he invested, at risk.

Chapter 3: The Profession and the Institution

1. Marvin Bower, personal files—speech on leadership, 1957.

2. *McKinsey: A Scrapbook* (privately published, McKinsey & Co., 1997), p. 8.

3. Marvin Bower, in discussion with the author, 2002.

4. Marvin Bower, *Perspectives on McKinsey* (privately published, McKinsey & Co., 1979), p. 5 and 6.

5. Ibid, p. 16.

6. Interview with John Stewart by author.

7. Marvin Bower, in discussion with the author, 2002.

8. Interviews for McKinsey's oral history, 1986–1988.

9. Marvin Bower, personal files (speech to McKinsey staff titled "Development of the Firm's Personality: Looking Back Twenty Years and Ahead Twenty," October 30 and 31, 1953).

10. Interviews for McKinsey's oral history, 1986–1988, p. 69 and 237; Marvin Bower, personal files (notes on his computer).

11. Interviews with Chuck Ames and John Stewart by author.

12. Marvin Bower, personal files (1953).

13. Interview with Gary MacDougal by author.

14. Marvin Bower, personal files ("Beating the Executive Market," *The Harvard Business School Alumni Bulletin,* May 1940); "Unleashing the Department Store— A Practical Concept of Department Store Organization" (reprinted from speech at Annual Convention of National Retail Goods Association, January 18, 1939); "The Management Viewpoint in Credit Extension" (reprinted from *The Bankers Magazine,* August 1938); "Untangling the Corporate Harness" (reprinted from presentation at the Annual Meeting of the American Society of Mechanical Engineers, December 5–9, 1938).

15. Marvin Bower, personal files (speech, 1951).

16. Interview with Warren Cannon by author.

17. Interviews for McKinsey's oral history, 1986–1988.

18. Marvin Bower, personal files (speech, 1953).

19. Ibid.

20. Marvin Bower, personal files (1974).

21. Interview with Don Gogel by author.

22. Interview with Andy Pearson by author.

23. Interview with Sir John Banham by author.

24. Interview with Joe Connor by author.

25. Anton Rupert, *Leaders on Leadership* (privately published, University of Pretoria, 1967), p. 37; interviews with Hugh Parker, Harry Langstaff, and Lee Walton by author; Marvin Bower personal files.

26. Interview with Harvey Golub by author.

27. Interview with Albert Gordon by author.

28. Interview with Quincy Hunsicker by author.

29. Marvin Bower, personal files (speech titled "Strengthening the Firm's Long-Term Position," 1953).

30. Interview with Warren Cannon by author.

31. Interview with Chuck Ames by author.

32. Interview with Ron Daniel by author.

33. Interviews for McKinsey's oral history, 1986–1988.

34. Interview with Jack Dempsey by author.

35. John Dewey, *Ethics* (New York, Henry Holt and Company, 1908).

36. Marvin Bower, personal files (memo titled "Sharpening Firm Objectives," 1941).

37. Marvin Bower, in discussion with the author, 2002.

38. *Perspectives on McKinsey.*

39. Marvin Bower, personal files ("The Challenge of the Next Fifty Years," October, 1960).

40. Marvin Bower, personal files (speech quoting Sir Charles Snow's *The Two Cultures and the Scientific Revolution*, 1950).

41. Marvin Bower, personal files, concept derived from James O. McKinsey's book, *Budgetary Control* (New York, Ronald Press, June 20, 1922).

42. Lyndall F. Urwick, *The Golden Book of Management* (London, Newman Neame Limited, 1956).

43. Interviews for McKinsey's oral history, 1986–1988.

44. Interview with Harvey Golub by author.

45. Marvin Bower, personal files (annual conference, 1953).

46. Marvin Bower, personal files (programmed management for McKinsey & Co., 1954).

47. Interview with John Stewart by author.

48. Interview with Fred Gluck by author.

49. Interview with Mac Stewart by author.

50. Interview with Quincy Hunsicker by author.

51. Interview with David Hertz by author.

52. Interviews for McKinsey's oral history, 1986–1988.

53. Marvin Bower, personal files (1941).

54. Interview with Harvey Golub by author.

55. Edgar H. Schein, 1967 McGregor Lecture referenced in Marvin Bower personal files ("Why McKinsey," undated).

56. Interview with Carel Paauwe by author.

57. Ibid.

58. Marvin Bower, in discussion with the author, 2002.

59. Interviews for McKinsey's oral history, 1986–1988.

60. Interviews by author.

61. Interview with Peter Drucker by author.

62. Marvin Bower, in discussion with the author, 2001.

63. Interview with Fred Gluck by author.

64. Interview with Lord Norman Blackwell by author.

65. Interview with Steven Walleck by author.

66. Interviews for McKinsey's oral history, 1986–1988.

67. Interview with John Stewart by author.

68. Interview with Don Gogel by author.

69. David Ogilvy, *Ogilvy on Advertising* (New York, Vintage Books, 1983), p. 54.

70. Marvin Bower, personal files ("The Challenge of the Next Fifty Years," October 1960).

71. Interview with Clay Deutsch by author.

72. Interview with Bob Waterman by author.

73. Marvin Bower, personal files (talk at Fiftieth Anniversary Conference, 1960).

74. Marvin Bower, personal files (article for *The Harvard Business Review,* "Nurturing High Talent Manpower," 1957); McKinsey's oral history, 1986–1988.

75. Interview with Don Gogel by author.

76. Marvin Bower, personal files (speech to American Boiler Manufacturers Association Annual Meeting, "Running a Business Well," June 1955).

77. Marvin Bower, personal files ("Preparing for the Next Stage of Firm Growth," October, 1958, draft of The Challenge Speech, 1959).

78. Interview with Mac Stewart by author.

79. In 2002, when asked who was the single most important person in helping him lead the firm, Marvin responded, "Everett Smith."

80. Interview with Mac Stewart by author.

81. *The Harvard Business Review,* September 1, 1975.

82. Interview with Theodore Levitt by author.

Chapter 4: Defining Moments of Leadership and Influence

1. Those 59 years include Marvin's time with the firm prior to the 1939 purchase of McKinsey & Co.

2. Interview with Warren Cannon by author.

3. Interview with Quincy Hunsicker by author.

4. Ibid.

5. Thomas J. Watson Jr., *Business and Its Beliefs* (New York, McGraw-Hill, 1963); interview with Marvin Bower by author.

6. Interview with Roger Morrison by author, interviews for McKinsey's oral history, 1986–1988.

7. Interviews for McKinsey's oral history, 1986–1988.

8. Marvin Bower, in discussion with the author, 2002.

9. Bob Allen, a partner at NYCP, in discussion with the author, 1995.

10. Interview with Fred Gluck by author.

11. Interview with Warren Cannon by author.

12. Marvin Bower, in discussion with the author, 1987.

13. Interviews for McKinsey's oral history, 1986–1988.

14. Ibid.

15. Marvin Bower, *Perspectives on McKinsey* (privately published, McKinsey & Co., 1979), p. 80–81.

16. Ibid, p. 66–67.

17. Interviews for McKinsey's oral history, 1986–1988.

18. Interview with Warren Cannon by author; interviews for McKinsey's oral history, 1986–1988.

19. Interview with John Macomber by author.

20. Interview with Roger Morrison by author; interviews for McKinsey's oral history, 1986–1988.
21. Ibid.
22. Ibid.
23. Interviews for McKinsey's oral history, 1986–1988.
24. Interview with Henry Strage by author.
25. Ibid.
26. Interview with John Stewart by author.
27. Interview with Ron Daniel by author.
28. Marvin Bower, personal files (McKinsey Partners' Conference, 1992).
29. Ewing W. Reilley and Eli Ginsberg, *Effecting Change in Large Organizations* (New York, Columbia University Press, 1957).
30. McKinsey & Co. internal files (foundation records reports, 1960–1972).
31. Marvin Bower, personal files (McKinsey Partners' Conference, 1992).
32. Interviews for McKinsey's oral history, 1986–1988.
33. Ibid.
34. Ibid; interview with Lee Walton by author.
35. *McKinsey Memoirs*, p. 10.
36. Interview with Jim Balloun by author.
37. Interviews for McKinsey's oral history, 1986–1988.
38. Ibid.
39. Gil Clee, quoted from speech to McKinsey management, 1954.
40. Gil Clee, "Expanding World Enterprise" (*The Harvard Business Review*, 1959).
41. Interview with Mac Stewart by author.
42. Interviews for McKinsey's oral history, 1986–1988.
43. Interview with Warren Cannon by author.
44. "Selling U.S. Advice to Europe" (*Business Week*, December 21, 1957).
45. *McKinsey: A Scrapbook* (privately published, McKinsey & Co., 1997), p. 29.
46. Salaries were equal at the partner level and scaled from the market rate for entry-level positions.
47. Interview with Lee Walton by author.
48. Interviews for McKinsey's oral history, 1986–1988.
49. Ibid.
50. John Loudon, quote from article in *The Director*, 1959.
51. Interview with Hugh Parker by author.
52. Interview with John Macomber by author.
53. Interviews for McKinsey's oral history, 1986–1988.
54. *McKinsey: A Scrapbook*, p. 34; interview with Sir Alcon Copisarow by author.
55. Interview with Lee Walton by author.
56. Interview with Mac Stewart by author.
57. Interview with John Macomber by author.
58. Harvard Business School Web site.
59. Interview with Harvey Golub by author.

60. Interview with Mary Falvey by author.
61. Ibid.
62. Marvin Bower, quoted in "McKinsey & Co. is Marvin Bower" (*Investors Business Daily,* January 7, 1999).
63. Interview with Linda Levinson by author.
64. *Memoirs,* interviews for McKinsey's oral history, 1986–1988.
65. Interviews for McKinsey's oral history, 1986–1988.
66. Jim Bowman, *Booz·Allen & Hamilton: Seventy Years of Client Service, 1914–1984* (privately published, Booz·Allen & Hamilton Inc., 1984).
67. Interviews with Marvin Bower and Walter Wriston by author.
68. Interview with John Forbis by author.
69. Interview with Peter Foy by author.
70. Interview with Henry Strage by author.
71. Marvin Bower in conversation with Bill Price, retired McKinsey communications department, 2001.
72. Interview with Hugh Parker by author.
73. Interview with Mac Stewart by author.
74. Ibid.
75. Marvin Bower, quoted in Geraldine Hines, "Step Down and Let Younger Men Lead" (*International Management,* 1968).
76. Jeffrey Sonnenfeld, *The Hero's Farewell: What Happens When CEOs Retire* (Oxford, UK, New York, Oxford University Press, 1988).
77. Interviews with Ron Daniel and Reg Jones by author.
78. Marvin Bower, quoted in BBC Interview, 1988.
79. *The Will to Lead,* (Boston, MA, Harvard Business School Press, 1997).
80. Marvin Bower, personal files (draft foreword for *The Will to Lead*); in discussion with the author.
81. Interview with Warren Cannon by author.
82. Ibid.
83. Interview with John Macomber by author.

Part II: A Leader's Leader
1. John W. Gardner, *Self-Renewal The Individual and the Innovative Society* (New York, Harper & Row, 1963).
2. Marvin Bower, personal files (*Every McKinsey Partner a Leader,* 1996).

Chapter 5: The Bower Reach
1. *McKinsey Alumni Directory* (privately published, McKinsey & Co., 1966).
2. Interview with Ron Daniel by author.
3. Interview with John McArthur by author.
4. Interview with Gene Zelazny by author.
5. Andrew Jackson.
6. Marvin Bower, *Memoirs* (New York, privately published, 2003).
7. Interview with Marvin Bower by author, 1979.

8. Interview with Terry Williams by author.

9. *Memoirs.*

10. Interview with Chuck Ames by author.

11. *Memoirs;* interviews for McKinsey's oral history, 1986–1988.

12. *Memoirs;* Marvin Bower, in discussion with the author, 2002.

13. Ibid.

14. Ibid; notes from Steve Walleck.

15. Marvin Bower, in discussion with the author, 2002.

16. Marvin Bower, personal files.

17. Marvin Bower, personal files (draft foreword for *The Will to Lead*).

Chapter 6: Inspiring Organizational Courage

1. Interview with Ron Daniel by author.

2. Interviews for McKinsey's oral history, 1986–1988.

3. Ibid.

4. Interview with Ron Daniel by author.

5. Interview with Steven Walleck by author; historical discussions with Fred Searby and author.

6. Ibid.

7. Ibid.

8. *McKinsey: A Scrapbook* (privately published, McKinsey & Co., 1997).

9. Interview with Hugh Parker by author.

10. Interview with Lee Walton by author; interviews for McKinsey's oral history, 1986–1988.

11. Interviews for McKinsey's oral history, 1986–1988.

12. Ibid.

13. Interview with Hugh Parker by author.

14. Interviews for McKinsey's oral history, 1986–1988.

15. Ibid; interview with Lee Walton by author.

16. Interview with Hugh Parker by author.

17. Ibid.

18. Ibid.

19. Interview with John Macomber by author.

20. Marvin Bower, *The Will to Lead* (Boston, MA, Harvard Business School Press, 1997).

21. Interview with Tom Schick by author.

22. Interviews with John Macomber and Lee Walton by author.

23. Marvin Bower, personal files (letters); *McKinsey: A Scrapbook.*

24. Interview with Hugh Parker by author.

25. "Organizing for Global Competitiveness: The Matrix Design" (Conference Board Report, 1983).

26. Interview with Joe Connor by author.

27. Ibid.
28. Ibid.
29. Ibid.
30. Ibid.
31. Interview with Joe Krovanski by author.
32. Interview with Joe Connor by author.
33. Interview with Robert O'Block by author.
34. Interview with Don Gogel by author.
35. Interview with Joe Connor by author.
36. Ibid.
37. "As Many of the Big Eight Centralize, Price Waterhouse Bucks the Trend" (*Business Week,* October 24, 1983).
38. Interview with Joe Connor by author.
39. Ibid.
40. Ibid.
41. Ibid.
42. Ibid.
43. Interview with Don Gogel by author.
44. Interview with Robert O'Block by author.
45. Interview with Albert Gordon by author.
46. Derek Bok, Annual Report to Harvard Board of Overseers, 1979.
47. Ibid.
48. Ibid.
49. Interview with Albert Gordon by author.
50. Marvin Bower, *Memoirs* (New York, privately published, 2003).
51. Ibid.
52. Jeffrey L. Cruikshank, *A Delicate Experiment* (Boston, MA, Harvard Business School Press, 1987).
53. Marvin Bower, personal files (1968).
54. John had had a previous relationship with Al from the time when John, as one of the trustees in bankruptcy, had successfully secured funding from Kidder Peabody to help turn around Penn Central Railroad.
55. Interview with Albert Gordon by author.
56. Ibid.
57. Interview with Richard Cavanagh by author.
58. Interview with Steve Walleck by author; Steve Walleck notes.
59. Ibid.
60. Ibid.
61. Interview with Albert Gordon by author.
62. Ibid.
63. Ibid.
64. Marvin Bower and Albert Gordon, "The Success of a Strategy" (Board of Direc-

tors, The Associates of Harvard Business School Task Force Report, December, 1979).

65. Ibid.
66. Ibid.
67. Ibid.
68. Ibid.
69. Marvin Bower, in discussion with the author, 2002.
70. Interview with Theodore Levitt by author.
71. Interview with John McArthur by author.
72. Ibid.
73. Ibid.
74. Ibid.
75. Ibid.
76. Joan Margretta and Nan Stone, *What Management Is* (New York, London, Tokyo, Sydney, Singapore, The Free Press, 2002) p. 15.

Chapter 7: Educating a Generation of Leaders

1. Theodore Roosevelt, *Theodore Roosevelt on Leadership: Excellent Lessons from the Bully Pulpit* (Roseville, CA, Forum, 2001).
2. Interview with Harvey Golub, 2002 by author.
3. Marvin Bower, in discussion with author, 2002.
4. Interview with Harvey Golub by author.
5. Ibid.
6. Ibid.
7. Ibid.
8. Ibid.
9. Ibid.
10. Ibid.
11. Ibid.
12. Ibid.
13. Ibid.
14. Ibid.
15. Ibid.
16. Ibid.
17. Ibid.
18. Ibid.
19. Ibid.
20. Ibid.
21. Marvin Bower, personal files (letter from Harvey Golub, March 7, 1995).
22. Interview with Harvey Golub by author.
23. Ibid.
24. Ibid.
25. Ibid.

26. Ibid.
27. Kenneth I. Chenault, *American Express Annual Report* (2000).
28. Marvin Bower, personal files (letter from Harvey Golub, January 2001).
29. Interview with Gary MacDougal, 2002 by author.
30. Marvin Bower, in discussion with author, 2001.
31. Interview with Gary MacDougal by author.
32. Ibid.
33. Ibid.
34. Ibid.
35. Ibid.
36. Ibid.
37. Ibid.
38. Ibid.
39. Ibid.
40. Ibid.
41. Ibid.
42. *Make a Difference,* (New York, Truman Talley Books, St. Martin's Press, 2000).
43. Ibid.
44. Ibid.
45. Ibid.
46. Ibid.
47. Ibid.
48. Department of Health and Human Services Administration for Children and Families, December 2002; Daniel J. Miller, Assistant Secretary, Illinois Department of Human Resources.
49. David Broder, "Welfare Reform Can Work" (*The Cincinnati Post,* January 27, 2000).
50. *Make a Difference.*
51. Interview with Gary MacDougal by author.
52. Ibid.
53. Marvin Bower, in discussion with author, 2002.
54. David Ogilvy, *Blood, Brains & Beer: The Autobiography of David Ogilvy* (New York, Atheneum, 1978), p. 61.
55. David Ogilvy, *The Unpublished David Ogilvy* (New York, privately published, The Ogilvy Group, 1986), p. 55.
56. Ibid., p. 99.
57. David Ogilvy, *Ogilvy on Advertising* (New York, Vintage Books, 1985), p. 52.
58. Marvin Bower, in discussions with the author, 2001, 2002.
59. David Ogilvy, *An Autobiography* (New York: John Wiley & Sons, Inc., 1997), p. 117, 130; Marvin Bower, personal files (memorandum).
60. Kenneth Roman and Jane Maas, *How to Advertise* (New York, St. Martin's Press, 2003); interview with Ken Roman by author.
61. David Ogilvy, *Confessions of An Advertising Man* (New York, Dell, 1964).

62. *An Autobiography*, p. 131; *The Unpublished David Ogilvy*.
63. *Blood, Brains & Beer*.
64. *Ogilvy on Advertising*, p. 48.
65. Ibid., p. 53; *Confessions of an Advertising Man*, p. 106.
66. David Ogilvy, quoted at McKinsey Training Program, 1987.
67. Interview with Ken Roman by author; Ken Roman correspondence file, November 1973.
68. Marvin Bower, personal files (memorandum to consulting staff, "David Ogilvy—Personnel Program," November 16, 1961).
69. Interview with Don Gogel, by author, 2002.
70. Marvin Bower, in discussion with the author, 2001.
71. Interview with Don Gogel by author.
72. Ibid.
73. Ibid.
74. Ibid.
75. Ibid.
76. Ibid.
77. Ibid.
78. Ibid.
79. Interview with Chuck Ames by author.
80. Interview with Sir John Banham by author.
81. Interview with Sir Roderick Carnegie by author.
82. Interview with Richard Cavanagh by author.
83. Interview with Ron Daniel by author.
84. Interview with Juliette Dively by author.
85. Interview with Roger Ferguson by author.
86. Interview with Michael Fleisher by author.
87. Lou Gerstner, quote from "Our Days with Marvin" (*Consulting Magazine*, February/March 2003).
88. Lou Gerstner quote from John A. Byrne, "Goodbye to an Ethicist" (*Business Week*, February 10, 2003).
89. Interview with Albert Gordon by author.
90. Bruce D. Henderson, *Henderson on Corporate Strategy* (Cambridge, Abt Books, 1979).
91. Interview with Herbert Henzler by author.
92. Interview with Jon Katzenbach by author.
93. Rob Spiegel, "Steve Kaufman: A Look Back" (*Electronic News*, February 27, 2002).
94. Interview with Steve Kaufman by author; Steve Kaufman in a speech, October 2003.
95. Interview with Linda Fayne Levinson by author.
96. Interview with John Macomber by author.

97. Leo Mullin, quote from "Our Days with Marvin" (*Consulting Magazine*, February/March 2003).
98. Interview with Andrall Pearson by author.
99. Interview with John Sawhill, 1998, by author.
100. Interview with Isabel Sawhill, 2003, by author.
101. Interviews for McKinsey's oral history, 1986–1998.
102. Interview with Klaus Zumwinkel by author.
103. Marvin Bower, *The Will to Manage*.

List of Interviewees

Person	Title/Relationship	Years at McKinsey
Frances Allen	Jim Allen's (Booz Allen) wife	
Charles "Chuck" Ames	Partner, Clayton, Dubilier & Rice, Inc.	1957–1972
Gerry Andlinger	Andlinger & Company Inc.	1956–1959
Jenny Bower Athanason	Granddaughter	
Phil Babb		1941–1978
Carter Bales	General partner, The Wicks Group of Companies, L.L.C.	1965–1998
Jim Balloun	Chairman, president, and CEO, Acuity Brands, Inc.	1965–1996
Sir John Banham	Chairman, Kingtirn DLL	1969–1983
Richard Baznik	Vice president executive compensation, Case Western Reserve University	
Jack Benfield	Retired chairman and inventor, Benfield Electrical Joint	
Jim Bennett	President and CEO, EmployOn, Inc.	1968–1998
Lord Norman Blackwell	Chairman, SmartStream Technologies Ltd.	1978–1995
James "Jim" Bower	Son	
Richard "Dick" Bower	Son	
Suzanne Bower	Great-niece	
Malcolm Candlish	Retired chairman, First Alert	1965–1977
Warren Cannon		1949–1988
Sir Roderick "Rod" Carnegie	Retired chairman, TRA	1959–1970
Richard "Dick" Cavanagh	President and CEO, The Conference Board, Inc.	1970–1987

Dr. Aphrodite Clamar-Cohen	Psychologist	
Don Clifford Jr.	President, Threshold Management, Inc.	1959–1984
Joseph Connor	Former senior partner, Price Waterhouse	
Ron Daniel	Former managing director, McKinsey & Co.	1957– Present
Brande Defilippis	Nurse, Florida	
Jack Dempsey	Director, McKinsey & Co.	1987– Present
Clay Deutsch	Managing partner, McKinsey & Co., Chicago	1981– Present
Juliette "Lilita" Dively	Wife of Marvin's good friend George Dively, chairman of Harris Graphics from 1939 to 1972	
Dr. Peter F. Drucker	Clarke Professor of Social Science and Management at the Claremont Graduate School	
Mary Falvey	Falvey Associates	1967–1975
Roger Ferguson	Vice chairman, Federal Reserve Bank	1984–1997
Mark Filippell	Sr. Managing Director and Co-manager, mergers and acquisition practice, Key Dane Capital Markets	1980–1982
Dan Finkelman	Senior vice president, brand and business planning, Limited Brands, Inc.	1981–1994
Michael Fleischer	President, Bogen Communications International, Inc.	1985–1990
John Forbis	Corporate vice president and general manager, Canon	1971–1983
Peter Foy	Chairman, Whitehead Mann Group L/P	1968–1973 1974–1996
Bob Garda	Executive in residence, Fuqua School of Business, Duke University	1967–1994
Candace Gaudiani	Gaudiani Associates	1973–1977
Fred Gluck	Former managing director, McKinsey & Co.	1967–1995
Don Gogel	President and CEO, Clayton, Dubilier & Rice, Inc.	1976–1985

Harvey Golub	Retired chairman and CEO, American Express	1966–1973
		1977–1983
Albert Gordon	Retired chairman, Kidder Peabody	
Rajat Gupta	Former managing director, McKinsey & Co.	1973– Present
Dr. Felix Haas	Author's father, coadviser to General Motors in the 1960s	
Dr. Alistair "Ali" Hanna	Executive director, Alpha North America	1974–1997
Dr. Herbert A. Henzler	Vice chairman, Credit Suisse First Boston	1970–2001
Dr. David Hertz	Chairman and CEO, Identification Technologies International	1962–1979
Randy Hogan	Chairman, President and CEO, Pentair Inc.	1981–1988
Frederik "Mickey" Huibregtsen	Former head of McKinsey & Co. The Netherlands	1970–1999
Quincy Hunsicker	Member, McKinsey & Co. advisory board	1961–1997
Reg Jones	Former chairman, General Electric	
Michael Jordan	Chairman and CEO, EDS	1964–1974
Nancy Karch	Advisory council member, McKinsey & Co.	1974–2000
Jon Katzenbach	President of Katzenbach and Associates	1959–1998
Stephen Kaufman	Retired CEO and chairman, Arrow Electronics, Inc.; Faculty of the Harvard Business School	1969–1980
Dr. Peter Kraljic	Member, McKinsey & Co. advisory board	1970–2002
Harry Langstaff		1966–1984
Mark LeDoux	Managing partner, Syzygy Consulting, Inc.	1982–1987
Linda Levinson	General partner, GRP Partners, Inc.	1972–1981
Professor Theodore Levitt	Professor emeritus, Harvard Business School	
Henry Lowes	Lowes stores	
Gary MacDougal	Chairman, Republican Party, State of Illinois; honorary chairman and CEO Mark Controls	1963–1969

John Macomber	Chairman, JDM Investment Group; retired chairman, Celanese	1953–1973
Bill Matassoni	Partner and director of marketing, Boston Consulting Group	1980–1999
Dean John McArthur	Retired dean of Harvard Business School	
Alonzo "Al" McDonald	Chairman and CEO, Avenir; former managing director, McKinsey & Co.	1960–1977
Ed Michaels III		1969–2001
Roger Morrison	Corporate director, Vector Command, Kinko's, Alliant Foodservice	1953–1991
Dietmar Meyersiek	Geschaftsfuhrender Gesellschafter, EXES Management information, GmbH	1970–1992
Margaret S. Neal	Secretary to Marvin Bower, Florida	
Bruce Nemlich	Director, Management Science, Pfizer, Inc.	1983–1986
Richard Neuschel		1945–1979
Robert O'Block	Former head of Boston office, McKinsey & Co.	1969–1998
Cherie Olland	Global director of business development and communications Jones Day	1982–1985
Stephanie O'Malley	Nurse, Florida	
Hein Onkenhout	Regional CEO Americas, Rexam Beauty & Closures	1981–1988
Carel Paauwe	Chairman, Rekkof	1970–1998
Hugh Parker	Former head of McKinsey & Co., U.K.	1951–1983
Andrall Pearson	Founding chairman, Yum! Brands, retired president, Pepsico	1954–1970
Don Perkins	Retired chairman, A&P	
H. Don Perkins Jr.	Partner, Zon Capital Partners	1985–1989
Bill Price	Retired editor, McKinsey & Co.	1980–2002
Sara Roche	Communications Consultants, McKinsey & Co.	1966–1998
Ken Roman	Retired chairman, Ogilvy & Mather	

John Rye	Former chairman, Lamb Machine Tool Company	
Thomas Schick	Retired head of R&D, Shell	
Norman Selby	CEO, TransForm Pharmaceuticals	1978–1997
Charles Shaw	Managing director, First Atlantic Capital, Ltd.	1965–2000
Barbara Sinclair	Administrative Assistant to Marvin Bower	1969–2002
Leif Soderberg	Senior vice president and director of global strategy and corporate development, Motorola, Inc.	1978–1993
Herman Stein	Retired provost, Case Western Reserve University	
J. Mac Stewart		1952–1996
John Stewart		1961–1998
Dr. Henry Strage	H.M. Strage Associates	1962–1991
John Tomb		1950–1975
Jack Vance	Managing director, Management Research, Inc.; Former head of Los Angeles office, McKinsey & Co.	1951–1989
Betty Vandenbosch	Professor, Case Western Reserve University	1983–1990
Joan Wallace	Housekeeper, Florida	
A. Steve Walleck	Former director, McKinsey & Co.; Former chairman and CEO, Magnetic Data Technologies	1971–1993
Lee Walton*	Former managing director, McKinsey & Co.	1955–1987
Robert "Bob" Waterman, Jr.	Chairman, The Waterman Group, Inc.	1964–1985
Howard "Terry" Williams III	Former head of Washington, D.C. office, McKinsey & Co.	1959–1997
Walter Wriston	Retired chairman, Citibank	
Gene Zelazny	Director of visual communications, McKinsey & Co.	1961– Present
Dr. Klaus Zumwinkel	Chairman of the management board, Deutsche Post AG	1974–1985

*Deceased since interview.

Index